Hilary Mantel is the author of fif... award-winning *Wolf Hall* trilogy, the memoir *Giving Up the Ghost* and the short story collection *The Assassination of Margaret Thatcher*. She has twice been awarded the Man Booker Prize.

Praise for *Mantel Pieces*:

'It shows the evolution in Mantel's style, which has been considerable. Some of the pieces are segments of memoir, some are deeply informed historical essays loosely attached to discussions of books. In the earliest reviews – before she is given subjects big enough for her to walk around in – Mantel is sarky and snarky as well as brisk and breezy . . . Mantel's own segments of memoir, which were published as diary pieces, are virtuoso performances . . . As a memoirist, Mantel is without parallel . . . It is only when her essays are laid out like this that we can see the inside of Mantel's huge head, bulging with knowledge and a million connections. 5/5 STARS'

Telegraph

'Remarkable selection of the essays and reviews that have constituted the other half of her creative life for the last few decades . . . The result has been a literary-critical relationship that has provided us with some of the most engaging and controversial writing in modern times. We are fortunate to have it collected here. Vast and various, the book offers the reader a fascinating vision of the restless intelligence that – in conjuring the *Wolf Hall* trilogy for which Mantel is most famous – has sustained and entertained so many. But it also functions as a heartening example of the rewards to be found in being undogmatic, curious, alert, roaming . . . this is a

work that is brisk and breezy, and further enhanced by her capacity to examine our hearts, register our feelings and bring up with tenderness the enduring question of our frail and vulnerable bodies'
Evening Standard

'Worth buying for the title pun alone, *Mantel Pieces* brings together three decades' worth of Hilary Mantel's criticism in the *London Review of Books* . . . her uncomplicated prose style is no less authoritative for being highly readable'
Sunday Times

'A volume of critical writing which often feels as if one is in the company of an exceptionally wise and generous friend, except very few of us have friends who can be as erudite on Madonna as they are on Anne Boleyn'
Sara Collins

'Bad girls. Ecstatic masochists. Housewives with hidden depths. Revolutionaries who rebelled all the way to the madhouse. These unruly women are her enduring obsession. Read those lines again and think of Mantel, smiling serenely in a billowing kaftan, sitting at her little desk near a tearoom town, inside a body which has betrayed her. This is a woman who gets her kicks, alright – on the page'
New Statesman

'Likely to leave readers in awe of the purity of Mantel's prose, the breadth of her interests and the sharp intelligence she brings to every topic . . . Reading it is like downing a cold, sharp glass of lemonade on a swelteringly hot day: crisp, tart and unbelievably refreshing'
i *Paper*

'Ferocious, witty and unapologetic'
Guardian

4th Estate
An imprint of HarperCollins*Publishers*
1 London Bridge Street
London SE1 9GF

www.4thEstate.co.uk

HarperCollins*Publishers*
Macken House, 39/40 Mayor Street Upper,
Dublin1, D01 C9W8, Ireland

First published in Great Britain in 2020 by 4th Estate
This 4th Estate paperback edition published in 2021

4

Set in FF Quadraat
Printed and Bound in the UK using 100% Renewable Electricity at CPI Group (UK) Ltd

Mantel Pieces

Royal Bodies and Other Writing from
the *London Review of Books*

Hilary Mantel

4th ESTATE • *London*

CONTENTS

Introduction
Hilary Mantel

WHEN my first novel, *Every Day Is Mother's Day*, was published in 1985, I had been living abroad for some years. Its sequel came out a year later, and at that point, returning from Saudi Arabia, I needed to work out whether I could make a living as a writer. The advance for my first book had been £2000. For my second it was £4000 – a good rate of progress, but not an income. Apart from my agent and publishers, I didn't know anyone in the media, or a single other person who was a writer. But I didn't think I was equipped for any other trade.

The first person to throw me a lifeline was Auberon Waugh, who had reviewed my novels and who asked me to write for the *Literary Review*: one piece a month, £40. Alan Ross at the *London Magazine* employed me; he was able to pay even less. But I decided I would say 'yes' to anything, especially if it frightened me. Soon Charles Moore at the *Spectator* became my patron, and offered me their film column. A weekly column made me visible, and led to more work than I could handle.

The reviewing scene was very different in those days. There were more daily papers and they made space for books. For a time, in the autumn of 1989 and the spring of 1990, there were five Sunday broadsheets, all of them eating up copy. There were periodicals that no longer exist, like *New Society* and the *Listener*. There was even one called *Books and Bookmen* – the title tells you everything about the world in which I started to publish.

Writing in 1938, Cyril Connolly identified journalism as one of his *Enemies of Promise*. He warns young writers against reviewing, identifying the danger of 'short articles for quick returns' – though in his day, two thousand words was considered short. He insists that 'any other way of making money would be better . . . reviewing is a whole-time job with a half-time salary.' The author runs the risk of losing energy, 'frittering it away on tripe and discovering that it is his flashiest efforts that receive most praise'. The only way to preserve yourself, Connolly advises, is to 'manoeuvre' so you never review a bad book.

It is true that reviewing eats up time. Even in the easier days in which I began, you had to become a workhorse if you wanted worthwhile returns. I was in awe of my paymasters, and at the same time I was uneasy. I recall having a batch of potential Booker winners fall out of a bag – four or five of them, and a scant two hundred words for each. I was offering opinions with no visible means of support, and with little scope for nuance. It is simple, if you have only a paragraph to spare, to swat a book like a fly. Even if you have more space, it is easier to write a bad review than a good one, or to locate the flaw in a book and become fixated on it. Young reviewers become fired with zeal against the established and the over-rated. They think they are doing justice, but it takes them longer to learn about mercy.

When I began to write for the LRB everything changed. I began my career during Karl Miller's editorship and continued with Mary-Kay Wilmers. My pieces became more expansive, the work became more challenging, and my unease dissipated, though only gradually. I still said 'yes' to everything. Mary-Kay speaks so softly that when she first called me I believed she was trapped inside a sofa. It's possible that I didn't always know what I had agreed to review. But I learned that the paper is skilled at matching contributors to a task. I almost never got a bad book – and if I did, I could send it back. At first I had qualms about my ability to rise to the standard. What I wrote was so plain that it felt exposed. I didn't have an arts degree, had never learned about literary criticism; in the theory wars, I was a non-combatant. But the paper had experts on tap, if they cared to call on them. If they wanted someone to stand in for the general reader, I was as general as they come. I didn't often review fiction, so I was not in danger of projecting my own perplexities onto someone else's work. And I welcomed the fact that all editorial changes were by negotiation. There was no danger of a sub-editor slicing off your last paragraph and changing the whole meaning of the piece. There were no particular space constraints. When I asked 'How many words?' the editors would say, 'Take what you need.'

That answer is a clever one, and more demanding than it appears. To fix a book in context needs background reading. When the paper unearthed my old letters – I had no idea they kept such things – I saw that I was always asking for time, more time to learn – and it was always granted. Sometimes I was slow because I was over-committed, but sometimes because I was fascinated. The editors forgave my occasional bouts of critic's block. They are forbearing with all their writers; sometimes it must seem unclear whether a piece is in progress or regress, or whether it will ever arrive at all. I am indebted to them for patience, and to Mary-Kay for encouraging me out of my shell. I had trained myself out of digression, but the paper was at ease with it. I was wary of jokes, but they didn't mind those either. And when I wanted to say something more personal, they were listening.

The pieces here were written over a long period, and fall into different categories. There are those where, as I have said, I stand in for the general reader. There are pieces on the early Tudors and on the French Revolution, where I have particular knowledge. There are diary pieces, offcuts of memoir. And then there is a category of one: my piece on royal bodies, which supposedly enraged middle England – or at least, left certain newspapers spitting and foaming and doubling up in ire.

'Royal Bodies' began life as an LRB lecture. Afterwards it was printed, and nothing happened for a while – and I didn't expect anything to result from a sober and harmless essay, although I did wonder if Buckingham Palace might be irked because I mocked their cocktail snacks. Ten days on, the press were on my doorstep – or somewhere near it. From my window overlooking the sea, I watched hopeless reporters range up and down, trying to work out how to catch me. They could not decide exactly where I lived, and the neighbours wouldn't help them – in Budleigh Salterton we don't engage with vulgarians. My husband came to tell me that the prime minister and the leader of the opposition were denouncing me. Neither, I believe, had read my lecture. Very few people had read it, but I was still Monster of the Month. If it had been bonfire season no doubt I would have been burned in effigy.

The ashes are frequently raked over, and I have to live with a traitor's name. But the prime minister of those days, and the leader of the opposition too, are shrinking into obscurity, while the LRB expands its readership and reach year by year, never shy of disputes and never trapped into faux-apologetic mode. I am proud to work for a paper so unafraid, so original and so current. The more books I turn out, the more I wonder how one ever finds the courage to begin, and the more I respect other people who write. So many volumes, so much toil, so much hope: the least we owe our writers is dispassionate assessment and considered response.

The LRB offers more than that. A literary journal must be a political journal, as we cannot detach from larger realities. The paper is at ease with controversy rather than consensus and will allow a contributor to be contrary, even unfashionable. I have felt no pressure to line up with the editors' views – just as I felt no need to become a Tory to write for the *Spectator*. Most imaginative writers are a party of one, and it is a riven and dissenting party, waging wars privately, silently. We do not like to be forced into confining self-definitions, or into consistency of response, or easy declarations of intent: or at least, we should not like it. Sometimes when I have written a piece for the LRB, I feel I understand less than when I started. What I knew, I have begun to unknow. I have not in fact finished, but begun a new engagement with a topic, an exploration that might stretch over years. There is, therefore, a temptation to write afterthoughts into these pieces, to embellish them with later and better thinking. I have not done that, but left them as they were – mantelpieces littered with to-do lists, and messages from people I used to be.

20a Trinity Place,
Windsor SL4 3AT

Dr Karl Miller
London Review of Books.

September 16th.

Dear Dr Miller,

My address from September 23rd will be:

36, Sandringham Court,
    Burnham
    Berkshire SL1 6JZ
    Tel: (06286) 65839.

If you would like me to do another piece, I
should be delighted to try. I have been writing
for Literary Review for the past year, and more
recently for London Magazine + Books; mainly I've
reviewed fiction, but for the Literary Review
also some books on Southern Africa, on French history,
+ on psychology. I have no critical training
whatsoever so I am forced to be more brisk + breezy
than scholarly. My background is: a law degree,

Letter from Hilary Mantel to Karl Miller,
1987

medical social work, 5 years in Botswana —
some of the time I taught English — then 4 years in
Saudi Arabia. My first novel came out from Chatto
in 1985, and my second last year. I am astonished to
find myself writing the Spectator film column, because as
I said to you on the telephone, I know hardly anything
about the cinema. John Lancester sent me 3 travel
books, which look interesting; I would be happy
to do a piece on them, or whatever — within my
limitations. Thank you anyway for sending me the
Saudi book — I've just finished my novel, so it was a
most opportune time to see the place through
someone else's eyes.

Yours sincerely,

Hilary Mantel.

Women in Pain
American Marriage
1988

S CRIBBLE, scribble, scribble, Ms Hite: another damned, thick, square book.* Shere Hite is a 'cultural historian'. She has already given us *The Hite Report: A Nationwide Study of Female Sexuality* and *The Hite Report on Male Sexuality*. Her work is an uneasy blend of prurience and pedantry; an attenuated blonde woman with curious white make-up, she has offended US feminists by making money out of sisterhood. She lives in some style, and has a young husband who, she tells us in a preface (there are many prefaces, a sort of philosophical foreplay), 'fills my life with poetry and music, more every day'. Well, that's all right then.

But sadly, it's not typical. What a picture of American marriage emerges from these pages! It is certainly a 'sad, sour, sober beverage'. (There is so much in these pages that Lord Byron said first, and better, and with merciful brevity, and without the advantages of sociological research.) The men are always off on a fishing trip, the women always masturbating in the bathroom. When he comes home, they fight; she rants, and he sits there 'like Mussolini'. Then maybe he smashes a

---

* *Women and Love. The New Hite Report: A Cultural Revolution in Progress* by Shere Hite (Viking, 1988).

little crockery. They have sex by way of reconciliation, but it's not too good: 'I have to remind him to remove his glasses.'

This is a book about emotional suffering. There is the odd woman who says she is happy. There is even a section called 'The Beauty of Marriage'. It occupies page 343 – but then a lot of page 343 is white space. Most of these nine hundred pages tell of disaffection, disillusion and incipient rebellion. 'Should Women,' asks one heading, 'Take a Mass Vacation From Trying To Understand Men?' Miss Hite's respondent tells us: 'Men's attitudes are so bad, so impaired, and they don't even realise how negative to women they are. They think they love women. It will take some massive reaction to make them start realising, start thinking . . . like a national strike, a boycott, a new Lysistrata.' Or as Shere Hite herself puts it, less dramatically: 'Women are suffering a lot of pain in their love relationships with men.'

Half the world's fiction is about this, but Hite wants to skewer it into a scientific fact. She is particular, though, about the definitions of science that she will admit. One thinks of the aperçu of the younger Amis: 'I don't know much about science, but I know what I like.' The basis of her inquiry was a questionnaire which runs to 127 pages. She eschews multiple-choice questions (quite properly, because they put a damper on things) and goes for the 'open-ended', which allows her respondents to answer in essay form if they wish. She distributed 100,000 questionnaires, and got 4,500 replies – not bad going, whatever her opponents say. Miss Hite's methodology has been attacked rather unfairly, and so often that she has buttressed her report with experts – professors all – who assure us of her probity and competence as a social scientist. Her opponents have picked up the term 'random sample' – a staple of saloon-bar wisdom – and have said she hasn't got one. What matters, she says reasonably, is to have a sample that is demographically matched to the population.

What is less reasonable, and more an act of faith, is Hite's contention that because her respondents were anonymous they must have been telling the truth. In the context of the study, the most one can hope is that they were telling the truth as interpreted by their feelings on the day that they answered. It is a characteristic of sociologists that they discount the grimly insistent nature of the human imagination. There is a chilling quality about Miss Hite's respondents which reminds one of all those people who say: 'I've got a book in me.' Of course, everyone has: what is a pity is that exercises like *The New Hite Report* give it the opportunity to come out.

The buttressing professors pose problems of their own. 'Hite,' says one, 'has rejected the silencing of women by recognising that a theory about women's ways of loving must be rooted in our own experiences.' You must do what you can with that sentence. You can read it backwards. You can try to put it out of your mind for a few days, and leave it in a room by itself, then spring back in and hope to take its meaning unawares. Probably it means that a good way to find out what people think is just to ask them. But then, you may object, their replies will be merely subjective – no use really, if you purport to be a scientist. Take back that 'merely'. *Wash your mouth out.* Feminist science is something quite different; subjectivity is of the essence. Until recently, women have been objects of study, and all the theories about feminine psychology, about how women think and feel, have been constructed by men. They have been constructed, very often, in the expectation of finding pathology, or at least a rather humiliating state of things: she is smitten by penis envy, by frigidity, if she can't have an orgasm from the Saturday Night Special she's some deeply unnatural woman. She's neurotic, and obsessed with one little bit of her anatomy that some civilisations delight in slicing off.

There is nothing controversial here. For controversy one must look a little further. Miss Hite belongs to the school of thought which rejects traditional, male-devised science; she says it is crampingly linear in its mode of thought, and mistakenly claims to be value-free, detached and neutral. Feminist science recognises its evaluative posture; it recognises that the observer is not neutral, for she has her position, her prejudices, her viewpoint; it values intuition. Hite takes comfort from vogues in literary criticism – text, not machine, as analyst's model – and from Heidegger: 'reason, glorified for centuries, is the most stiff-necked adversary of thought.' An essay appended to the book says that white male thinkers (it is a puzzle to know how skin colour gets in) are uncomfortable with hermeneutics: 'for them it raises the spectre of total relativity, the fear that we will never be able to know anything in an absolutely objective and certain way.' It is possible, of course, that many scientists – physicists especially, and white and male at that – have been living with this 'fear' for many years; that it is now a necessary part of whatever understanding of the universe we have. But they have not entirely been frightened out of the scientific method; it has its uses, and when Shere Hite wishes to be sure that she will be taken seriously, she displays an old-fashioned masculine zeal for quantification. The questionnaire asks: 'How happy are you, on a scale of 1-10?' It's a question which – if we accept Shere Hite's views up to this point – incorporates the worst of both 'masculine' and 'feminine' science; its only merit is that it makes us laugh.

The truth may be that *The Hite Report* is science, but not of the mould-breaking sort its author thinks it is; that in fact it's just the usual kind, which offers incomprehensible explanations for what everyone knows. Sociology has never made it into the gentlemen's club of the 'hard' sciences; many people have suspected that it is simply a higher form of gossip.

Considered as gossip, though, this book has a grave defect: all Miss Hite's anonymous respondents sound alike. She insists that women of all classes were well represented, that the less educated were not deterred from writing essays on their lives; in some cases, she says, the misspellings were 'very appealing'. But they did not find their way into the finished product, because, Miss Hite says, 'it seemed that in print these misspellings sometimes looked demeaning to the writer, or might be seen as trivialising that respondent.' Then, too, some of these women adore jargon: as if all their lives have been a preparation for a survey; perhaps it is because they have 'therapists' to contend with, as well as their families. Their range is small, their vocabulary often restricted, and there is a huge gulf between their emotion and their capacity to convey it: being a lesbian, says one, 'is the most comforting identity I've had since I was a cheerleader in junior high school'. The book's tone is homogeneous, dull, flat: all these thousands of women sound like one woman, one awful person, droning on and on. If only Miss Hite were not so contemptuous of pop sociologists, she could have given her informants fictitious names, and to each one accorded a little pen-picture, to encourage us into her narrative: 'Mary Lou, a much tattooed redhead of 43 . . .'

Yet the book does have its fascination. Between the lines are the sagas, the epics, the unwritten histories, a novel condensed into a throwaway phrase. It is not that what the women have to say is very original: it is that their reports, by their weight, their mass, offer such resounding confirmation of the absurdity of life. The relationships Shere Hite surveys are so painful, and so achingly comic, that one wonders how anyone came up with the notion in the first place that men and women might live together: whoever thought it might be possible?

Language is the first problem. There are men who seemed biologically programmed to avoid it. 'My clue that something is bothering him is when he grinds his teeth when he sleeps.' If they do talk, it might be about the weather: one woman says acidly that after 31 years she finds the weather is no longer interesting. They say, these men: 'What is the baseball score? Put on the basketball game!' Women like talking – about everything. According to men, they always choose 'soap-opera topics'. While they are indulging in these, the men 'whistle and sing and slam doors'. Sometimes they absent-mindedly walk off into other rooms. If they answer, it may be completely at random. 'I will ask,' says one misunderstood soul, 'two or three questions at once – example: "Do you want milk or coffee?" And he will answer: "Yes." He feels,' the woman explains, 'that I should ask them one at a time.' Another describes her marital small talk as 'like pulling teeth'.

Ninety-eight per cent of these women say they want more 'verbal closeness' with men; and they want to offer emotional support when they see that life is getting to their partners. When their offer is rejected, they feel baffled and useless. (One man lost his job, his father, and the wheels off his car. His wife expressed sympathy, so he slapped her.) The men repress their feelings, and deny that women have any; one of the gay women, who has opted out of the whole thing, says that she can't imagine falling in love with a man, because men are so alien, 'as if they all come from the East Coast and women from the West'. For the women who decide to stay in heterosexual relationships, there is one ultimate uncertainty: 'I wonder if he has any emotions at all?'

Almost all the married women who replied said that they believed in monogamy: but of those who had been married for five years or more, 70 per cent were having affairs. There is a lot of deception around; some of it self-deception. Eighty-two per cent of women believed that their husbands were faithful: but earlier Hite research showed that 72 per cent of men who had been married for over two years were seeing other women.

These statistics do seem to contradict one's belief and everyday experience. But then, to judge by this sample, few extramarital adventurers ever tell, or are found out. Some are most adroit at juggling their relationships; one woman admitted to 12 lovers since her marriage, some concurrent, and affairs that had lasted between two months and 33 years. These lovers are 'dear men', 'precious men', willing to talk about their deepest feelings, and with a thorough working knowledge of female anatomy. They are generally, of course, someone else's husband.

Single women joined in the survey too: on her lecture tours round the colleges of the United States, Shere Hite has collected examples of the chat-up lines they have to endure. Attempts to manoeuvre women into bed range from the manipulative ('There's a rumour round school that you are a lesbian') to the circumlocutory ('Ever heard the "1812 Overture" on CD?') to the pathetic ('My balls hurt'). The women feel pressured to marry: it seems that twenty years of the women's movement has not changed society's expectations in this or in many other matters. 'Sometimes I think even if I were a new Mozart it wouldn't be enough. All my friends and family would still be saying: "And when are you getting married? Are you seeing anybody?"'

At first glance, it seems that it is the lesbians who are most satisfied with their relationships. 'I believe a love relationship between two women is far more serious than one between a man and a woman. Women run on a higher emotional level than men will let themselves, and they get to deeper levels with each other.' But when you read on, the same old complaints emerge. There are people who can't or won't talk about their feelings, and people who go too far in the other direction and plunge a relationship into what one respondent calls 'introspective shit'. Some partners are philanderers; others are violent. There are some over-familiar, melancholy anecdotes: 'I was sitting there with a flashlight, inside the car, trying to read the map, and she was screaming at me, because I can't read it properly.' Why can't a woman be less like a man?

The New Hite Report raises all the difficulties and dilemmas that have beset women for years. Should women fight for change, or lower their expectations? Should they fight for their rights in a man's world, or make a world of their own, with values they find more congenial? Is there some way in which men can be educated to set greater value on loving relationships? Or should women cut their losses, and accept that heterosexual relationships, and traditional marriage especially, provide limited emotional satisfaction? The hardest thing to accept about Shere Hite's book is that she believes there are answers to these questions; and for her of course the solutions are not within the individual's grasp, but are, in the feminist sense, 'political'. She is an optimist: she looks forward to an era of 'Feminist Enlightenment'. And she has nothing to say about the current backlash against the women's movement; nothing to say about Beverley LaHaye and the Concerned Women for America, preaching the virtues of 'submission', and campaigning against equal pay.

This is not a comfortable book. You may disagree with Shere Hite's methods, and with her conclusions, but no one could believe that she has seriously misrepresented what many women feel about their lives. It is no relief, however, if you feel as the Hite respondents do, to know that your problem is multiplied by millions, that you are part of a national trend. And the more one reads, the more one loses the flavour of real life, and the more one despairs of it: the more one feels like the unlucky one of three, waylaid on the way to the wedding by the Ancient Mariner. Miss Hite's glittering eye is not easily avoided, her skinny hand not to be shaken off. But does she know, one wonders, that the perfect relationship is not to be had? It is not a bad thing to go on looking for it, but as one woman puts it, in the bleakest terms, 'people will always be separate. That's how we're born and that's how we die, one at a time, one per body, alone.'

London Review of Books

Tavistock House South, Tavistock Square,
London WC1H 9JZ
Telephone: 01-388 6751
Advertising and Distribution: 01-388 7487

Hilary Mantel
36 Sandringham Court
Burnham
Berkshire SLI 6JZ

18 October 1988

Dear Hilary,

I have been thinking, and worrying, about Sex
Work since our conversation at the Viking
party; and the more I think about it, the
more I think that you have produced an
admirable review of a book we shouldn't have
sent out. Could you bear it if we pay you
for it and look out for something more worth
your while? We value your contributions to
the paper a great deal and I am extremely
contrite.

Yours ever,

Mary-Kay

6   60-80-07

National Westminster Bank PLC

18th October 19 88

Tavistock Square Branch
British Medical Association House, Tavistock Square, London WC1H 9JA

Pay Hilary Mantel.   or order   V

One hundred & fifty pounds.   £150-50

                                                        FOR LRB LTD

Mary-Kay Wilmers

Letter (and kill fee) from Mary-Kay Wilmers
to Hilary Mantel, 1988

19

Diary
Bookcase Shopping in Jeddah
1989

WHEN the Salman Rushdie affair broke, the first thing I thought of was the day we tried to buy a bookcase in Jeddah. Jeddah is Saudi Arabia's most sophisticated, cosmopolitan city. Compared to the capital, Riyadh, it is liberal and lively. It is also of course very rich. Its shopping malls, with their icy air-conditioning, are temples of marble and glass, of lush greenery and tinkling fountains. They are something like the Muslim vision of Paradise; only the houris are missing. You can buy a fox fur, if you like, or a portrait of King Fahd, or an American-style donut; a king-size sofa with a stereo built in, if that takes your fancy. But you couldn't, in 1983, find a bookcase anywhere. No call for them.

When I first went to Jeddah I thought I had arrived in some ultimate abomination: the Bookless City. The supermarkets had racks of newspapers and magazines in various languages, and sometimes a little stack of doctor-nurse romances. There were things called bookshops, but they sold stationery. Of course, there was the book, the Holy Quran. The shelves that contained it had an untouched air, and the big volumes in the stiff cheap-looking bindings put me in mind of the sets of children's encyclopedias once found in the homes of the aspiring classes. The censors were active, but it was images, not words, that they seemed concerned about. The newspapers from America and Europe came with sections blacked out with broad felt-tip pens. But it was the photographs and not columns of type that were mutilated. It was Joan Collins's bosom, Zola Budd's legs.

Saudi Arabia is a video culture. Housewives whose mothers sat in tents spend the days in their urban apartment blocks watching Egyptian soap operas on TV. Students at the university would not buy books, their European teachers said: it was necessary for a department to buy enough copies of the standard texts, and place them in the library. My closest Muslim friend, a well-travelled and articulate woman, had a degree in English from a college in Pakistan. She mentioned one day that since her marriage, three years previously, she had read only one book.

During my four years in the Kingdom the supply of books began to improve. It was possible to buy a limited selection of paperbacks. People going out on vacation would be given a list of books to bring back – but they would have to get their purchases through the Saudi customs. Some governments publish lists of prohibited books, but if the Saudis had an Index I never saw it: it was only rumour that told you what had most recently given offence, and your fortunes might depend on how pious or touchy was the customs officer who turned out your cases. We believed that the customs men could not read English; that if they could, they wouldn't; that a book would be judged by its cover. My copy of Robert Lacey's monumental work *The Kingdom* travelled safely inside the dust-jacket of Vincent Cronin's *Louis and Antoinette*. Perhaps it was not the wisest choice, since Saudi Arabia has a few things in common with the Ancien Régime: but I was confident that the customs men wouldn't see the connection.

However, it soon became clear that the censorship was interested in words after all. The word 'pork', for instance. The censorship had its catering corps. It was someone's duty to go through consignments of imported food and check out such items as dehydrated sauce mixes, in case they had recipes on the back; and then to strike out that dreadful word wherever it appeared. After a time I realised that far from being unimportant in this society, as I had thought at first, words were in fact the most important thing of all. You cannot abolish the concept of pork from the world, but if you are assiduous you can unsay the word; if your felt tips are busy enough, and numerous enough, you can take away its name and thus gradually take away its substance, leaving it a queasy, nameless concept washing around in the minds of unbelievers, a meat which will gradually lose its existence because there is no way to talk about it.

In the holy city of Qom, it is said, the Iranians have a Quran with pages two metres square, each vellum sheet illuminated by hand. The Saudis would despise such a display; they would think it a piece of showing-off, the kind of thing that Shi'ites go in for. They favour contests at which the Quran is recited, with much public fanfare and the award of large cash prizes. I learned that the Holy Quran had little to do with the book on the shelves of the stationery stores. It was a living book, and its very language was sacred. Its verses were charged with power; they could heal the sick. Each word was a little fighter in a daily war.

Okaz, Jeddah's Arabic daily, carried in March 1986 a doom-laden, prescient column about the power of words. 'The war of words,' the writer said, 'is more harmful than World War Two. Words are forcing the world to World War Three. Words – written in newspapers, magazines, books, uttered on radio and television – are tools to massacre the souls of people.'

The world conspiracy against Islam of which Tehran now speaks is not the fantasy of one elderly paranoiac: in the Kingdom it was a fantasy purveyed as fact to the whole nation. Talented young Arabs, the newspapers alleged, went to Europe to study, and by their abilities excited the envy of their hosts, who would quickly set about ruining them by addicting them to drugs and introducing them to prostitutes. In Marks & Spencer's London stores, specially trained agents of Zionism lurk, ready to pounce on Arab shoppers, accuse them of shoplifting, throw them into jail and publicise their disgrace worldwide through Reuters and UP.

In November 1986 the *Saudi Gazette* reported a pronouncement by 'the General Presidency of the Departments of Religious Researchers, Ruling, Call and Guidance', warning against certain Italian floor tiles that had been imported into the Kingdom. These tiles were aimed at 'purposefully offending the sentiments of Muslims'. Hidden away in their swirl of pattern – not obvious at a casual glance, but evident on close inspection – were the words 'Allah' and 'Mohammed'. Or so the authorities said. The eye of faith is formidably sharp. If a floor tile can offend Islam, what chance has a novel?

The Saudi response to *The Satanic Verses* has been low-key; the ayatollah, who refers contemptuously to their faith as 'American Islam', has stolen their thunder. But it is not difficult to imagine the depth of outrage. The first popular reaction in the West to the death threat was, I think, amazement, tinged by what came near to a disbelieving hilarity: 'But it's only a novel.' We could not believe that people would riot about a story.

Novelists have various tricks for concealing what they are about. If they want to use a real person as a character they can, if competent, cover their tracks well enough to avoid being sued for libel. If critics call their work 'brutal' or 'offensive' they can smirk and say that they were spinning a metaphor, forging a conceit, creating an allegory. They can, like Salman Rushdie, allow their characters to dream. Writers no longer talk about their muse, but they are willing to talk about how their characters take over, about how the author himself is a minor part of the process, carried along on some irresistible creative tide. It is all part of the mystique; authors enjoy it. In the West, it does not matter whether they slide away from the implications of their work in this way.

Elsewhere, of course – in the Eastern Bloc or in South Africa – a novel is taken perfectly seriously as a vehicle for ideas. Its writer is forced to stand behind the points he makes, and is given no particular privilege. The censor will peel the novel's defences away and say, so this is what you really meant; and penalise and punish the author accordingly. But elsewhere the censor may not bother to strip away the conventions; he may not even recognise that they exist. Art for art's sake will mean nothing to him. *The Satanic Verses* may be a great work of art, the pattern on the floor tiles may have been aesthetically pleasing: but both are political acts. The defences of merit and of good intention that we are accustomed to erect around a persecuted work of art cannot help Rushdie's book, in countries where they are not recognised as defences. In Tehran, malice is understood. It is taken for granted. There is a worldwide conspiracy against Islam, and Rushdie is its 'mercenary'.

If his defence cannot be made in artistic terms, it must be made in political terms, but it is hard to feel pleased with the politicians. When the British government says that it understands that Muslims are offended by the book, it means it understands that offence has been taken. It is not near to understanding the nature of the offence. The prime minister says that great religions should be strong enough to withstand criticism, and her remark is alarming because it is so wide of the point. Unlike modern Christianity, Islam does not make a virtue of tolerance. In theory it accommodates the faith of Christians and Jews, the 'people of the book', but the Kingdom, at least, does not permit any form of worship other than the Islamic; projecting their own intolerance on the outside world, the faithful in Jeddah found it hard to imagine that in Britain their co-religionists could go freely to a mosque, and they only half-believed it. If you are in Britain, Islam appears an inward-looking and self-protective faith, but when you are in the East it appears vital, active and proselytising. Not long ago, the same could be said of Christianity. Unless we are prepared to think about our own history, enter into it a little, we cannot know what the Muslim writer is talking about when he speaks of 'spiritual torment and torture'. The silly and the secular do not understand the God-driven. Fundamentalists look at our cheerful modern notion of live-and-let-live, and find it immoral and incomprehensible.

In the first few days after Iran issued the death threat, the support for Salman Rushdie was heartening and unanimous. But we are so used to intellectual consensus and compromise that when we meet an intransigent opponent, with whom no meeting of minds seems possible, we immediately doubt our own case and our own values: politeness may be the ruin of the West. The backtracking has been an unpleasant spectacle. It was unpleasant to hear a young Tory MP say recently that 'two or three' of his friends had told him that the book was 'very second-rate', and announce that since Rushdie had made so much money he should pay for his own police guard: we do not expect our legislators to be able to read, but we do expect them to be able to distinguish between a private man's private difficulty and a matter of vital public interest. And just as unpleasant is the defection of those who now cast doubt on Rushdie's integrity, or urge the withdrawal of the book. Perhaps it is understandable that the authors of children's books and light social comedies should decline to defend *The Satanic Verses*. Their freedom of expression is not at issue.

Back in Jeddah, the same woman who had read only one book since her marriage explained one day with great eloquence the consolations of living among believers, in a solidly Muslim society – the feeling of security for the faithful, the freedom from the constant bombardment by alien values. Muslims in Britain live under such bombardment, and they have to accept it and survive as best they can. But their faith still has its consolations, and some good would come of this sorry business if the spokesmen of the Muslim community, and the enlightened and educated Muslims who must be offended by Iran's decrees, could explain to a sceptical and ignorant Britain what these consolations are.

Hilary Mantel 36 Sandringham Court, Burnham, Berkshire SL1 6JZ
Tel (06286) 65839

Mary - Kay -

Nicholas Spice left a message to say that an American university wants to reprint the Diary column I did — please would you tell him that's fine by me?

I have to get my new novel underway, so I'm not going to do much reviewing

for a while — but do keep in touch, won't you? Fludd is coming out in September from Viking, so proofs should be around in a few weeks.

I'm glad you liked this piece. The funniness book filled me with mirth because I grew up quite near Oldham, so I know all about it. Love,

Hilary.

Postcard from Hilary Mantel to
Mary-Kay Wilmers, 1989

29

Looking Back in Anger
John Osborne's Memoirs
1991

O NE OF THE more extraordinary revelations in *A Better Class of Person*, the first volume of John Osborne's memoirs, was the fact that the author was proposed as the leading man in the 1948 film *The Blue Lagoon*. The teenage Osborne by his own account had a hollow chest and acne, and a loincloth would not have shown these off to advantage; the opportunity to loll among the palms with Jean Simmons went to the Welsh actor Donald Houston. Houston was blond and wholesome, and had a long career, much of it in B-movies; it's interesting to think that John Osborne might have enjoyed it in his stead. Osborne as the fourth intern in *Doctor in the House*, alongside Dirk Bogarde, Kenneth More and Donald Sinden . . . Osborne as a Spartan, as a rugby fan, as Dr Watson . . . He would, you feel, have snarled a hole in the screen.

A *Better Class of Person* is written with the tautness and power of a well-organised novel. It is a ferociously sulky, rancorous book, remarkable for its account of a lower-middle-class childhood on the fringes of London, and for its vengeful portrait of a mother who had 'eyes that missed nothing and understood nothing'.

Osborne's father worked in an advertising agency. He was a semi-invalid for most of his son's youth; his mother was a barmaid – or, as she put it, 'a victualler's assistant, *if* you please'. They moved often, from one rented suburban house or flat to another. Until he was sent away to a third-rate boarding school, the boy had virtually no education; his mother preferred to keep him at home to go window-shopping with her, or to the cinema. These were the days of the double-feature, and he saw, he estimates, two hundred films a year. He had a crowd of relatives who were, in his view, spiteful, greedy, stupid and pathetic. They manifested 'a timid melancholy or dislike of joy, effort or courage . . . Disappointment was oxygen to them.'

It is an atmosphere in which effort is despised, and anyone who has the temerity to try to advance in life must bear the complacent smirking of those who predict that it will all end badly. His mother, Nellie Beatrice (so he calls her – the family called her Dolly), dominates his life and shapes the picture of himself which he gives to the reader. The whole book bears witness to the grown man's failure to separate himself emotionally from a woman he despises – from Nellie Beatrice with her flaking face powder and her Black Looks. The consequences of this failure are played out in the second volume: they are a disabling misogyny, a series of failed and painful relationships, a grim determination to spit in the world's eye.* He is not loveable, he knows; very well, he'll be hateful then.

It might, the reader thinks, have turned out quite differently. Throughout both books Osborne reproduces letters sent

---

* *Almost a Gentleman. An Autobiography: Vol. II 1955-66* by John Osborne (Faber, 1991).

to him by his mother and relatives. Uncle Jack writes to him: 'There is nothing to report, only I have lost the sight of one eye.' If the Osborne family had lived, say, in Lancashire instead of London, such a letter would have made Jack a local celebrity; a turn of phrase like that would be a family treasure. But Osborne's humour is aggressive, not black, not self-deprecating, not tolerant; it makes the world a harder place. The letters make the memoirs easier for the reader, however: one looks forward to them. In the days of heady fame – of Broadway and the Royal Court, of pursuit by the press, of 'love-nests' and 'hideaways' and CND celebrity rallies – the letters still wing their way. 'Sid is upstairs in Bed. He had all his bottom teeth out on Wednesday.'

How did our hero escape Nellie Beatrice, Sid and the rest? He had a footling journalist career on *Gas World* – and, briefly, on *Nursery World*. Primed by his success at the Gaycroft School of Music, Dancing, Speech, Elocution and Drama, he tried the theatre. Talent seems to have been less important than the ability to live on almost nothing and endure insults from management and patrons. Jobs in rep were advertised in terms like these: 'No fancy salaries, no queer folk.' Queer folk appear on almost every page of both volumes of memoirs, and Osborne is at pains to point out – many, many times – that he has no homosexual proclivities. He'd rather a doss-house than a warm sofa where his timid virtue might be imperilled; and indeed many of his theatrical lodgings didn't rise much above the dosshouse level.

He toured the provinces in melodramas about 'middle-class girls compromised in their cami-knickers' and in 'northern comedies' where he failed to see the joke. Between jobs, he learned to subsist on evaporated milk and boiled nettles. His Hamlet was a 'leering milk rounds man'; he featured in a production of *Aladdin* so bad that the child amateurs who formed the chorus were abducted from the theatre by their furious parents, so that the 'Big Spectacular' had to be cancelled. His first play got its world première in Huddersfield, and lasted for a week.

The first volume left Osborne in 1956, at the point where – in 17 days – he had completed *Look Back in Anger*. George Devine, the first artistic director of the English Stage Company, arrives in his life (in a rowing boat) and makes him 'preposterously famous'. Osborne vehemently denies claims that the play was first entitled 'On the Pier at Morecambe', but a photographed page of his notebook shows that several titles were contemplated. They include 'Angry Man', 'Man in a Rage' and 'Close the Cage Door behind You'. Only one strikes you as false to its begetter: 'Farewell to Anger'.

For in this second volume, it's hello to some more. Fame makes Osborne savager than ever. What is wonderful is how the years have deepened the ire, how memory has mauled his wounds so that they open again before the reader's eyes. When he was a boy, a hospital messed up an appendix operation, leaving him with a hole in his side; they gave him a special pencil with which he could cauterise the wound and help it to heal. If you could wish the playwright one thing, it would be a styptic pencil for his psyche. Self-mutilation is, however, a riveting spectacle.

On the cover of *Almost a Gentleman* Osborne wears a miscellanea of camp togs, and an expression at once quizzical, combative and prissy. As with the first volume, frail jokes and bad puns decorate the text. We know the writer is on form by page 20, when we read of 'Binkie Beaumont, most powerful of the unacceptable faeces of theatrical capitalism'. There is some repetition: the comedian Max Miller is once again 'a god . . . a saloon-bar Priapus', and various people are 'a sphinx', or, in the case of his second wife, Mary Ure, 'not a sphinx'. The spite, though, comes up new and fresh.

When *Look Back in Anger* opened at the Royal Court, the warmest reaction was Philip Hope-Wallace's 'spinsterly condescension' – Osborne has always at his command the exact, skewering phrase – but then the Sunday papers came out. Ken Tynan called it a 'minor miracle' and praised it in these peculiar terms: 'I doubt if I could love anyone who did not wish to see *Look Back in Anger*.' Some critics said: 'It calls out for the knife.' All these years on, Osborne will not take the point. '*Hamlet* is too long,' he says grandly.

Thereafter the hostility of his audiences fuelled his talent; so did rows with the Lord Chamberlain. The list of cuts required to *The Entertainer* has a strange poetry of its own: 'Page 30, alter "shagged" . . . page 43, omit "rogered" (twice) . . . Act III, page 21, omit "balls".'

If the balls were omitted, this book would be nothing. It is essentially a book of vitriolic gossip. It does not pretend to be a history of the Royal Court – which is just as well, or we'd never hear the end of the disputes about who said what to whom. (Did Lindsay Anderson really try to ban critics from the Royal Court? Lindsay Anderson doesn't think so.) It tells very little about how Osborne and his contemporaries went about freeing themselves from the constraints of the theatre as they found it; Brecht's influence barely merits a nod.

Indeed, the book tells us less about Osborne's work than about other people's reactions to it, and less about applause than condemnation. After the opening of his musical satire *The World of Paul Slickey*, the *New Statesman* said with restraint: 'It has almost every fault.' Playgoers, less circumspect, chased him up Charing Cross Road.

His attitude to his audience is always uncompromising: 'Their pleasure inflames my prejudice, their indifference stirs my rage.' In hindsight, Osborne takes a gloating pleasure in trashing his best efforts. Yes, there was a theatrical revolution – the barricades manned by lecherous petty-minded egotists. Yes, the Angry Young Men were political radicals. But this radicalism, he tells us now, was a gigantic self-deceit. They were duped by traitorous fanatics. When, the reader wonders, did Osborne become so discerning? When did he become able to see the true nature of things? It is only the development of some cooler qualities that gives a point to retrospection: since he is as angry as ever, is he any more likely to be right now than he was then? There is no particular reason, of course, why people who write their lives should be fair to themselves or other people. It is more diverting if they aren't. But when revenge seems the major motive for writing, diversion soon becomes mixed with disgust.

His portraits of colleagues and contemporaries are bilious. Tony Richardson's 'duplicity was so sinewy and downright that he was able to deceive friends and adversaries effortlessly'. Freddie Ayer had an 'organ-grinder's monkey's brain'. Olivier gets off comparatively lightly: he is chronically adulterous and manipulative, but so is everyone else Osborne knows. At one point Olivier sings, to the tune of 'John Peel', a merry song about buggery.

Women come off worse: Vanessa Redgrave, for example, 'Big Van' with her incontinent Yorkshire terrier. 'Loyal' is often the best adjective he can find for a woman; it is a trait more often valued in dogs. He may despise the women who cross his path, but doesn't refuse them. George Devine, who was such an influence on his career, would 'pull on his pipe lingeringly at the sight of a pretty girl'; Osborne was also a pipe-man. Back in his Gaycroft School days he had run away from a fiancée who worked in a building society – run away from the £12 Bravingtons engagement ring, and the Saturday promenade to look at furniture in the High Street. He married Pamela Lane, who he met in rep in Bridgwater, but their work took them to different parts of the country, and the relationship expired from lack of interest.

His next wife was Mary Ure, who played Alison in *Look Back in Anger*; even in his description of the wedding ceremony, Osborne is sneering at the bride. She is accused of having a large family, and of having bought a going-away outfit which would 'photograph pretty disastrously in the departure lounge'. When once again it is time to 'pump out the blocked drain of matrimony' he moves on, via mistresses, to Penelope Gilliatt. 'Why do you keep *marrying* these women?' the agent Peggy Ramsay asked him. 'I'm sure they can't possibly want to marry you.'

It is not long before moaning and sneering again dominate the text. Gilliatt is accused of nothing much worse than 'dumb pedantry', self-importance, spending too little time on her husband and too much on her *Observer* film column –

and of not knowing how a writer works because she is not a proper writer herself. The actress Jill Bennett arrives on the scene. Osborne doesn't like her much – but why should that impede his career as what he likes to call a 'cocksman'?

Here the reader's mind may go back to *A Better Class of Person*. Early in his acting career Osborne worked with Lynne Reid Banks, who went on to write *The L-Shaped Room*. Pronouncing her 'unspeakable', he saved up his hatred until 'some time later at an improbably posh party in London I offered her a sandwich. I had taken some trouble to insert among the smoked salmon and cream cheese . . . a used French letter. The unbelieving repulsion on her face . . . was fixed for ever for me.' An unbelieving repulsion steals over the reader too, who begins to wonder whether Osborne is – and one must phrase this delicately – faintly deranged. Through this new book, the question is constantly posed, and for some people it will answer itself when Osborne in a 'fast forward' takes us to 7 October 1990, the day after Jill Bennett's death. Falling upon her newspaper obituaries, shredding them line by line, he denounces 'this whole rotting body of lies and invention which was her crabbed little life'. He tells us that she 'was a woman so demoniacally possessed by Avarice that she died of it', and quotes Tony Richardson's judgment that she was 'the worst actress in England'.

At this point, the pious reader may wish to pray, the queasy reader vomit, the prudent reviewer consult the libel laws. Adjectives stored up – 'fascinating' perhaps, or 'scurrilous' – don't seem worth using. It no longer seems possible to make a literary judgment on this second instalment of Osborne's life; the author forces from his reader the moral judgment which he has worked so hard to elicit.

Harold Hobson, writing about him in the Sunday Times at the peak of his fame, said: 'Self-loathing appears to be the driving force of his art. He should control it; he is not as bad as he thinks he is.' I don't know about that.

Cover: Madonna on her last world tour.
Hilary Mantel, who writes about ~~her~~ Madonna
in this issue, ~~doesn't like her very~~ compares
her to Mike Tyson — a ~~remark~~ insight which Madonna
~~which~~ some of the ~~feminists~~ women written about in this issue
might quite like. Her former boyfriend would
Warren ~~Beatty~~ Beatty has spoken of her hate her for
as 'someone' who doesn't want to live it①
off-camera'. Much of the present issue is
taken up with ~~questions~~ of gender or of representation ~~of this kind~~
~~that have to do with aggression~~ with
whether things happen in life as well as
texts
in ~~words~~ or on television① '1991,' W.J.T.
Mitchell writes, 'was a year of war & publicity
— not just the publicising or representing of
war, but the waging of war by means
of publicity and representation.'
~~Later in the issue Elaine Showalter~~
~~Later~~ in the issue / Elaine Showalter
writes about

Draft caption by Mary-Kay Wilmers for a
(rejected) cover for the 23 April 1992 issue
of the 'LRB'.

Plain Girl's Revenge Made Flesh
In Bed with Madonna
1992

C HRISTOPHER ANDERSEN'S book begins, as it should, with the prodigal, the violent, the gross.* But what do you expect? Madonna's wedding was different from other people's. The plans were made in secrecy, and backed by armed force. 'Even the caterer . . . was kept in the dark until the last minute.' You also, you may protest, have been to weddings where the caterer has seemed to be taken by surprise. But we are not talking here about a cock-up with the vol-au-vents. We are talking about something on the lines of Belshazzar's feast: but more lavish, and more portentous.

When Madonna married the misanthropic actor Sean Penn, 'reporters were stopped at the kerb by a guard armed with a .357 magnum handgun . . . an army of journalists descended on 6970 Wildlife Road, the palatial $6.5 million cliff-top home of property developer and Penn family friend Dan Unger. Armed security guards scanned the horizon with infrared binoculars.' Overhead, press helicopters competed with the ocean's roar. Inside the steel gates, sushi and champagne were served – sometimes by journalists impersonating waiters. No writing appeared on the wall. Instead, Penn ran

---

* *Madonna Unauthorised* by Christopher Andersen (Joseph, 1991).

down to the beach, and scrawled his message to the world in twenty-foot letters in the sand: FUCK OFF. Madonna wore a ten-foot train and a bowler hat. They exchanged vows on the brink of a cliff: 'Prophetically,' says the author. He is not a man to let a symbol give him the slip.

The unblushing bride was born in 1958. Her mother, also called Madonna, was a French-Canadian X-ray technician; her father, the son of Italian immigrants, was an engineer. The family was large but affluent, and Madonna grew up in pleasant suburbs: the blue-collar upbringing she claims for herself is one of her inventions, it seems. Andersen makes Madonna's early years sound like those of St Thérèse of Lisieux. Surely Catholic childhood in 1960s America was not quite so stifling and bizarre? We can be sure it featured crucifixes and rosary beads, all the jolly props which Madonna would later find so useful, but when the author quotes Madonna on her formative influences, he doesn't try to discriminate between what she thought then and what she says now. 'Crucifixes are sexy; there's a naked man on them.' If Madonna went to a postmortem, would she find the corpse sexy too?

Is there any point in trying to write about Madonna's life in the conventional way? One thing everybody knows about the woman is that she has invented herself: it is a commonplace. When constant revisionism and reinvention is under way, what does it profit a biographer to drag the weary 'facts' before us? Something sterner is required: whole blank pages, paragraphs of exclamation marks. Andersen's mode is conventional, his style good enough for his subject matter and appropriate to it. His technique, though, is sneakier than at first appears. You may grow infuriated by what seems an un-critical, gormless narrative: but if you stop reading for five minutes and rehearse what you have learned, you realise that anything you now know about Madonna is entirely to her dis-credit. Yet this is as it should be. Didn't the girl herself, in high school, ask her friends to call her 'Mudd'?

Still, let's truffle with Andersen on his dogged path. When Madonna was five years old, her mother died of cancer, and her father married again. Cue self-examination on the super-star's part: 'Like all young girls I was in love with my father, and I didn't want to lose him. I lost my mother but then I was the mother; my father was mine.' Andersen refers us – as he often must – to the film *In Bed with Madonna*, in which his sub-ject explains how she would often crawl into bed with her father. 'I fell right to sleep after he fucked me.' Inane giggle. 'Just kidding.' The pause is fractional, not long enough for a reaction from the viewer. The girl knows when she's gone too far. At the age of six or so she would say to Papa: 'If you ever die, I'm going to get buried in the casket with you.' This Donne-ish sentiment Tony Ciccone found 'really disgusting'. Poor man! His disgust threshold will have to rise. When he reaches 59 his daughter will drag him onto a stage to sing 'Happy Birthday', her navel exposed and a pattern of laces, like evil stitching, covering her private parts.

The pages concerning Madonna's childhood are far more interesting than those which follow: but is this not often the case with biography? The relation of mature achievement, in any contemporary life, becomes a dreary procession of dates and places and figures; even the potential excitements of a life like Madonna's seem to melt away under scrutiny –

another day, another million dollars. *Madonna Unauthorised* is full of names of people who were forgotten by the time they reached the page, or which belong to people who were never more than a footnote in the subject's great narrative. And most people are a footnote to Madonna, who is no nurturer of other people's reputations. A great many people who have passed through her life have been famous for 15 seconds; or less, if she could manage it.

It would be good to feel human while you read her life; it would be good to feel pity where pity's due. But you are prevented. Here is Madonna on her mother's death and its implications:

> It was then that I said, okay, I don't need anybody. No one's going to break my heart again. I'm not going to need anybody. I can stand on my own and be my own person and not belong to anyone.

Each line of this sounds like a trawl for a song title: sounds like some awful, thumping, monotonous chart-topper.

Until she was 12, Andersen tells us, Madonna wanted to be a nun; and he tells us in a way that makes it clear that he expects us to throw up our hands and say 'Lawdie me!' In fact, most intelligent Catholic girls go through a phase in which they would rather be like Mother than like mother: but then their eyes are opened to wider possibilities. (Besides that, Madonna naturally feels that 'nuns are very sexy.') One feels that Madonna's onstage antics with Romish paraphernalia have never brought her quite the odium she craves. Perhaps we all recognise that the faith lends itself readily to vaudeville productions. Catholic vaudeville is divisible: Waugh and

Greene purveyed the intellectual version, and Madonna has done it for simple souls.

In her early teens, by Andersen's account, Madonna gives up on Thérèse of Lisieux and turns into a Tyson. When she chases a boy, it's no figure of speech. 'At one point she ripped off her blazer and blouse and began pursuing a boy named Tommy around the playground.' Still, sex and religion are very much confused, as she tries to fathom the still unfathomable riddle of her gender. 'You know how religion is . . . Guys get to do everything. They get to be altar boys . . . They get to pee standing up.' Determined to do something about this Vatican-sponsored inequity, Madonna 'experimented with ways to urinate without sitting down'. Andersen does not go into much detail, or tell us what success she had. But he describes with diligence her early sexual relationships with boys and girls: in one case, a beau 'asked her if she wanted to take a walk through Samuel A. Howlett Municipal Park'. And she did, it seems; she did not deem it too exciting. One of her swains reports: 'I realised I'd actually kissed a girl, though in my case it happened to be Madonna.' However, when party-going, 'she guarded her virginity by sometimes wearing a purple turtleneck leotard.' There is a point where the reader loses interest in Madonna, and becomes ambitious only to meet the man who can paint such a word-picture.

There is nothing else in Andersen's book that comes near to the pleasure he gives the reader in these early pages. The account of Madonna's defloration is an anti-climax in every way. Notoriously, she has described the loss of her virginity as a 'career move', which one took to mean that she had preserved her hymen until she met someone prepared to pay to shred it. But if Andersen is to be believed – and why not? – the fateful evening began at Knapp's Dairy Bar, and Madonna yielded to the caresses of a 17-year-old schoolboy who had trouble with her bra strap; a veil is drawn over what he made of the rest of her. He is quoted as saying: 'I had this great urge to laugh, but Madonna was pretty methodical about it.'

Madonna was now missing Sunday Mass in favour of trysts at Dunkin' Donuts. Soon, too, she would meet the gaiety, in the shape of a dance teacher, who took her to museums, concerts, art galleries, and also to places where 'she felt strangely at home as the only female among hundreds of writhing men.' Andersen may mean they were dancing, but perhaps it depends at what point in the evening she arrived. Madonna has a prurient fascination with male homosexual activity. The film *In Bed with Madonna* (the film, if you need to know, of her 'Blonde Ambition' tour) shows how she likes to encourage it amongst her friends and co-workers. One of her other biographers, Douglas Thompson, quotes her as saying that she thinks of homosexual men as her 'alter ego'. This is interesting, but Andersen does not pursue it. He is more concerned at this stage to describe her intellectual development. She had decided to grow the hair on her legs, he tells us, believing that this indicated a bohemian cast of mind. She won a dance scholarship to the University of Michigan: 'Keeping herself to herself, Madonna devoured the dark poetry of Sylvia Plath and Anne Sexton.'

An axe-murderer couldn't carve up the girl more efficiently. But is it a case of diminished responsibility? One would like to think Andersen is of sound mind, that he writes with premeditation and intends the consequences – but then again, who wants to brand a family man a killer? The blurb tells us that the author 'lives in Connecticut with his wife and two daughters'. He has previously written 'highly praised' works on Katharine Hepburn and Jane Fonda. This does not seem adequate preparation. Perhaps life's ambiguity has passed him by, or he has come by praise too cheaply?

So: Madonna went to New York. Her dance teacher persuaded her she needed the larger stage, and so she took herself off in search of fame, living in slums and foraging in dustbins for her food. Andersen brings tears to the eyes with his account of her early struggles, but does not feel for her so much that he suppresses the verdicts of her various teachers and colleagues. No one seems to have liked Madonna, or seen anything in her, or thought she had much talent. But – unaccountably – she was taken up by two French music producers, who spirited her off to Paris in the hope of turning her into a disco queen. But Madonna wanted to be a punk: so when they gave her a car, a maid, a secretary and a voice coach, she sulked and sulked until she found herself back in New York.

And then . . . but come now, if we go at this pace we'll be here all day. When Madonna got back to New York she joined a band. There was a female vocalist who performed in her underwear. Madonna got her sacked, and took her place. From there she made the progress of which we are all aware. The received wisdom is that even if you have talent, you still need luck; even if you're lucky, without talent you'll be found out. Madonna shows that energy can be a substitute for talent; and she has made her own luck. She is thorough: 'she asked me,' says one of her friends, 'to teach her how to spit.' And spit and spit she did, over and over, till she spat like a veteran. Someone else taught her how to smoke. From Michael Jackson she learned how to grab her crotch. Are these not accomplishments, hard-won for a girl from a nice family? So often Andersen seems to miss the point. He will, persistently, describe Madonna as a transcendent beauty, when, as everyone can see, she's the plain girl's revenge made flesh. Madonna has cultivated ardently – apparently without humour or irony – her identification with Monroe: he mentions that she is said to have purchased an adjacent crypt, so that their dust may mingle, but he does not insist on this as fact.

If he recognises pastiche, he never says so. If he identifies id-in-boots, he doesn't let on. His book has photographs, but he is almost perversely unable to set down, in words, what Madonna is like. And the truth is that three hundred pages, however well composed, could not convey what three minutes of *In Bed with Madonna* make explicit. Our heroine is charmless, foul-mouthed, will admit the camera and the sound-recordist everywhere, except into a business meeting. We know that in this film we are seeing the real Madonna – for we know from her other films that she cannot act. And also, that she sees no need to: for she has tapped, somehow, into a rich deep vein of fantasy and cash, and all she needs to do is mine it. A proper inquiry might be instituted into what Madonna means: perhaps a joint inquiry, to look into the question of Michael Jackson too, for they seem of a kind. Their appeal is to children ten or twelve years old, too young to know who or what they are, aware of sex as a waiting, empty arena, desperate perhaps to burrow back into a childhood of fantasy and irresponsibility. Madonna has always wanted to be black, if we are to believe Andersen, and she looks like a female impersonator. Michael has transformed himself from a black man into a white-ish female child. They have dined together ('vegetarians are paler,' Madonna says) and appeared together at award ceremonies. But it seems they are locked in competition, about who has the more formidable publicity machine.

The most interesting moment of *In Bed with Madonna* shows the star before a mirror, her make-up lady hovering at her shoulder. Face white, blank, hairpiece cosied on her skull like the top of a cottage loaf, she waits for experience to be layered over the impersonation of innocence; she could, you think, become anything at all. Madonna says: 'I will be a symbol of something . . . Like Marilyn Monroe stands for something. It's not always something you can put a name on, but she became an adjective.' For anyone who wishes to become an adjective, Madonna is an inspiration. On stage, her little muscly body twists itself in a parody of sensuality: her mini-soutane rides hip-high, her voice wavers on and off-key; up and down she dips, over the supine body of a spreadeagled semi-man. It all happens too fast for words, and it repels or excites at too deep a level for any writer who has offered his services so far. Madonna is not a subject for easy writing. She is a commentary on something, but God knows on what. Andersen doesn't, that's for sure.

IAN HAMILTON ON DAMON RUNYON
IAN HACKING BITES BRYAN APPLEYARD

London Review
OF BOOKS

(USPS 709–250)

VOLUME 14 NUMBER 10   28 MAY 1992   £1.95   US & CANADA $2.95

Hilary Mantel:
Théroigne
de Méricourt

'LRB' cover, 28 May 1992

Rescued by Marat
On Théroigne de Méricourt
1992

I N 1817, at the asylum of La Salpêtrière in Paris, a long-term inhabitant died of pneumonia. Her malnourished, oedematous body was taken away for autopsy. For some years before her death she had been intractably and violently psychotic. She had crawled on the floor like an animal, eaten straw. She stripped off her clothes in freezing weather, and did not mind (her keepers noted) if men saw her naked. She threw icy water on her bedding and her person, and on the floor of her cell.

Her madness was not without eloquence. Until the last years of dementia, she talked all the time. She denounced her keepers as royalists, and spoke of decrees and government measures, addressing her words to the Committee of Public Safety. But the great committee was long since disbanded, its members guillotined or in exile. For Théroigne time had stopped sometime in 1793. Trapped in the rat-infested cell that was her last home, she spoke always of liberty.

The woman whom the press called Théroigne de Méricourt was born Anne-Josèphe Terwagne, in the village of Marcourt, not far from Liège. She was therefore not a Frenchwoman, but a subject of the emperor of Austria. Her family were of peasant stock, but comfortably-off. The train of disasters in her life began when she was five years old, with her mother's death. She and her two younger brothers were parcelled out to relatives. (About the same time, in Arras, four motherless children called Robespierre were being bundled from one household to another.) Théroigne was taken in by an aunt, who appears to have treated her as a servant. She returned to her father, and got short shrift from his new wife; through her adolescence she trooped from one family to the next, often with her younger brothers in tow, always hopeful of being wanted, and doomed to disappointment.

The family drifted into money troubles, and its most vulnerable member slid sharply down the social scale, spending a year as a cowherd. After this, she secured a post as a governess, Elisabeth Roudinesco claims – though she goes on to tell us that at this stage Théroigne had not learned to write.[*] More likely, as her 1911 biographer Frank Hamel says, she earned her living as a seamstress. But then in 1778, when she was about 16, her luck changed. She met a Mme Colbert, who engaged her as a companion, arranged music lessons for her, and took her around Europe.

Théroigne had considerable musical talent. She was a pretty young woman, petite, with blue eyes and chestnut hair, and a sharp intelligence to make up for her lack of formal education. She had, in fact, all the qualifications for a romantic heroine, or romantic victim. Accordingly, four years after her stroke of luck, there came along a fateful Englishman. Something between an elopement and an abduction occurred. The

---

[*] *Théroigne de Méricourt: A Melancholic Woman during the French Revolution* by Elisabeth Roudinesco, translated by Martin Thom (Verso, 1991).

cad took her to his estate, procrastinated about the marriage he had promised; then they flitted back to Paris, where between them they ran through his money. 'Yet she knew neither carnal passion nor genuine affection,' Roudinesco sighs. After that she seems to have taken up with a number of men, including an elderly marquis who gave her an annuity. Roudinesco describes her as 'uneasily suspended between literary bohemianism, polite society and moral degradation'.

Elisabeth Roudinesco (a pupil of Lacan and a historian of psychoanalysis) is concerned not just with Théroigne's life history but with revolutionary feminism; with Théroigne's madness and what it means, and with how historians have treated this baffling and intriguing woman. Her book is intelligent, original and deeply felt, but it is written, or perhaps translated, in a strained and artificial idiom which makes Théroigne's story sound even more bizarre than it really is. Throughout the book, errors and inconsistencies pass without editorial intervention; the index is waste paper. But however badly you tell Théroigne's story, you cannot take away its fascination. The cowherd became an opera singer. The opera singer became a rabble-rouser. The rabble-rouser became a madwoman. It is inevitable that the poor, starved body on the postmortem table should have become a battleground for theorists. No doubt it is useless to complain that the subject's humanity has slipped away. Even her contemporaries were quick to turn Théroigne into a symbol.

Théroigne had a daughter; we do not know her date of birth or the name of her father, but we know that she died in 1788. Théroigne also contracted syphilis. In the light of her later illness one would like to hear more about this, but perhaps it is as well that we don't hear more from this author; it is impossible, for several reasons, that a surgeon should have told Théroigne that 'the virus had entered her bone marrow.' Medical matters are not Roudinesco's strong point; it is only in legend that the murdered Marat was still bleeding on the day of his funeral.

Théroigne was restless and ambitious; she wanted to make a professional career as a musician, so she left her old marquis and went in pursuit of success. She crops up in London, Naples, Genoa, Rome; we can follow her, just about, by a paper trail of pawn tickets and letters and legal agreements. In the spring of 1789 she took lodgings in Versailles, and attended every day the debates of the newly convened Assembly.

On the eve of the revolution, women did not regard themselves as an interest group. Throughout the century poor women had taken to the streets in times of shortages and high prices. But few people in 1789 thought that women should be allowed to vote – or indeed, that all men should be allowed to vote. Suffrage was dependent on economic status, and few women had enough of that. Besides, as Roudinesco shows, few Enlightenment thinkers could conceive of any role for women beyond the domestic. There were exceptions, like the Marquis de Condorcet, who believed that either no human beings had natural rights, or all had the same rights. But the biology-is-destiny school of thought had the upper hand: women were weak, irrational, subject to cyclical indisposition, unfitted by providence for any part in the political process. The Declaration of the Rights of Man did not extend to women; it was enough if their fathers and brothers and husbands had rights. Théroigne called this attitude 'supremely unjust'.

At some stage Théroigne acquired not only the language of political discourse, but also the famous riding habit – white, black or blood red – in which she sweeps through the imagination of her contemporaries and of romantic historians; at some stage, this neglected, abused little girl puts on her plumed hat and picks up her pistols. What was she then – a feminist pioneer, a street-fighting woman? Any close account of her life is a process of debunking. Though she haunted the Palais-Royal in Paris, she was perhaps not present on 12 July, when the crowd turned into a mob; she was not present two days later, when the Bastille fell. She did not lead the women of Paris on their October march to Versailles, to bring back the royal family, 'the baker, the baker's wife, and the baker's little apprentice'. What she did do was to make herself pleasant to various up-and-coming deputies and journalists, to attend little discussion groups; to be seen, once or twice, on the streets when notable events were occurring. Her greatest moment came when she delivered a speech to the men of the Cordeliers Club, and was enthusiastically applauded. But would the left-wing club make her a member? Ah, well: that was another matter.

Elisabeth Roudinesco has a number of interesting things to say about the nascent political power of women, but she tends to make simple ideas sound very complicated; Olwen Hufton, in her study of women and citizenship, is a model of clarity.[†] Hufton has produced a vigorous, well-argued, level-

---

[†] *Women and the Limits of Citizenship in the French Revolution* by Olwen Hufton (Toronto, 1992).

headed book, written with a nicely sardonic wit. She handles theoretical issues with ease, makes them concrete; Roudinesco makes them vaporous. Théroigne is peripheral to Hufton's narrative; her interest is in more ordinary women, women who (by and large) have neither faces nor names, but who, as the revolution progressed, arrogated to themselves an increasing share of informal power. But did the revolution advance women's rights, or retard them? Both these authors show how feminism and progressive politics came adrift from each other. Urban women rioters did not want the vote, but price controls on bread, candles, soap. Their interests and those of peasant women did not coincide. And rural women, as their men complained, clung to their priests: to their madonnas and village virgins, to the hope of a better life after this.

As Théroigne became better known, she became the target of a ruthless campaign in the royalist press. She had tried to keep herself to herself – Roudinesco, who presumes to go to bed with her subject, assures us that 'it was not hard for Anne-Josèphe to renounce the pleasures of the flesh, for she had never known them.' But inevitably, stories about her background leaked out. A certain deputy had the unfortunate surname of Populus. The satirical right-wing news-sheets nominated him as Théroigne's lover, thus implying that she was mistress to the people, a very busy prostitute. She was depicted as having given birth in the chamber of the Assembly – her labour brought on by excitement at one of Robespierre's speeches.

In the imagination of the era – and of later eras, too – a public man is one thing; a public woman quite another. A woman who leaves hearth and home for the wider world is a streetwalker. She is a locus of disease; she victimises men, infects them. A number of historians have described the revolution as a spreading infection, a disease running out of control. Roudinesco shows us the painful metaphorical weight the woman revolutionary had to bear. She tends, however, to write as if Théroigne had a harder time than her female contemporaries. In fact, sexual slur and innuendo was the established, pre-revolutionary weapon of anonymous but aristocratic pamphleteers, who portrayed Marie-Antoinette as a predatory lesbian. During the revolution, the journalist Hébert would portray the ferociously respectable Manon Roland as a slut, and Antoinette as a seducer of her own pre-adolescent son. Any woman who put her nose above the parapet received the same treatment. Right-wing journalists like Suleau, one of Théroigne's persecutors, employed language offensive to a 20th-century ear. Did people in fact believe what was written in the press? Were they blind to satire and exaggeration and sheer silliness? Roudinesco writes as if the left-wing press of 1790 was quite different from the royalist press – as if it was sober and responsible, and employed legions of fact-checkers. But abuse was in the air. The press was free for the first time. The fine art of vituperation was flourishing, on every side. There was no divide between the personal and the political. Théroigne's friend Camille Desmoulins once wrote a theatre review so ruinous to business that the leading man called him out.

The men who traded insults had means of settling their disputes: rapiers and writs. Théroigne had no platform from which to reply. Towards the end of 1790, heartsick and in debt, she left Paris. She wanted to see her family – she was always loyal to them, despite their treatment of her. Unfortunately, her reputation as a political activist followed her. Three émigré officers kidnapped her from a rural inn. One of them attempted to rape her. She was handed over to the Austrians, and imprisoned in the Tyrol, in the formidable fortress of Kufstein.

Her captors had swallowed her legend. They did not ill-treat her physically, but they put her under a great deal of mental pressure. They believed that she was on intimate terms with the men who were now shaping events in Paris. They had amassed a formidable amount of documentation about her – some of which has misled Elisabeth Roudinesco. But it soon became clear that while Théroigne was a singular and eloquent woman, a great enthusiast for revolution, her actual influence had been very limited; she had no particular knowledge of the inner workings of the Jacobin Club or of the private opinions of revolutionary leaders.

Théroigne coughed blood. A doctor said her mental state showed cause for concern. Her interrogators took her to Vienna, where she was taken to an interview with the emperor, who ordered her release. Escorted halfway across Europe by her captors, she resurfaced in Paris. Most people had assumed she was dead; besides, the world had changed.

In republican France, Théroigne would grow into her popular persona, go halfway to meet her violent legend. Did she, on the day the monarchy was overthrown, kill the journalist Suleau? Certainly, she was at the centre of a mob which did so. Roudinesco does not concern herself too much with sifting through the available accounts, and this seems a loss. So many of the revolution's leaders remained aloof from the violence. It seems important that Théroigne did not.

At least there was no longer a royalist press to spread rumours about her private life. But she was further away than ever from real power. Manon Roland – who was disdainful of women's role in public life – exercised covert power when her husband was minister of the interior. Pauline Léon and Claire Lacombe – mysterious, marginal women – seized the initiative in the political societies. By 1793, the women sansculottes were on the streets, calling for price controls. Théroigne did not fit in anywhere. Whatever she was, she was not a woman of the people: her superior if patchy education, her cosmopolitan experience, marked her out. She attached herself to the Brissotin faction in the Convention, to the people who were later called Girondins; she backed their pro-war policy, and campaigned for the right of women to bear arms.

It was not an astute move. Théroigne and other women campaigners invoked the image of the Amazon. Myths were well understood, in those days. As Roudinesco reminds us, the Amazons killed half their male children at birth, and kept the rest as emasculated slaves. It is hard to think of an image more calculated to strike panic into the male psyche. Théroigne campaigned among the women in Saint-Antoine, claiming that her views had the backing of prominent revolutionaries like Robespierre. But Robespierre had never met her, and said so. He was unlikely to favour her notion of women's battalions, since he did not favour any battalions at all – he was opposed to the war. He had his own constituency among the women of Paris, who came to sit in the public gallery at the Jacobin Club and worship him. As Hufton says, a pattern had been established: on their day off, men went drinking and women went to church. The women of Paris may have had little time for the priests the old regime had foisted on them, but they preserved the image of a male saviour who was gentle, celibate and ready to die. They cherished at the same time, Roudinesco says, the image of Marat, but for a different reason. He was everything the political woman was said to be. He was ugly. He was irrational. He was a political embarrassment.

Théroigne's opponents in the press were now on the left, not the right. They depicted her as wearing a false moustache, which tended to drop off at moments of crisis. Predictable male grumbles were beginning to surface. When a man got home from a hard day's patriotism, he wanted his dinner on the table; he didn't want to find that his wife was three streets away, attending a political rally. In the summer of 1793 the power of the women's clubs would be broken. A series of personal and peculiar contingencies – which Hufton describes very clearly – identified them with the enragés, the anarchistic looters of grocer's shops, the populists whose views, in time of war, became a luxury the republic could not afford.

Théroigne was not a clubbist, though, or an enragé's mistress, or anything much any more, just a woman washed up on the revolution's inhospitable shore; her vision of women's role was becoming utopian, at a time when only the bleakest pragmatism could take one safely from day to day. In May 1793 she turned up at the door of the Convention to take her usual place in the galleries reserved for Girondin supporters. A crowd of women ambushed her, stripped off her clothes and whipped her. The incident was very violent; it was not a token humiliation. She was rescued by Marat, who called off the women, put an arm around her and took her to safety. It is one of the doctor's few recorded good deeds.

The following spring, one of her brothers asked the authorities to take her into protective custody, and declare her insane. This may, Roudinesco thinks, have been an attempt to pre-empt her arrest. She was said to be suffering from delusions of persecution – but, during the Terror, who was persecuted, and who was deluded? She wrote a letter to Saint-Just: 'I have neither paper nor light, I have nothing . . . I must be free so that I can write.'

The letter seems more desperate than mad, but it was used against her. She was transferred from one asylum to the next, ending up at the terrible Salpêtrière. Roudinesco shows how proposals for the reform of the place had come to nothing – other considerations had elbowed out the issue of how the mad were treated. It is clear that, if she was sane when she was shut up, Théroigne could not have remained sane for long, under the stress of mistreatment. She was not forgotten after the revolution – far from it. She became a well-known curiosity. The doctors who treated her did not trouble to inform themselves of the facts of her life. They embraced the legend. She was the killer, the emasculating Amazon. It was considered that the revolution had driven her mad. What was the revolution, after all, but an outbreak of mass psychosis? The monarchy restored, this view seemed persuasive.

After Théroigne was dead, a cast of her head was taken. The tiny face is avian, chilling. She had withered away, Roudinesco says, 'through a slow extinction of the organs, arising from the depth of melancholia'. If we are to be Freudian, melancholia is induced by mourning for the 'lost object'. Théroigne's lost object was the revolution. The language of her madness is simpler than Roudinesco will concede. Enemies said she was filthy, hot, demanding. For twenty years she washed herself in ice.

Olwen Hufton writes very cogently of the decline of the female militant, and of the counter-revolutionary woman. Roudinesco devotes her later chapters to historiography: her subject seen by Michelet, by Lamartine, by the Goncourts. Théroigne becomes thinner, more shadowy: an ideological nullity, a ghost. Yet she was real, wasn't she? In her postscript Roudinesco describes her journey to Marcourt, the village where Théroigne was born. She finds 'nothing, no shadow or shade'; almost nothing to demonstrate that the woman or her family ever existed. There is only a baptismal certificate, preserved under glass. The author is overtaken by that haunted malaise common in those who try to make sense of the revolution: 'I feel that I have invented everything.'

Hilary Mantel
46 Percheron Drive, Knaphill, Woking, Surrey GU21 2QY
Tel: 01483 798910   Fax: 01483 798912

Dear Mary-Kay,
I'm delighted that you like my story,
and that it's you who will be
publishing it. I'm now almost
finished the first draft of my radio
adaptation of A Place of Greater
Safety, so have dwelled extensively
with the dead — and hope to
finish my gruesome novel over the

summer. In the circumstances, I
am indecently cheerful,
shuttling between here and the
Nottingham branch of Guillotine
Enterprises.
I hope you're well & thriving.
All love,
Hilary.

Postcard from Hilary Mantel to
Mary-Kay Wilmers, 1997

Blame it on the Belgians
On Christopher Marlowe
1992

'YOU DON'T WANT to see him,' said the porter at Corpus, when Charles Nicholl went to Cambridge to look at the portrait that is probably Christopher Marlowe.* 'He died in a tavern brawl.'

Nicholl viewed the putative Marlowe, in his opulent slashed doublet, and wondered how he could afford the outfit. He looked at his buttery bills too, and noted when the shoemaker's son had money to spend; noted when (unless he was starving himself) he was absent from college. His conclusion? There was no tavern. There was no brawl. It is an old lie that Nicholl has set out to nail, but he is unable, he admits, to substitute a new truth. All he can hope for is a 'faint preserved outline where the truth once lay'. In Elizabeth's England, men lied to their reflection; and Marlowe belonged to a shadow world of espionage, where every straight action is mirrored by treachery, where the agent provocateur is king.

Charles Nicholl has previously written on alchemy in the Elizabethan age. 'As above, so below': this was the maxim of alchemists. It works in the real world too. The factious giants

---

* *The Reckoning: The Murder of Christopher Marlowe* by Charles Nicholl (Cape, 1992).

of Elizabeth's court are supported by a vast root system of con-men, of prison informers, of spies, 'projectors' and 'ambodexters'. Marlowe was part of this underground world: this is not in contention. But his reputation is surrounded by rumour, misinformation, disinformation. Shady and unpleasant he may have been, Nicholl says, but we owe him something – not simply because he was a great dramatist and poet, but because his death was murder, and the crime is unsolved. Nicholl is an investigator with a compelling sense of duty to the past and the people who inhabit it. To accept an untruth, to assent to a lazy version of history, is not just negligent but immoral.

Charles Nicholl writes vividly, without the academic's compulsion to cover his back; but where he is speculating he says so clearly. Part of the success of his book comes from the fact that he has focused sharply on his central incident. He begins with an account of Marlowe's death; he leads us away from it, into the thickets of European politics and the literary and political underworld; then he leads us back, by ways digressive but sure, to the Widow Bull's victualling house in Deptford, where in spring 1593 four young men spent a day drinking wine in the garden.

Mrs Bull's house was not a tavern, nor was she a sort of Mistress Quickly, half-expecting a fight to break out as the sun declined. She was a bailiff's widow, with some court connections; her house was a respectable one. Nicholl evokes the Deptford evening: the scent of apple orchards mingling with the reek of fish and sewage. At about six o'clock, the young gentlemen came in for their bespoke supper. A short while later, Ingram Frizer put the point of his dagger into

Christopher Marlowe's right eye socket. He inserted it to a depth of two inches. Marlowe died quickly, with no great fuss.

The inquest produced a tidy, emollient version, which the coroner accepted. It had been self-defence, said the two witnesses, whose names were Skeres and Poley. Marlowe and Frizer had quarrelled over the bill, or reckoning. Marlowe had picked up Frizer's dagger and slashed at him, Frizer had wrested it away (presumably while the witnesses stood as if turned to stone) and had inflicted the fatal wound. No other version was available to the court; these were the only witnesses, and their account could not be contradicted. Four weeks after Marlowe's death, Frizer was pardoned. One of the rumours that went about town was that there had been a quarrel over a boyfriend. Nicholl is quite certain that whether or not Marlowe was a homosexual, it had no bearing on his death, and we cannot know what bearing it had on his life: 'We do not know what it meant to be gay in Elizabethan England.' As for the row about the bill, it is plausible enough, as an explanation, until you know there was a greater account to be settled. At the time of his death, Marlowe was under investigation by the Privy Council, suspected of being part of a plot to incite the citizens of London against the immigrant Dutch merchants. His friend Kyd had already been arrested and tortured, and the fact that Marlowe was not in jail suggested that some powerful interest was protecting him. It was not the first time he had been in trouble with the authorities. In Cambridge in 1587, his college had taken fright at a report that Marlowe was planning to skip the country and join the ranks of the would-be Catholic martyrs, the seminarians at the English College in Rheims. The Privy Council had taken the unusual step of intervening on his behalf: young Marlowe was a good boy, he should be given his degree. Then in the late January of 1592, he had got into a more spectacular kind of trouble: he was deported from the Dutch town of Flushing, accused of coining. In London he was interviewed by Burghley, the lord treasurer; though coining was a capital offence, he cannot have served more than a short term of imprisonment: in May that year he was on the streets again, brawling in Shoreditch and attracting the attention of the constabulary.

Leave aside for a moment all speculation and suggestion. Just these two (well-documented) incidents seem to show that we are dealing in a business of spectacular complexity. They went back a long way, Marlowe and Frizer and Skeres and Poley, much further back than the 'feast' at Mrs Bull's. In *As You Like It* Shakespeare made a reference to Marlowe's death, cryptic but pointed: he called it 'a great reckoning in a little room'.

What sort of man was Marlowe? Nicholl is not primarily writing a work of literary criticism, but he presents us with a picture of an author who is congruent with what he writes. Marlowe is flamboyant, sceptical, a vivid schemer, with plenty of 'stomach' – that is, he is ambitious, impulsive, noisy, prone to violence. Not the best sort of recruit for the secret services, by modern standards – but patient undercover work was not his forte. Nashe wrote:

> His pen was sharp-pointed like a poignard. No leaf he wrote on but was like a burning-glass to set on fire all his readers . . . He was no timorous servile flatterer of the commonwealth wherein he lived. His tongue and his invention were foreborn: what they

thought they would confidently utter. Princes he spared not, that in the least point transgressed.

At some level, however, he must have been in the service of princes; everyone was. Poetry wasn't a living. So, in 1587, Nicholl tells us, he was acting as a recruiter for the Catholic seminary at Rheims, working on the young men within his university, and reporting back to some important Protestant about what success he had. Some recruits were from crypto-Catholic families; some were just romantic boys with a relish for danger and for being on the wrong side of the establishment. Christopher Marlowe was – no doubt – not intrinsically evil or depraved; probably he was not particularly anti-papist, and perhaps indeed he had flirted with Rome himself. His own beliefs are unknowable, but at an early age, it seems, he found work he could do, the kind of work that keeps you in doublets you can wear to have your portrait painted. He was the kind of man whose rashness, in speech and action, might provoke an answering rashness in others. He was articulate, where others fumbled for words. He was ingenious, where others struggled to find the mechanism of a plot. The weak, the wavering, the disaffected would be drawn to a man like Marlowe.

In the Europe of the late 16th century, Nicholl shows, 'intelligence' was a massive industry. Of course it was different from the modern idea of intelligence, because ink and paper and the spoken word were the only means of communication, and news could travel only as fast as a courier. Every government department needed its sources of information, and so did every great man; networks of couriers and foreign correspondents were maintained. And when it came to understanding what your opponents were up to, you could not tap their telephones or monitor their radio communications: your only course was to insert some man of yours among their men. Thus, the two-faced man flourished – and at state expense, since Francis Walsingham had set up in England the world's first professional secret service.

Subversion was an industry. You can feel, reading Nicholl, that every second seminarian at Rheims must have been a spy; indeed, that seems quite possible. The history of Elizabeth's reign has a thin, friable top surface: the Protestant virgin of England, standing alone against Catholic France and Spain; the Queen of Scots nourishing her assassination schemes, knotting them to a vast papist conspiracy that creeps throughout Europe. Yet if you look at these conspiracies – at the Throckmorton plot, the Babington plot – they melt away. Deluded, muddled, inefficient young gents have their plans firmed up for them by whatever brisk agent provocateur Walsingham has put in place. 'Farewell, sweet Robyn,' writes Anthony Babington to Robert Poley, who was one of the men who stood by as Marlowe was stabbed. 'Farewell, sweet Robyn, if as I take thee true to me.' Poley was anything but true: and Babington, briefly strung up but fully conscious, was shortly afterwards castrated and disembowelled by Elizabeth's executioner.

Nicholl is adept at tracing the cross-connections, the processes by which sedition was manufactured; and he has plenty of persuasive case histories, of agents turned double agents turned triple agents. He leaves us in no doubt that Marlowe was on the edge of the secret world, then later at its heart.

Why did the secret services bother with the young literati? Because they were clever, and good at understanding plots; because they always needed money; because they were footloose and willing to travel; because they had the entrée to great households, and could be induced to spy on their patrons. Marlowe's patron was Thomas Walsingham, the great spymaster's nephew. Beyond this, he had the friendship of powerful men.

One was Lord Strange, who became earl of Derby. He belonged to the Stanley family, whose power base was in Lancashire, a part of England famous for clinging to Catholicism. His cousin Sir William Stanley was a notorious traitor, who after years of stalwart military service to Elizabeth had handed the Dutch town of Deventer over to the Spanish and formed a regiment in the king of Spain's service. Lord Strange was a problem for the government. As a Lancashire official he did his job of naming and fining recusants. Ostensibly, he was loyal. Yet he was high in the line of succession, and Catholic exiles saw him as a likely figurehead in the event of a coup. The Earl of Northumberland, too, was very near the throne. He was an occultist and scholar, and collected the works of Giordano Bruno. Northumberland's friend was Walter Ralegh; their coterie was sceptical, intellectual. They had the kind of inquiring minds a precarious regime detests.

One of Nicholl's most interesting lines of investigation follows the work of Frances Yates, and concerns Giordano Bruno's visit to England in 1583. Bruno was protected by Henri III of France; while in England, he may have proffered a distinctive Valois solution to Europe's problems. On the one hand was an intransigent, narrow-minded Protestantism; on the other, the Jesuitical, proselytising Catholicism of the Counter-Reformation. Might there be a third way – another way of looking at God? Bruno's dream was of something more spiritually and intellectually attractive than the aggressive dogmas which dominate the age. There is no space, in his tightly constructed book, for Nicholl to explore Bruno's mysticism, or the shifting frontier between mysticism and science; nor can he do more than advert to John Bossy's theory that Bruno was spying for Walsingham. If he was, Nicholl argues, it did not help his notions gain currency; Walsingham was interested in the man and his links with the French embassy, not in Bruno's wider message. Nicholl suggests that it was in the Northumberland-Ralegh circle that Bruno's ideas lingered on, after his extravagant presence was withdrawn. They may have lingered on, too, in the mind of a playwright looking for a model for Dr Faustus.

One cannot say that the government was simply too hardheaded for Bruno's ideas to take hold. They were alchemists, too, when it suited them. Edward Kelley, a famous spiritmedium and an assistant of John Dee, the occultist, geographer and mathematician, was one of Lord Burghley's agents in Prague, where there was a set of expatriate, feebly plotting Catholics. Burghley applied to him hopefully for some of his 'tincture', for it would have been very useful for the war-weary economy if the lord treasurer had a starter potion for turning base metal into gold. 'Our gold is not the common gold,' the alchemists used to say. But Burghley had missed the spiritual dimension of the science. Common gold was what he was after. He also asked Kelley for a cure for his gout.

To men of this mentality, religion was the servant of the state. It kept the masses quiet – such men acknowledged, in that respect, the atheist's objection to faith – and it also provided a touchstone of allegiance. It was said that Ralegh, for instance, belonged to no religion. Kit Marlowe, informers said, had 'read him the atheist lecture'. And Marlowe was a well-known scoffer, who would say (in his cups, perhaps) that Jesus and Saint John were lovers, that 'the first beginning of religion was only to keep men in awe.' Where church and state are in alliance, atheism is treason.

It was not a private matter, whether a man believed in God. A man of no religion might soon be a man of any religion: that is, he might become a papist, a subversive, if talked to in the right tone or approached with a big enough bribe. Again, to the conventional mind, atheism was incomprehensible: if you did not believe in God, might you perhaps believe in the devil, and might you not, if you were a slippery occultist like one of the Northumberland set, have the means of communication with him? The devil had, notoriously, more spies than any lord treasurer, or Mr Secretary Walsingham; more battalions than the Earl of Essex, the old queen's toy-boy. Atheism would be a neat charge to stick on that contentious man Ralegh, if you were ill-disposed to him. It was vague, too vague, perhaps: but suppose you could associate him with the popular discontent against 'the beastly brutes the Belgians', the French and Flemish refugees, the rich Dutch merchants – against whom, it seemed, his man Marlowe had made placards? Would that not (at least) tend to get Ralegh into more trouble than he was in already?

Once you have praised The Reckoning for its sharp focus, it seems ungracious to carp at it for not taking an overview. To get the best from the book you need to understand about the succession problem, about Elizabeth's constant equivocation, about the efforts of her ministers to stampede and panic her into action; you need to know why the secret service was necessary. Could Nicholl not have provided a swift, synoptic background? Of course, specialists would have quarrelled with it, but it would have supplied the one lack in his fascinating book. He doesn't usually make the mistake of assuming the reader knows everything he knows, but there are areas of obscurity. He refers, in a phrase, to the Lopez affair. Has he explained it somewhere? The book is, necessarily, one-paced and choked with detail; you might blink and miss something. But 'Lopez' is not in the index: so perhaps he hasn't explained.

Lopez was a Portuguese Jew, one of Elizabeth's court physicians. He plotted in a pale and extensive way, took money from here and there, from so many masters that any intelligence he ever supplied was cancelled out by counter-intelligence. But it is unlikely he plotted, as the Earl of Essex alleged, 'a desperate and dangerous treason' to poison the queen. Even Elizabeth did not believe it, but – because Essex sulked, and manufactured evidence – the old man was hanged, drawn and quartered, just the same. His real crime, possibly, was to have laughed at Essex with two Portuguese drinking cronies, and to have insinuated that he had cured him of a certain discreditable disease. The point is that both Lord Burghley and his son Robert Cecil believed Lopez innocent. That was no reason to assert themselves on his behalf. They were dispensable, these little, paid-for consciences, these bought bodies.

Nicholl explains that after Walsingham's death the secret service divided. Some agents were bought by the Earl of Essex, and some by Robert Cecil. This split may have been fatal for Marlowe. Essex and Ralegh were old enemies, implacable opponents; they fought a naval campaign together, but they also fought for the favours of the old woman who was the fount of all power. Nicholl sees Marlowe's end as part of a conspiracy to bring down Ralegh; he makes persuasive connections. But finally, he cannot explain what Marlowe was doing in the 'little room': with Poley, who was Robert Cecil's man, with Skeres, who was Essex's man, and with Frizer, who was anybody's man, perhaps, if the sum were agreed beforehand. What pretext was given to Marlowe for this strange meeting; what proposition was put to him, in those long hours in the garden; why did he not sense the drift of events, and get out of that little room in time? Nicholl does not claim he can supply the answers, but rather puts us into a frame of mind where we see that there can be none. What stays with the reader – when he has forgotten the smaller details of the intelligence network so minutely described – is a sense of frustration and futility. If it were otherwise, the author would not be true to his subject. The secret services of that time, and maybe of more recent times, existed largely for their own 'inward' reasons, and were governed and kept in business by their own distorted logic. They were the great school and refuge of opportunists, cynics – and of poor poets, no doubt – and operated not so much to serve the state as to serve themselves. Despite his scholarship, Nicholl's aim is humble enough. 'I am not trying to argue that Marlowe's death has to have a meaning. My reading only extends to a more complex kind of meaninglessness than that of a tavern brawl.'

Is the book pointless, then? Not at all. It tells us, if we needed telling, that poetry and cynicism may co-exist, flourishing in one heart, that great writers may be the dupes and servants of small regimes – and that writers will do most things for the promise of hard cash.

Date 23rd Aug.

Number of pages including cover sheet 1

TO: Mary Kay Wilmers
LRB

FROM: Hilary Mantel
        142 Chobham Road
        Sunningdale
        Berkshire SL5 0HU

Phone
Fax Phone 071 404 3337

Phone   0344 22838
Fax Phone 0344 21502

Dear Mary-Kay,

Could I please have some more time for my piece on _The Unredeemed Captive_? You may remember that I wanted John Demos's 2 earlier books, but only one has come so far. I'm going to Holland for a few days, and I thought that if it hadn't turned up by the time I get back I should just start in anyway, + let you have a piece by mid-September. Is that okay?

All love.

Hilary.

Fax from Hilary Mantel to
Mary-Kay Wilmers, 1994.

Eunice's Story
A Mohawk Captive
1994

THE INDIANS attacked in the dead of winter, before dawn.* The first the minister knew of it was the sound of axes breaking open his windows and doors. Moments later, twenty painted savages were in his house. Bound and helpless, he watched them kill his six-year-old son, his new baby of six weeks and his black woman slave.

This, properly discerned, is an incident from the War of the Spanish Succession. The thread of history stretches from Charles II, last of the Spanish Habsburgs: from his dead hands across an ocean, to the bound hands of John Williams, a minister of religion in Deerfield, a small settlement in New England. Europe's conflicts are echoed and mimicked in this precarious, snow-bound frontier territory. The winter of 1703-4 had been a season of ugly rumour, of a defensive huddle in the stockade, of a phoney war. And in the small hours of 29 February, the French and their 'mission Indian' allies descend. They kill, they slaughter the livestock, they fire the houses. Then they round up their prisoners – it is the Indians who do this work, not the French – and march them out into the freezing wilderness.

---

* *The Unredeemed Captive: A Family Story from Early America* by John Demos (Knopf, 1994).

'Most of all, I wanted to write a *story*,' John Demos says. It was the stories that first drew him to the study of history, when he was a child. The tide of the times ran against narrative, and he became a pre-eminent analyst, interpreter. His earlier book *A Little Commonwealth* is a study of Plymouth colony in the first two generations after the *Mayflower* settlers. It gives a vivid picture of an emerging society, and of the kind of habits, assumptions and ideals from which John Williams and his surviving family were so brutally torn.

In that book Demos was careful not to focus on individuals; he wanted to improve on the anecdotal method. He made an aggregation of the settlers' lives, for the sake of a wide and general picture which is not distorted by the idiosyncrasies of personal predilection and personal fate. This is valuable work, and his book is a swift, informative read. He is not some sultan of statistics, conferring the largesse of knowledge only in tables at the back of the book. But it is easy to see why the generalising method seems deficient to a man of imagination. What is true of everybody is true of nobody.

'Biography, psychology, sociology, history,' he has written: 'four corners of one scholar's compass, four viewpoints overlooking a single field of past experience.' This compass guided him through *Entertaining Satan*, his 1982 study of witchcraft in New England. Once you have decided on such a multi-disciplinary approach, where do you stop? How wide do you open your arms? One could argue his study would be more informed, complete, if he had read the relevant papers on Huntingdon's Chorea, the dreadful inherited disorder traceable in the families of some pre-eminent New England 'witches'. So, to psychology, one should add neurology. If you opt to be eclectic, there is no limit to scholarship, no end to your book. Yet you know you are working closer to some sort of truth . . . One might argue that in his new book Demos has done the risky, the necessary thing. He has embraced imagination, and yielded – in a controlled and chary way – to its delights. So he has written certain interposed passages of reconstruction, of supposition, of – let us spit the word out – fiction. Like Simon Schama he is dealing in 'dead certainties' and 'unwarranted speculations'. But within the text the line is clearly drawn. The critic cannot claim to be confused.

On the afternoon of 29 February, John Williams and the other Deerfield prisoners were marched five miles through deep snow. From a height, they looked down on the ruins of their town. The second day was worse – perhaps the worst day of John Williams's life. He may have understood his own significance to his captors; he was an important man, respected in his community and throughout New England. He could be exchanged for some prisoner valuable to the French; but why these innocents, these babies and women? What use were they? The answer was simple and nasty and would have occurred to him as he tried to stay on his feet on that second day. Prisoners were money.

There was a flourishing system for exchange and ransom. Prisoners were the Indians' bonus, for fighting in settlers' wars. In times past, the frequent fate of Indian captives was to be used as slaves, to be adopted by the tribe, or to be tortured to death. Recently, perhaps under the influence of the Jesuits who had converted them, the Indians had become more pragmatic and a little less bloodthirsty. If they took English prisoners, the French authorities in Canada would buy them for exchange. Sympathetic French individuals would 'redeem' the small children. Any buyer might sell on his captive – and the chain would lead, eventually, to a New England extended family who would pay almost anything, fulfil any demand, to get the prisoners back from among the savages and the papists.

On that second day, John Williams's wife was killed. She was six weeks out of childbed. Her baby daughter was already murdered. As they forded an icy river, Eunice Williams went head over heels. She swam out, alive. An Indian killed her with one blow from a hatchet. Later that day, another baby was killed; so was a girl of 11. These killings were a sort of mercy, John Demos suggests, to those who were too weak for the trials ahead. Their end was swift; otherwise, they would have been left by the trail to die of exposure. Why the Indians now killed the minister's black male slave is not known, but one doubts the explanation is palatable.

In four days they covered 65 miles. The Indians recovered their stores and their dog sleds. They killed eight women who could not keep up. One week after the massacre, the captives were split into small groups. John Williams was marched away with a party of Indians and two children of his former neighbours. He had lost sight of his own children; but perhaps at some point he looked back and noted that his seven-year-old daughter, named Eunice after her mother, was being carried on the broad shoulders of an Indian who did not seem to mind her weight.

Of the 112 Deerfield captives, it is believed that twenty died on the trail. John Williams survived to reach Montreal, and was 'redeemed' by the governor, the marquis de Vaudreuil.

Three of his children were bought out soon after – Samuel, who was 15, Esther, who was 13, and Warham, who was four – the latter 'wonderfully preserved', for on the journey he might have been killed many times. But there was one child, Eunice, whom the Indians would not sell back.

They held her in a fort near Montreal, called Kathnawake. The mission Indians lived cheek by jowl with the French, preserving much of their traditional way of life, and preserving too, Demos suggests, many traditional beliefs under a Christian veneer. The women farmed, the men hunted, made war on each other, and traded in furs. Adoption, even of adult prisoners, was not a rare practice. The fertility rate was low and infant mortality very high. Adoption brought another pair of hands into an extended family. But to the families left behind, it seemed a cultural and psychological catastrophe. As soon as John Williams was home, he and his community began the strenuous, complex negotiations that they hoped would lead to the 'redemption' of Eunice. They were to last, in one form or another, for eighty years.

A year on, her father saw her, but though she begged him to take her away with him he was unable. She still remembered her catechism, and how to read. She said her captors made her say prayers in Latin. She didn't understand the prayers; she hoped they wouldn't harm her. These are her reported words. Direct evidence of Eunice is lacking. Her father, her brothers, were great diary keepers, great correspondents. Eunice has just one letter to her name – and that is transcribed from her words spoken in the Mohawk language, taken down in French and then translated into English so that her family could read it. The facts of her life are scant and debatable, so that she scarcely emerges from the shadow of history; but in John Demos's hands her story is powerful, resonant and moving.

Eunice grew up among the Indians, married, had children. Within two years of her capture, she had forgotten how to speak English. She was baptised into the Catholic Church, and took an Indian name. Years on, when their negotiating skills – and the power of prayer – had been tested to the utmost, her family had to face the awful, unimaginable truth. Eunice did not want to come back. Wrenched from the 'Land of Light', she had made her home in the dark.

The case of Eunice Williams stirred up the English settlers' deepest fears. They were the fears of all colonialists. They had come to America with two projects – to tame the land, and to 'help' the native inhabitants by converting them to Christianity. From the farming of the wilderness, from the compliance of savages, all the benefits of civilisation would flow. But what if the process somehow went into reverse? Each year nature fought back, with droughts, blights and epidemics. Was it possible that the settler might become decivilised, become primitive, be drawn into the wilderness and vanish? Demos extends the point: 'The "frontiers" between New England and New France, between Protestantism and Catholicism, between Euro-American and Native American people: all were clearly drawn and carefully patrolled. To travel across them was costly and dangerous – and potentially transforming. Some who set out would not return.'

Captivity was the deepest fear. It seemed to go against the natural order; the Indian became master, the settler his slave. That one might elect captivity, as Eunice Williams did, seemed a kind of blasphemy. How did her family and the wider society come to terms with what had happened? They prayed. Every day, year after year – a great network of beseeching, stretching across New England. Her family's eloquent letters show that she was never out of their thoughts. And if the prayers were not answered, what did that show? That they were unworthy. They must reform their lives.

Some of the most interesting insights in The Unredeemed Captive concern the Christian response to suffering and loss. The settlers had various psychological methods for coping with their capricious deity. When John Williams was first a captive in Canada, the Boston minister Cotton Mather told him in a letter: 'You are carried into the land of the Canadiens for your good.' His patience and resignation would glorify God more than 'ye best Activity in any other Serviceableness'. In addition, 'Your calamities are useful . . . they awaken us.' The Puritan God was thirsty for glory, and his subjects had to seek out any opportunity to slake this thirst. Pain and suffering were a punishment for man's evil deeds, but they were also a test for the individual. They would bring out the best in the person concerned, give him the chance to display all his virtues. So the perennial question 'Why me?' is answered. Your punishment is also your opportunity.

Over the years there were various sightings of Eunice. Her Indian husband tried to persuade her to visit her relations, but explained that she was 'exceedingly afraid of ye English'. A rendezvous in Albany was negotiated, and two of her brothers saw her and spoke with her through an interpreter: 'We had ye joyfull, Sorrowfull meeting of our poor sister yt we had been sepratd from fer above thirty-six years,' wrote

Stephen. It was only after John Williams's death that Eunice came down to New England. John Demos suggests that his helplessness on the long march, his inability to rescue her, had made him a feeble, untrustworthy figure in her eyes, and that very soon she had responded to the warmth and strength of her Indian captors, and identified herself with them.

Her first visit caused a sensation. It seemed a turning point for everyone concerned. She and her husband would not stay indoors, but camped out in the orchard. It is clear that her surviving family found her strange, impenetrable. But would she stay? No. Yet Stephen wrote, hopefully: 'And when I took leave of her I do think her affections were movd.'

On subsequent visits she sat in church with her family, wrapped in her blankets, while prayers for her and about her passed over her head: mere gibberish, as far as she was concerned. On each occasion the family raised their hopes: this time, surely she would stay? The authorities attempted bribery, offering the family a lump-sum payment and an annual allowance to settle back in New England. But Eunice's world was elsewhere, in the longhouse and cornfield, among her tribe. When it became clear that she would never be redeemed, the community performed a face-saving psychological manoeuvre. According to one sermon, she was living 'in the Thickness of popish darkness and superstition'. She did not perceive her own misery. She had not really rejected her home and family and community. She was simply not responsible for herself.

Why would she not return? John Demos suggests that in many ways she may have been better off among the Indians. Their child-rearing practices were indulgent. Casual observers would often describe the squaws as little better than slaves, but those who lived among the Indians for some time remarked that women had power and influence in the tribe's affairs as well as in household matters. Eunice herself gave a reason that her family would not have wanted to hear: she said that 'living among heretics would endanger her and her children's salvation.'

The family visits ceased when Eunice and her brothers became too old to travel. She died at the age of 89: an object lesson, a focus of fear, an awesome study in psychological malleability. Her story, told in John Demos's spare and disciplined prose, goes straight to the heart of the puzzle of personal identity. He has drawn the meaning from what few facts we have about Eunice Williams, by an exercise in scrupulous scholarship and imaginative sympathy. Trying to convince himself that his daughter's apostasy would end, that her true faith was preserved beneath papistry and savagery, John Williams wrote: 'God can make dry bones, very dry, to live.' So can historians; that must be their job, and it is seldom performed so successfully as here.

TO: Mary-Kay Wilmers
LRB.

Phone
Fax Phone 0171 209 1102

FROM: Hilary Mantel
            46 Percheron Drive
            Knaphill
            Woking
            Surrey GU21 2QY

Phone   01483 798910
Fax Phone   01483 798912

Dear Mary-Kay,

Is there any chance of a little extra time on my review of Blake Morrison's book? (A day would help!). I've sent for Gitta Sereny's book on Mary Bell, which is pertinent, plus I'd like to muddle around in Rousseau a little more, as one does. But I don't want to impose stress on your schedules, so let me know what you think. Also, may it be fairly personal in parts? When I wrote the Leila Bey review you seemed to be giving me a licence I didn't take. But the way Blake begins his book resonates very much with my own memory. He's writing about the 'Children's Crusade,' and the impression it made — recall reading about it and where, + how uneasy it made me, & how I disbelieved it + thought I was being manipulated by this story. It <u>might</u> be interesting.

Tomorrow I am out with my Jacobin sweetheart turning over the contents of a picture library — I pity the curator — so if you could fax a word, that would be good.

All love,

Hilary.

Fax from Hilary Mantel to
Mary-Kay Wilmers, 1997

Boxes of Tissues
The Murder of James Bulger
1997

BLAKE MORRISON begins his account of the murder of James Bulger with a delicate diversion into the story of the Children's Crusade.* The year 1212: at Saint-Denis, a boy of 12 begins to preach. He has received word from God that it is the mission of Christian children to free the Holy Land from the infidel. He draws crowds, draws followers: boys and girls swarm from street and field. God is their pied piper. They march the roads of France, exalted, unstoppable, expecting a miracle at every turn in the road. They reach the sea and set sail for – what?

The grown-up Blake Morrison dwells on a darker version. Was the crusade exploitative, a lawless migration of unwanted children who would end by being sold into slavery? Disconcerted, he researches. It seems certain that the story has some basis in fact. Why has it stuck with him into adult life? Did he entirely believe in it, when he first came across it? And where was that? Was it a school history lesson? Henry Treece's novel, published 1958?

Fine prose makes the memory work. I myself first read about the Children's Crusade in a weekly magazine called

* As If by Blake Morrison (Granta, 1997).

Look and Learn. This publication was approved by adults; it was better than *Bunty* or *Judy*. When you turned one of its stiff, highly coloured pages, you crackled with rectitude inside. And there it was: a child-hero gathers his forces for the Holy Land. There was a large illustration. After one reading they haunted me, those notional peasant faces – naive medieval eyes upturned under pudding-bowl haircuts. I found them in library books, I found them everywhere; the girls in the pictures were always younger, and their faces were unformed, less decisive. Why everywhere? Was someone arranging it? Was it a piece of knowledge directed especially at me? As *if* adults were sending me ceaseless information about it, as some sort of test of my moral courage. As *if* I were obscurely at fault for not having joined the crusade myself. As *if* . . . It was the first 'fact' I decided to disbelieve. I thought it was a myth, and you can decide whether to take myths into your life; this one was not in my best interest.

Further research convinces Blake Morrison that scepticism is in order. It seems the word used of these crusaders was *pueri*, which can mean not a child but a youth, any male between 12 and 28. A more convincing picture emerges: runaway apprentices and landless younger sons, big lads on the loose, on the road . . . It sounds more likely. Still, the original, uneasy picture gnaws in the psyche: children lost and wandering, lost and gone for ever. Reading the early pages of Morrison's book, I go back to an earlier age still, when my body registered symptoms of fear whenever I heard the phrase 'far and wide'. It was the title, as my luck would have it, of a series of graduated reading books. I heard it again and again, with the same stir of panic. It's what every child fears:

to be far, to be flung wide, to be lost without hope of gathering-in.

And so the mind arrives at the blocky geometry of that defective video screen; the toddler's arm stretched up, the older child in step with him, and the other form – the third point of the triangle – moving weightily ahead, purposive, as if in a hurry to arrive at the obscenity being prepared.

Two ten-year-old boys, truanting from school, go to a Liverpool shopping centre. They stole, or may have stolen, 'a pen, a packet of batteries, Humbrol enamel paint tins, sausage rolls, party poppers . . . a troll . . . a packet of iced gems, a balloon, a plum, a pear, a banana'. Think of the young Jean-Jacques Rousseau, trying to steal apples; standing rapt before a fruit stall, gazing at ripe pears. Today it's Robert and Jon who are on a spree: they steal a yoghurt, a milkshake, two cartons of Ambrosia rice. Finally they steal a child, blond-haired, not quite three. One of them takes him by the hand. They lead him into the city.

They walk some busy roads, they are seen many times, remarked by passers-by. At intervals the baby shows distress, and adults do stop, ask questions; after all, this is Liverpool, where mouths are not zippered and concern is not frozen and a child is everyone's concern. But the big boys are plausible: he is lost, but they're taking him to a police station. And at times the child looks happy, trotting along quite trusting and contented. They walk him two miles. Two miles away from the mother who momentarily took her eyes off him. They take him to open land, beside a railway line. It is now almost dark. They strip off his lower garments. They . . . what comes next, we do not know.

They beat him to death. They leave his body to be cut in half by a train.

Some time later, Blake Morrison, poet-about-town, leaves London for Preston to attend the trial. For this is a rare crime – children killing children. Twenty-seven incidents in two and a half centuries is one suggested figure. One can't think the statistic will be very sound. Still, it's not like ripping off car stereos, is it? Or beating up prostitutes. Or any instance of workaday murder. This is a special crime, requiring the attention of special people. An aristocrat among crimes, which requires aristocrats of sensitivity to interpret it. We are all waiting to know what this killing *means*. Moral panic has set in.

Already the poet is wondering about his motives and his stamina for the enterprise, anticipating the day when he will feel 'guilty, collusive, voyeuristic'. He has no intention, at this stage, of writing at length; he has been commissioned by an American magazine to cover the trial. He packs two books. One is Rousseau's *Confessions*. The other is Rousseau's *Émile*. What would he have felt if, at an early stage, his journey had stalled on some platform: and out of boredom he had flicked through *Émile*'s preface, to hear Jean-Jacques say: 'I had at first planned only a monograph of a few pages. My subject drew me on in spite of myself, and this monograph imperceptibly became a sort of opus, too big, doubtless, for what it contains, but too small for the matter it treats.'

It is hard to think of a more just description of *As If*. Too small (though well-padded); too big (because well-padded). It is a memoir and a meditation, not a polemic, not reportage; it is beautifully composed and beautifully shaped. No one writes more tenderly than Blake Morrison about parents and children, about the fear and responsibility of parenthood. No one could write with more compassion about the god-forsaken events he describes. His imagination is supple, he casts the net of allusion wide. He opens his heart to us, and he opens his diaries: his own baby's battle with meningitis, bad moments in his marriage. And back to childhood, adolescence. That girl of 14, drunk at a party, who went into a cloaks-cupboard a virgin and came out, trembling and crying, with as much experience as the Wife of Bath; his mates had her, he didn't, but could he have helped her? Could he have stopped them? Again, is it a form of child abuse, to be sensually aroused by the creamy body of his infant daughter? Male guilt implodes in his bloodstream.

He is at the trial. The accused are two small boys, both podgy, pale, unlikeable. He would prefer to like them, warm to them, but cannot. The judge is an unknown quantity. The barristers are caricatures. The early witnesses are those who saw the baby on his death march. They are stiff, uneasy, conscious that they passed by on the other side; the setting intimidates them, the language is alien, they talk in stereotyped phrases as if they have picked them up from the newspapers, or from each other. And the small defendants, Robert Thompson and Jon Venables, seem to belong in some other reality.

Again, the book's cadences and concerns go to work, drawing out a reinforcing memory. Our legal system can seem divorced from reality, estranging; the people in a courtroom can seem to live in separate dimensions. Long ago, in 1972, being then a law student with a sort of social conscience,

I spent a summer placement with the probation service. Nothing I saw of adults was new to me, but a day in the juvenile court disturbed me profoundly. I took my concerns to our senior officer, a no nonsense (I'd thought) and rather stern woman; she would have passed nicely as a county councillor, standing in the Conservative interest.

The juvenile court, I don't like it, I said. It's not working.

At once, the stern face softened. Did you feel it was too formal, she asked, did you feel the children didn't understand? Was the language too difficult, were they intimidated?

Mutual incomprehension. Give her a minute, and she'll push me a box of tissues.

But no! It didn't scare them enough. It didn't touch them, it didn't reach them, they may as well have been somewhere else. They don't give a — (better abdicate from this sentence, I thought).

Her dark gaze, behind her glasses, welled with distaste. What have we here, a trainee fascist, eh?

And they remain in my imagination, the 14-year-old shoplifters whose rubber faces were stamped with a sneer. They were untouchable, these offenders. They had perfect confidence that no one could do anything to them that would matter. Because, what matters? The adults in court were agonising over them, the lawyers, social workers, magistrates. But they were merely bored. They were impatient. They wanted release – the release they knew was coming. To get back on the streets. To do it again and again. That was 1972. A liberal age. They say the world is getting worse . . .

And they do say it. It is natural to compare Blake Morrison's book with Gitta Sereny's book, *The Case of Mary Bell*, reissued with an appendix about the Bulger murder.[†] Mary Bell and Norma Bell – neighbours, but not related – were girls of 11 and 13, tried in 1968 for the killing of two little boys, three and four years old. Norma was acquitted, and Mary was convicted not of murder but of manslaughter, on a plea of diminished responsibility. What did Mary do? She 'squeezed their necks'. A quiet death interested her, a tactile death; not the stoning, the kicking, the bleeding. I remember how in the winter of 1970, at a conference of lawyers and social workers in a snow-bound grand lodge in the inappropriate setting of Windsor Great Park, I heard someone who had been involved in the case speaking of Mary Bell: of her early life, the many deaths she nearly died, the poisoning, the accidents, the attempts to dispose of her. This was a young woman co-opted onto a discussion panel, her eyes downcast, gnawing her lip, alluding, just alluding, to all the facts that had not been admissible as evidence in court – not knowing whether it was decent to reveal this knowledge, and yet feeling that everyone should know.

Should everyone know? How can we know what is 'normal'? 'Families operate in camera,' Blake Morrison says. 'It's hard to know what happens behind closed doors.' True, up to a point. True, if you're middle class. If you're working class, anyone may stare in: social workers, journalists, Blake Morrison. Children who kill children might be found in any stratum of society, but you can be quite sure that if Thompson and Venables had been the offspring of accountants, and Mary Bell had been a doctor's daughter, Morrison and Sereny and the other investigators would have been quietly shown the door.

[†] *The Case of Mary Bell: A Portrait of a Child who Murdered* by Gitta Sereny (Pimlico, 1995).

There are times when As If takes on the air of a set of writing exercises. Blake Morrison goes to a restaurant alone, watches three couples, makes up stories about their relationships. We've all done it, but it's slightly indecent to do it cold on the page. It's not that you fear they will read his book, and be upset by it; they probably wouldn't recognise themselves. The offence is rather that he is confusing their imaginative reality with his, deliberately wiring them into some fantasy of his own. There is a name for this activity; it is called writing fiction. So do it then, the reader wants to say. Stop lurking in the shadows with that notebook. Step into the novelists' playground. You'll like it. We're well hard.

It would not serve any purpose to summarise what Blake Morrison has discovered about the family life of the two young accused – except to say, that with its run-around fathers and suicidal mothers, it is not too different from the home life of our own dear queen. Deprivation, neglect, violence: there is a monotonous circularity to it, it hasn't the shape of a good story. Sometimes, in order to find enough story to tell, Morrison has to invent naivety in himself. He has to spend pages misunderstanding, refusing to accept that the legal system isn't going to change in mid-trial. It is not difficult to grasp the essentials. The court had to ask two questions. One: did the boys kill James? Two: did that killing amount to murder? Morrison blames social services for not bringing forward evidence that would anyway have been inadmissible. He hacks about wildly with the blunt knife of his indignation. He blames the police and prosecution 'for so vehemently pursuing a murder conviction against two damaged and half-formed boys'. How then should murder be pursued?

Every decent person will suffer some disquiet about the way our legal system treats children who are accused of serious crimes. Sereny particularly is exercised by the belief that had there been a mechanism to explore the background of the case, a way to understand the children's mindset, there might – just might – have been a manslaughter verdict rather than a verdict of murder. (The sentence – detention for many years – would inevitably have been the same.) But ever since the murders took place, the bandwagons have been sagging under the weight of those who advocate a radical shift in the way we treat young offenders. Everyone does it better than Britain, it seems. There were even commentators from the US who criticised the way the British try homicide: it is like a man up to his neck in a cesspool scolding another for having mud on his boots.

There are questions here that need to be addressed in the language of human rights, not the language of pity and empathy. Nothing that Blake Morrison adduces can convince the reader, or would convince a court, that the boys were incapable of forming the intent to murder. To insist that they were so incapable diminishes them as moral beings. For the most humane of reasons, Blake Morrison wants to take away part of the responsibility from Thompson and Venables. But to do that is to take away part of their humanity. If two ten-year-olds of normal intelligence cannot tell right from wrong, and do not know killing is wrong – then what is the worth of a ten-year-old? Blake Morrison confuses the concept of 'the age of reason' with the fact of 'the age of criminal responsibility'. (The latter is 18, he says, in Romania – a country notoriously concerned with child welfare.)

It is strange that people think – and many people do think it – that the way to protect children is to deprive them of status, to reduce them to something less than adults. It is possible that to adopt the kinds of system Morrison and Sereny advocate would effect this reduction, and create a system where children have fewer rights than at present and are even less protected.

Consider Sereny, in her new preface to *The Case of Mary Bell*. 'Can it be right to subject young children to the awesome formality of a jury trial? How can a jury be expected to understand the thought processes, the emotions or language of children?' But why should they not? Have they not been children? Have they not memories? Can only psychologists and social workers understand children? Is the whole concept of childhood to be medicalised? Is childhood a pathological state?

Later, Sereny says she prefers the European systems of 'having family or juvenile courts deal with these cases after the social inquiry has been completed and therapeutic treatment substantially advanced'. So, before the facts are established, the interpretation of the facts is made? Treatment is begun before we know the nature of the wound? In this brave new world, adults charged with a serious crime have open court, a jury and the rules of evidence to protect them; no one may detain them or treat them or in any way interfere with their lives unless they are guilty 'beyond reasonable doubt'. But children charged with the same crime are tried in secret by a tribunal which admits what evidence it likes, a tribunal which, however constituted, calls on experts who all have their theories to push, and which is likely to be much less rigorous in separating certainties from probabilities than a judge and jury. We may find children 'treated' not for their crimes, but for their tendencies – for their proclivities, not their proven offences. We should hesitate, I think, before diminishing children's rights in this way.

It is very hard to accept that the death of a small child has no meaning. It is natural to try to find an explanation for it which goes beyond the individuals concerned. But to try to deduce anything about the state of society from the Bulger killing is probably a mistake. Blake Morrison has John Major in his firing line, for his statement that 'we must condemn a little more, and understand a little less.' An 'epitaph to a brute culture', he calls it. Not even his worst enemies would believe John Major is a brute. His statement can be read otherwise – simply as a plea for us to redirect our attention. To face reality – face the fact of what is done. Because, if you strip away the 'why', the murder remains. To understand all is to forgive all, it's said. That is, as Shaw pointed out, the devil's sentimentality.

Blake Morrison seems to be pessimistic about the future of Thompson and Venables. (We are not allowed to know their present whereabouts, how they are coping with detention.) But Mary Bell has been rehabilitated, and there is no reason to suppose they will not be released, with new identities, when they are young men. It is probably not necessary to re-shape the administration of justice in the light of the very rare set of circumstances that led to the Bulger murder. It is possibly unwise to take any action that further diminishes the status of children, divides them from the blessings of adulthood. It is certainly undesirable to make the lives of poor people into public property; why is it that from those who have least, and have suffered most, even privacy is taken away? Blake Morrison's plea is for understanding, more understanding, more understanding still. What if I am the object of all this understanding? What if your understanding looks to me like interference, like expropriation, like colonisation? I am not sure that we should indulge ourselves in our favourite pastime of exploring the nature of evil. Perhaps all we need do is to say, with Rousseau: 'There is no man so bad that he cannot be made good for something.' And to know that everything can be salvaged, this side of the grave.

24th Jan.

Dear Mary-Kay,

I have to admit at last that I have got hideously bogged down in the Evelyn Waugh piece I was writing for you, and I think it would be better if I dug myself out + lurched off on some other path. I have never heard of critics block, but I am sure I have got it. Interruption is one factor, I think, and too many projects at the stage where they need attention, many of them related in some way — and Waugh marooned + grumbling. I have never failed to complete a review before, & it is very humbling. I would be enormously grateful & relieved if you could start me off on something else. My sincere apologies,

Hilary.

Postcard from Hilary Mantel to
Mary-Kay Wilmers, 1999

FAX

	Date **Friday**
	Number of pages including cover sheet 1

| TO: | Paul Laity |
| | LRB. |

FROM:	Hilary Mantel
	46 Percheron Drive
	Knaphill
	Woking
	Surrey
	GU21 2QY

Phone	
Fax Phone **0171 209 1102.**	

Phone	01483 798910
Fax Phone	01483 798912

Dear Paul,

Thank you for your fax. I have 5 portraits of Robespierre on my study wall*, and I think the likelihood of critic's block recurring are minimal in these circumstances. I would like to do the Antoinette book too, if you want both. Would they go together, or would that be silly?

But I don't think I'm the person for Rushdie.

I will explain more fully to Mary-Kay what happened with Daniel — insofar as I understand it myself.

All good wishes,

Hilary.

* Nor, you understand, that I like just anyone to know this...

Fax from Hilary Mantel to Paul Laity, 1999

Fatal Non-Readers
On Marie-Antoinette
1999

IN JUNE 1999 the BBC showed a documentary called *Diana's Dresses*. It was about the auction which took place at Christie's in New York two months before the princess's descent into the Paris underpass. The purchasers spoke reverentially of Diana when she was alive, but her death turned glad rags into relics. 'I wanted to have a part of royalty,' one explained. 'I am in awe of the dress,' said another.

When the clothes are turned inside out for the camera, you can see the bones and secret skin of them, second dresses built inside so that a princess's mortal underpinnings wouldn't show. Only superficially do they bear a resemblance to clothes worn by ordinary women. They seem constructed rather than sewn, durable as stone with their elaborate frosting and beading, and capable of standing up on their own. But their owners worry about their survival. One appears on display only under armed guard. When a Boston shop-owner bought three of them and put them in her window, passers-by made a pavement shrine to them, with mourning bouquets and tearful messages. One owner described his prize as 'historically, one of the most important dresses Diana ever wore'. It is clear that the garments can hardly be picked apart from the flesh. And there is one dress that leads a double life: two people claim to have the original. Bilocation is an attribute of saints – and of their party frocks too.

With this in mind I searched in the Carnavalet museum this summer for a scrap of cloth from one of Marie-Antoinette's dresses, which Chantal Thomas mentions in her lively and imaginative examination of the public personae of the French queen.* This fragment of cloth was carried to the scaffold, she says, by Barnave, who was first seen as an extreme revolutionary but later became an adviser to the court. I looked hard but could not find it among the royal souvenirs: curls of hair, the dauphin's lead soldiers, chess pieces, the king's geometry set, shaving bowl and razor, and fragments of his waistcoat, whimsically made into butterflies. Perhaps, like one of Diana's dresses, it has gone on tour. Even more than Diana, Marie-Antoinette *was* her frocks. They defined her and betrayed her. Madame Roland reported that when Marie-Antoinette tried to eavesdrop on a conversation between Pétion and the king, Pétion detected her presence by 'the rustle of silk'.

'It is she who invented the modern princess,' says Chantal Thomas. She was the prototype: blonde, blue-eyed, with porcelain skin. Until Marie-Antoinette, the queens of France had been of interest only as breeders. With her appetite for dresses, jewels, parties and public entertainments, she was more like a favourite than a queen: more like Madame du Barry, Louis XV's mistress, the frequent target of lampoonists. She imposed her style on Versailles, and it was a style of contrived, artful, expensive simplicity, of model dairies and muslin; it

* *The Wicked Queen: The Origins of the Myth of Marie-Antoinette* by Chantal Thomas, translated by Julie Rose (Zone, 1999).

was a charade of private life. Invited to the Petit Trianon to walk in the gardens, Gouverneur Morris, an American in pre-revolutionary Paris, at once saw the hopeless ambiguities of her situation: 'Royalty has here endeavoured at great expense to conceal itself from its own Eye but the attempt is vain.'

When Antoinette left the Austrian court for France she was 14 years old and, according to the Duchess of Northumberland, looked about 12. In a dreadful ceremony on an island in the Rhine, every stitch of Austrian clothing was taken from her, and she was handed over naked to be dressed as a French-woman. Louis, still the dauphin, had not yet seen her, and asked a courtier whether her breasts had developed. The courtier responded with praise of her rosy complexion and bright eyes. 'That's not what I mean,' said Louis doggedly. 'I'm talking about her breasts.'

Thereafter she was a virgin in a nest of vipers. Every party and faction at court scrutinised her for whimsies and gaffes. She had very powerful enemies. Provence, the brother next in age to Louis, was deeply resentful of his secondary position. Among the constant intriguers and gossips were the king's unmarried aunts, Adelaide, Victoire and Sophie (who had been known to Louis XV as Snip, Piggy and Rag). For the anti-Austrian party, Antoinette was the power to be destroyed, the natural target of attack. Her mother the empress kept her under double surveillance. Each month a courier left for Vienna with a letter from the princess and reports from the ambassador. But the ambassador sent a second, secret report for the empress alone, filled with minute unofficial detail about what her daughter had said and done. As Thomas says, it must have seemed to Marie-Antoinette that her mother was clairvoyant.

Fatal Non-Readers

It was not surprising that she sought allies outside the usual royal circles. Her favourite dressmaker, Rose Bertin, was given free access to the royal apartments, and was known as 'the female minister'. Choosing what to wear was Antoinette's waking duty each day. With her first cup of coffee came a catalogue of samples from her wardrobe. Though the fashions of the court were widely studied in the outside world, there were aspects of them that could never be emulated. Madame de la Tour du Pin spoke in her memoirs of the strange gliding walk that the ladies of Versailles developed to prevent them from treading on each other's trains. Rouge, also, had a peculiar function as caste mark. It was applied with a heavy hand and in a circular pattern. It was worn most lavishly on the day of a woman's debut, when she was obliged to simulate the flush of the contrived orgasm bestowed by royal favour.

For outsiders, the court ladies were targets of satire rather than envy. The use of feathers in head-dresses had the unfortunate connotation of fetishism, as well as stigmatising their wearers as bird-brained. Similarly, high hair excited public derision and a quasi-sexual disgust. It required one to kneel, not sit, inside a carriage. It required hairdressers who stood on ladders. Indeed, hairdressers were exalted as never before. Until Marie-Antoinette's day, only noble ladies had touched the royal head. But she employed a man and a commoner, Léonard, and thought so highly of him that she took him with her in 1791 when the royal family tried to escape over the border.

Marie-Antoinette's chief talent was for amusing herself, which she did with some style. She was grandly conscious of the effects of her good looks, and enjoyed performing in amateur theatricals. 'She was fond of charity,' Thomas reports, 'and never tired of the spectacle of her own goodness.' Instances of her benevolence had the flavour of a pageant about them. Sometimes her initiatives went badly wrong, as with her forcible adoption of a peasant child who, having been almost run over by her carriage, was taken back to Versailles to have his lot in life improved. Despite the advantages conferred by his new white suit and his pink scarf with a silver fringe, the child screamed constantly for his sister. Later he went to the bad, hung about with revolutionaries and would die for the Republic at the battle of Jemappes.

Thomas's book is not a biography but 'a history of mythification', the narrative of Marie-Antoinette's representation in the pamphlet press between the 1770s and her execution in 1793. What the historian Antoine de Baecque calls 'the unmasking of politics through the scandalous chronicle of the bed' had been a widespread practice in the age of Louis XV, but now there were fresh young targets and, as the revolution approached, a more beleaguered censorship. In the early pamphlets, beginning in 1770, the focus was Louis and his presumed impotence. The source here was gossip and perhaps leaked correspondence, and it seems likely that the first lampoons came from the court. The queen did not become pregnant for seven years, but diplomatic bags grew fat with anecdotes from doctors and valets and confidantes. The king's nightshirts were studied for stains, and the nature of the stains debated. The goose-queen, writing to her mother, did not know whether her marriage had been consummated or not. She always hoped to be pregnant, but was vague about whether it was a possibility; much had been omitted in her education. All the rumours trickled down from the royal household through the clandestine press to the streets. The Parisians sang: 'Some say he can't get it up! Some say he can't get it in.' The king's limp organ and the queen's bodice-ripping frustration were portrayed in copperplate engravings. The pamphleteers, mysteriously, knew every bitter word the couple exchanged.

From 1789 the number of publications directed against the queen rose rapidly. Some denounced Marie-Antoinette's political crimes: being an Austrian, spending too much money, corrupting the king with her notions, favouring this party or that. Some ribald tracts were concerned primarily with her alleged promiscuity. She was an adulteress, given to 'uterine furies', who prevented herself from having children by indulging in lesbian practices or aborting her pregnancies; later, she was an adulteress who gave birth – but to bastards. A great number of pamphlets were hybrids of satire and pornography in which political and sexual innuendo swirl in a pantomime mix of scenes of copulation and conspiracy, endless unbuttoning and tupping and frotting and plotting.

'All our calamities, past, present and to come, have always been and will always be her doing' was the constant theme of the pamphlets. Like a Sadean heroine, she tries her hand at every crime. Louis is portrayed in the pamphlets as a snoring booby, not just a cuckold but a drunk; his physical impotence has become moral impotence too, and the king who was once a cipher, 'a naught', is fitted out in verse and engraving with gross animal characteristics. The queen's sexual style is crude and voracious: 'If all the cocks that have been in my cunt were put end to end, they would stretch all the way from Paris to Versailles.' She sucks men in and spits them out, symbolically castrating them. In 'The Royal Bordello' the queen copulates with a knight, and 'the baron, the marquis and the bishop bugger each other while awaiting their turn.' After several bouts of copulation, the queen exclaims: 'Get off now. It's time for soup; we've had enough bawdiness.'

Early in the 20th century the historian Hector Fleischmann found 126 pamphlets against Marie-Antoinette in which the main theme was 'libertinage'. But this figure does not give much idea of the way the pamphlets multiplied, edition after edition, and disseminated their libels through all levels of society. A particular title often had different authors at different stages of its life, and was reissued with supplements and up-to-date slurs. There were forgeries of the most popular titles, so that libels bred shadow libels. The pamphlets took various forms: songs, burlesque playlets, mock biographies with the appurtenances of cod scholarship. They often purported to be fragmentary manuscripts found by innocent passers-by and made public by their scandalised readers for the good of the realm. The Palais Royal was a favourite place to 'find' these manuscripts. The public gardens were owned by the Duke of Orléans, the king's cousin and rival. They were full of brothels and gambling joints, and a centre for the un-respectable opposition to the regime; writings were 'found' there because it was there that they were created. Others were 'found' in the captured Bastille.

Chantal Thomas is not interested primarily in the source of the pamphlets or how they were distributed. Robert Darnton and Daniel Roche, among others, have made extensive studies of the underground press, of the mechanics of clandestine production and distribution. Some of the pamphlets are translated here for the first time, but of course there is nothing new in the observation that the Old Regime was undermined by slander and pornography. Few biographers of the queen have tried to avoid reference to or quotation from these pamphlets. But Thomas thinks there is a problem with the way they have perceived them. They have interpreted the writings 'as though they had a direct relationship with the personality of Louis XVI's wife'. They judge the queen in as far as they believe, or disbelieve, the pamphlets. They trace a particular slander to an innocent mistake by the queen; or they believe that exaggeration always contains the germ of a reality; or they believe 'she brought it upon herself.' Louis is seen as well intentioned but weak, she as the stronger character, who leads him astray and makes his people hate him. Even the gushing sentimentalists who have made Antoinette their special study are quick to point a moral, saying she should have been sweeter to her spouse. History is reduced to a highly personal analysis of cause and effect; the 'character' of both spouses and of the marriage itself is picked apart and Antoinette is castigated, more in sorrow than in anger, for being light-minded.

Struck by the 'awesome monstrosity', the 'flagrant unreality' of the figure represented in the pamphlets, Thomas approaches them as a student of Roland Barthes, seeing them 'not as testimony but as an autonomous system endowed with its own rules, its own rhetoric, its particular function'. For her, myth is a system of communication, not an object or concept in itself, and the function of the pamphlets was to elaborate a mythology, but 'the symbolic violence of the pamphlets cried out to be made real by action.'

It was the misogyny of contemporaries and historians that, Thomas believes, made possible the traditional approach, whereby the pamphlets are given the status of evidence. Both the pamphlets and historians' responses to them reveal the hatred and fear engendered by 'the dark continent of the feminine'. It has become a commonplace to say that the revolution mobilised intense anxiety about the role of the father and to claim that in the course of the revolutionary years the role was redefined, from that of tyrant to that of nurturer. At the same time, it is said, the role of mother was explored and in some senses exalted; women become good patriots not by direct action but by being fecund wives and dutiful mothers. Thomas is conscious that this is a complex and much explored area, and is content to point out that revolutionary feminists (of both sexes) had to contend not only with deeply embedded and irrational fears of the feminine but with the revolution's own sacred texts: with Rousseau's horror of women in public life and Diderot's conviction that women together are always up to no good. The women about Marie-Antoinette, as portrayed in the pamphlets, are sniggering helpmeets to her festering schemes. They introduce her lovers to her presence and arouse her physically in preparation for them. Reproductive sex gives way to sex as libertinage. Antoinette is undermining the dynasty, first by failing to have children, then by presenting Louis with bastards. She is unnatural, denatured; the journalist Louise Robert says 'a woman who becomes queen changes her sex.' All the men in the news copulate with Antoinette: the king's brother Artois, the cardinal Rohan, Lafayette, Axel von Fersen. But times are changing. Suddenly, the 'man in the street' is the man in the news. 'You have to be Swedish to mean anything to me,' the 'queen' says, thinking of Fersen; but then adds, democratically: 'or you have to be a great strapping man.' The people itself can copulate with Antoinette; the Declaration of the Rights of Man, rolled into a sheaf, is the people's phallus. But what can be born of this union? What can come from the stranger's womb other than monsters?

In *The Family Romance of the French Revolution* (1992), Lynn Hunt explored the pamphlet literature in detail and observed all its contradictions. How can a vain, half-educated and frivolous woman become a 'political tarantula', and exercise a demonic cleverness in affairs of state? But no one at the time was concerned with consistency; the pamphlets have only the logic of fantasy. What sprang into existence, Thomas says, was 'a caricatured double who lived her own life and developed according to the internal logic of a genre that required "ever worse" as a law of necessity'. She compares Marie-Antoinette to Sade: 'The condemnation of each arose from the same lack of distinction between person and text.' Sade, in her view, paid the penalty for the crimes of his characters, and Antoinette for the crimes of the characters she incarnates.

For in the underground literature Marie-Antoinette exists in various personae, ancient and modern. She is Messalina; she is Eve, facilitating the work of the devil. Not only is she the daughter-agent of that other atrocious feminine ruler, the empress of Austria, she is the malign spirit of all the queens who went before her; Catherine de' Medici appears in her dreams and urges her to 'let rivers of blood flow.' The wombs of these wicked queens are poisonous caverns, like feudal fortresses or the lairs of fabulous beasts. Antoinette is the bad mother of fairy tales. She is compared to the wicked Queen Fredegond, 'executioner of humankind', of whom Louise Robert reports that one day she showed her daughter a chest containing rich fabric and jewels, and when the daughter bent over to examine them, slammed the lid on her head.

What did the real-life Antoinette make of these pamphlets? Early in her career, Thomas says, she was oblivious to the danger, referring lightly to the libels in a letter to her mother. The police took them seriously, because they were about personalities, and court politics was about personalities too. But Marie-Antoinette was a 'fatal non-reader', as Sue Townsend described Diana. No one had ever known her to finish a book. Perhaps, Thomas says, it was because she did not want to know the ending. If you are not armoured by the vicarious, by the pleasures and pains of imaginative experience, all that occurs will seem new and personal. It appears that people outside the palace thought about the queen constantly, but she never thought about them. She had barely travelled outside her palaces. Her public was 'presumed to bear good will'. She had no language in which to negotiate with the new order; she was accustomed to banter, not dialogue. She did not witness her own mythification, but performed the process in her turn; she called the legislators of 1791 'beasts' and dreamed of revenge.

How did the people of the time understand these pamphlets? Did they believe them? It is evident that the writers did not believe themselves, and often seem to be winking at the reader, inviting complicity in myth-making. One pamphlet of 1789 says in its preface: 'the incredible things you are about to read were not invented for pleasure; even if they are a little bit exaggerated for fun, at least the foundation is true.' The writer then goes on to say: 'anyone can add what he knows to what he is about to read – and who hasn't heard something?' This suggests that the public of the time believed/disbelieved in the crimes of the queen just as people now believe/disbelieve in aliens. They think there may be something in it, though they know the stories don't bear looking at too closely; anyway, believing in aliens is more fun than not, and at the root of the whole problem is a restless intimation that 'they' are keeping something from us, that in dark palaces and laboratories something is going on that 'they' think we ought not to know about. But relentless exposure to even the most ludicrous stories breeds a sort of popular wisdom, a spirit of 'everybody knows.' An *Essai historique sur la vie de Marie-Antoinette* appeared in 1789 and in its final form ran to 146 pages. It was a summary of most of the accusations levelled at the queen over the previous dozen years or so, and some early authorities believe Sade wrote part of it. Marie-Antoinette speaks in the first person, unabashed, calling herself 'barbarous queen, adulterous spouse, woman without morals, polluted with crimes and debaucheries'. Unlike her real-life counterpart, this mythic Antoinette has no illusions: 'My death is the object of the desires of an entire people.' She needs no denouncing; she does it herself.

So what was to be done with her? The pamphleteers have various suggestions. She could be shut up in a convent, but that doesn't make much of a show. More humiliation and pain is desired. Her offences have been not just against law but against nature, and a fate is called for that will distinguish her from the ordinary criminal. Perhaps the guillotine is too good for her? She should work in the Salpêtrière, or sweep the streets. Her corpse should be eaten by dogs. The fantasies were not confined to the public realm. Lucile Desmoulins jotted in her notebook a violent fantasy called 'What I would do in her place'. Pray for three days in public, she suggested, go through a process of public mourning and penance, then burn oneself alive on a pyre. Such a death, she said, would 'overawe the whole world'.

The reality was more sordid, and deeply strange if you stand back to look at it afresh. It is easy, if you have read many accounts, to forget how disturbing the events of the queen's trial became, as the dream logic of the pamphlets invaded the legal process. Her trial was different from the king's: she was not brought before the Convention, but the Revolutionary Tribunal, supposedly like any private citizen. She had aged – no doubt the Parisians thought that she had the face she deserved – but the focus on her sexualised body was intense. The Tribunal moved from the descriptions of the pre-revolutionary orgies at Versailles to her 'intimate liaisons' with the forces of counter-revolution. She was also accused by the journalist Hébert of incest with her small son. It is unlikely that anyone believed this charge, and it was superfluous to the proceedings. But France was two countries, where the queen was concerned; there was a separate realm in which anything could be true, in which no accusation could be too monstrous. Her sexual body had corrupted the body politic. It was a whited sepulchre, ready for her own bones. 'Myth has a life of its own, based on an internal logic,' Thomas writes. 'It is independent of its support: the latter may die the physical death of the body, but the myth still hovers over the cadaver.'

When Marie-Antoinette was imprisoned, she worked hard to keep the clothes she had respectable, mending and patching. When her scissors were taken away she broke the thread with her teeth. After her death, her clothes were sent anonymously to a hospital. The women who wore them would never know the name of their first owner.

From:	██████████████
Sent:	03 January 2001 09:41
To:	edit@lrb.co.uk
Subject:	news and greetings for Mary-Kay

Dear Mary-Kay, I hope you've had a good Xmas and send warmest good wishes for 2001.

I am now working on a proposal for a Profile book - 3 linked essays on women and the French Revolution - and hope to get it to you and Andrew Franklin within a week or two.

I've been reading page proofs of a book which comes out in April, called Hellish Nell, a study by a historian called Malcolm Gaskill of the medium Helen Duncan, who was gaoled in 1944 after being convicted under the Witchcraft Act of 1735. If you mean to review it, will you think of me? It is quite an interesting sociological study and he is good on the nature of evidence.

Love, Hilary.

Dear Hilary

It was great to hear from you.

I very much look forward to the book proposal — and of course to the essays.

As for Hellish Nell, how cd we resist it?

love

M-K

1

Email from Hilary Mantel to Mary-Kay Wilmers,
2001, with a draft response in Wilmers's hand.

The Dead Are All Around Us
Britain's Last Witch
2001

A PRIL 1944. Winston Churchill sent a memo to Herbert Morrison at the Home Office:

> Let me have a report on why the Witchcraft Act, 1735, was used in a modern Court of Justice. What was the cost of this trial to the State, observing that witnesses were brought from Portsmouth and maintained here in this crowded London, for a fortnight, and the Recorder kept busy with all this obsolete tomfoolery, to the detriment of necessary work in the Courts?

The person tried and convicted at the war-damaged Old Bailey was a stout and ailing Scotswoman called Helen Duncan, whom few people loved and many exploited. She was not a witch in any popular sense of the word; she did not fly, wear a pointed hat or have congress with the devil, and neither she nor her followers imagined that she did. She was a witch only in the sense that she was convicted under an old statute, as a convenience to the court. If the attention-grabbing title can be excused, it is because the author has a strange and pitiful tale to tell.*

---

* *Hellish Nell: Last of Britain's Witches* by Malcolm Gaskill (Fourth Estate, 2001).

Rumours of Churchill's indignation, and of his own spirit-ualist leanings, have been enough to make the case bob back into public consciousness every few years. As Malcolm Gaskill says, 'we inherit ancestral tales reworked by each generation to make their truth powerful rather than precise, moral rather than empirical.' Among the majority today, reverence for Chur-chill survives surprisingly intact; it is a folk-tale Churchill who intervenes in the case, incisive and on the side of the under-dog. In fact, as Gaskill shows, Churchill took no further part in either vilifying or vindicating Helen Duncan. If he was superstitious, that made him like many soldiers and ex-soldiers. If, as a young man, he had consulted an astrologer, then he was a natural leader for a nation that employed state stargazers to track the forecasts of their Nazi counterparts.

Helen's trial lasted eight days, and ended with a jail sent-ence of ten months, which (less remission) she served in Holloway. Prosecuted psychics often elicited public sympathy, especially when the police were suspected of entrapment. Helen's tabloid image henceforth was as the 'St Joan of Spirit-ualism'. The charges against her arose from a police raid on a séance in Portsmouth, where informers were planted in the audience. Though Helen was a well-known medium who commanded a troop of followers, her deceptions on this oc-casion were no more florid, distasteful or ludicrous than the tricks she had been getting away with for years. Fortune-tellers were usually dealt with summarily under the Vagrancy Act of 1824: not hauled before judge and jury, flattered by the attentions of King's Counsel and the national press. So why was the silencing of Mrs Duncan considered so vital by the state?

Her partisans, and conspiracy theorists in general, looked back to 1941, when at an earlier séance in Portsmouth Helen had raised the spirit of a young sailor. In life, he had served in HMS *Barham*. News of his materialisation soon spread among the families in the port. This was a source of dismay to the Admiralty, which had not yet admitted that the warship had gone down. Malcolm Gaskill explores this legend, which is central to the strange life of Helen Duncan. There is a question-mark over how specific Helen's identification was, and whether its precision increased in the retelling. Did Helen actually name the ship, or did she extract the name from an anxious audience member, and produce an apparition to suit? Had there been some security leak which had brought her the knowledge by ordinary means? However it may be, it does seem that MI5 was involved in building the case against her, and it is clear that she was seen as a security risk – damaging to morale, at least. However she got her peculiar knowledge, it was best to lock her up and teach her a lesson.

Malcolm Gaskill has undertaken to tell the life-story of Helen Duncan, placing her in the context of her time and class. The book is also in a wider sense an inquiry into 'how we know the things we know' and how what we can know or choose to know is circumscribed by our culture. As far as Helen and her trade is concerned, he will try for a position of observant neutrality: 'I do not seek to exonerate her, any more than I am committed to a rationalist crusade against superstition.' A Cambridge historian, he is generally a prosaic and stable guide through what Freud called 'the black tide of mud of occultism'. Sometimes his material tempts him into a tweedy sarcasm, and sometimes he strays into twopenny-coloured mode; the people who queued to see Helen's trial were 'curious citizens, successors to the Londoners of Hogarth's day who had gathered there to follow the condemned to Tyburn, jeering and sharing the latest from the Grub Street presses'. Anyone who explores the issue of the paranormal is vulnerable, both to accusations of crankiness and to a sort of self-disgust about the sensationalism involved; and it is hard to sift out an acceptable truth, given the human tendency to confabulate, the fallibility of memory, the wide scope for interpretation, and the prejudice which invests the whole subject. As a good historian should, he insists, he is going to try to vanish in the presence of his subject. He would not like to think that, like some spirit guide made of papier-mâché, he is now Helen's announcer, her mouthpiece, and that his dematerialisation amounts to crouching in the half-light behind a torn curtain on a rickety rail.

He writes very well about Helen's background and her upbringing in the small Scottish town of Callander. Like much else about her, the date of her birth is uncertain. She was the fourth of eight children in the family of a skilled man, a slate-worker and builder. The family were not very poor, but their circumstances were modest and their outlook austere. At the age of seven or so Helen began to report clairvoyant experiences, which her mother warned her not to speak about outside the family. It was a part of the country where folk belief in second sight, omens and ghosts had simply slid underground, and her mother's warning was perhaps designed to protect her less against scepticism than unhealthy interest. The name of Hellish Nell, however, had nothing to do with preternatural abilities: she got it because she was a noisy, boisterous tomboy.

But as she grew up, she developed what Gaskill describes as a 'crippling diffidence, timidity and passivity, punctuated by sudden outbursts of hysterical rage'. It was a passivity which allowed her to be strip-searched before her séances, tied to her chair, enveloped in sacks, sewn into shroud-like cocoons intended to prevent fraudulent limbs from emerging; which made her agree to swallow dye for test séances, and allow her body cavities to be probed by doctors appointed by those who had an interest in proving that she was a cheat. One could argue, too, that it was this passivity which made her choose her trade in the first place, made her earn her living as the mouthpiece of dead people: travelling the roads of Britain, sustained by tea and endless cigarettes, her parasitic husband in tow, her paying public always fresh and expectant, the thought of her needy children ever in mind, and her heavy body always sicker, and apt to take on the sicknesses of other people. It is no wonder that the rage burst out from time to time, causing her to curse out loud, and lunge at sitters who upset her, and try to knock sceptics down with chairs. In the early 1930s, one witness described her as 'by no means a magnetic personality . . . rather a repellent one that aroused one's critical faculties'. There was nothing otherworldly about her coarse features and plain speech, and yet perhaps she was not so unattractive as the self-righteous and brutal busybodies who tried persistently to expose her. If there was money to be made from raising the dead, there was also a profit to be shown from proving the dead to be made of old newsprint and cheesecloth. With credulity on the one hand, bigotry on the other, and greed everywhere, the history of spiritualism shows humanity in an unedifying light.

The town where Helen grew up was a poor community, with low wages and high unemployment. The average age at which women married was 26, which attests to the difficulty of setting up a separate household; the choice for many men was between migration and emigration. When the Great War broke out, the boys queued down the street to join up. But Hellish Nell, 16 years old, pregnant and disgraced, had already been banished to Dundee, and would seldom return to Callander. In Dundee she lived in a working-woman's hostel and worked in a jute mill. She applied for munitions work, but was found to have TB, and sent to a sanatorium. Discharged, she took a post as an auxiliary at Dundee Royal Infirmary, where the sights and sounds of the psychiatric wing worked on what was already, no doubt, a morbid imagination. Her baby was a girl, and would be the first of eight children. Helen's pregnancies were perilous, and some of her children had birth defects. She suffered from a complex of conditions which exacerbated one another: she was hypertensive and diabetic, had kidney damage, and suffered from pleurisy and abdominal pains, which cannot have been helped by her self-punishing habit of ingesting carpet tacks and cigarette ends; it was not just her audience who swallowed rubbish.

Her husband, Henry Duncan, was a Dundee boy who enlisted at 16. His very poor family had a history of hauntings, and Henry seems to have been superstitious, sensitive and intelligent. Later, he would become the theoretician, while Helen attended to the practical business of raising spooks.

Most mediums were women, and the men – with revered exceptions like the great Victorian D.D. Home – were seedy afterthoughts with inferior talents. There was perhaps something degradingly feminine in the pursuit, in the helplessness, the physical indignity of being the plaything of the deceased; gifted men preferred to be impresarios, and manage their talented wives. Henry Duncan emerges from Gaskill's account as a manipulator and a liar, but his early life was sad beyond bearing. Invalided out of the army with rheumatic fever, he would never regain good health. He met Helen through his sister, who was a workmate of hers, and they had no doubt that they were soulmates. They married in 1916, and their early years together were wretched, with one or other of them too sick to work, though Henry took on casual labouring where it was offered and Nell would turn her hand to anything. Henry started a furniture business which failed, seemingly not through his own fault; he had a heart attack, and Helen engaged herself to crippling work in the bleach-fields to feed them, at the same time taking in washing and mending, and organising the sale of stock to pay the creditors. In the end Henry became too ill to work, and spent his time reading spiritualist books; though Helen was widely known to be psychic, she had not yet embraced – if she ever did – the corpus of cult belief.

Spiritualism thrived on disaster, and on poverty. The comfort of 'proved survival' was superior to the airy assurances, given over the years by the orthodox churches, that the deficits of this life would be repaired in the next. For the working classes it had this advantage: it did not operate *de haut en bas*. A practising and proficient medium was likely to arise in any stratum of society, and if you lived in one of Britain's cities you were likely to find one a few streets away. Spiritualism was a neighbourly, engrossing business, offering a particular and home-grown comfort. It thrived in the Mechanics Institutes and the philanthropic and self-improvement societies of the industrial towns. The Great War gave it impetus: all kinds of occult belief flourished, among the fighting forces and among civilians. In the trenches, among men facing death minute by minute, chance incidents were blown up and acquired a magical dimension. When death is dealt out so randomly, the notion of cause and effect is lost. Phenomena like the Angel of Mons, invented by a popular writer, were subsequently 'seen' by thousands of soldiers.

Peace brought little respite to the bereaved imagination. It was as if there was a widespread feeling that somewhere, just out of reach, the young men were still alive. Returning spirits were always in favour of world peace and brotherhood; they were never bellicose or revengeful. Trite though their messages were, one can hear in them the voices of the living, battered by disaster, pitchforked into quarrels of their masters' making. Where did the revolutionary impulse go, in British society? In the 18th century it went to sing hymns at Methodist meetings; in 1917, to bawl spiritualist anthems and sit tight, once again, in the hope of a fair deal in the hereafter. A great strength of Gaskill's book is that it provides, by the way, a piece of working-class history: he makes spiritualism comprehensible in the context of the utter bleakness of the lives he describes. The night Henry Duncan's mother died – a diabetic, worn out, an old woman at forty – Henry and Nell saw her disembodied hand tapping at their window; they recognised it by the marks of her trade, the scars across her palm made by her herring-gutter's knife. The bitterness of imagination that could give rise to such an image, the poverty that bred it, the pity it inspires: all these are part of Helen Duncan's story, and part of a common story which suggests a hunger for consolation that only a new religion could assuage.

If the context is tragic, however, the daily practice of spiritualism was a theatrical spectacle that, as Gaskill says, drew on 'farce, burlesque and vaudeville'. Spiritualism, in its modern form, began in 1848 in upstate New York, where the teenage Fox sisters heard rapping noises in their farmhouse, found human bones in their cellar, and soon afterwards struck a deal with the showman Phineas T. Barnum. Gaskill has a whole catalogue of comic and grotesque manifestations which could only have fooled the most suggestible of sitters, or those determined to get value for money. Performing mediums were hated by magicians and illusionists who, having laboriously copied their feats, would expose them as frauds; some of these illusionists, like Houdini, were disaffected believers for whom the spirits had declined to perform. It would be natural to assume that the spiritualist movement was a branch of the music hall, a low-class amusement, reactive even: washed in on a tide of irrationality, lapping against the stony convictions of Victorian science. But, as Gaskill describes, the opposite case is true: the rise of spiritualism coincided with the high point of scientific materialism, and the assumptions of one creed fed the other.

If you attended a séance, you were not asked to open the eye of faith, but to trust your direct experience; all the senses were to be gratified and convinced. You did not have to accept the truth of the Bible or swallow sermons about the existence of a spirit world: all you had to do was turn up and pay your money, and you would see and hear for yourself. Immortality was sold as a fact, not a pious hope; it was not just the soul that went on after death, but the body and the hands and the feet. Dead fingers stretched out to touch and pat the cheeks of the living, or chalked their messages on slates, or plucked at spirit harps. Discarnate lungs puffed at wind instruments. Bouquets of roses – thornless – were 'apported' into the séance room, and dogs, cats, rabbits and parrots attested to the fact that the inhabitants of Victorian pet cemeteries would rise too. Sequestered behind a curtain, protected by the half-dark, the medium would pass into a trance state and soon the voices of the dead would come through, wanting to be recognised. Masks, wigs, wires, beards and rubber gloves were the props the mediums employed, and for the voices they used their native histrionic ability; a daughter of Nell's once remarked bitterly that if all her mother's manifestations were self-engendered, she was a loss to the acting profession. It was, and is, extremely difficult to reconcile the evidence of witnesses of psychic phenomena. Many séances were becalmed, with long stretches of non-event, so that when a sudden dramatic event did occur the sitters were not sufficiently focused to report on its nature. The same 'manifestations' could leave an audience divided, half of them sneering and half of them moved to tears.

Helen Duncan was a classic 'materialisation medium', and central to her act was the production of ectoplasm, a substance for which there is no recipe, and which now has vanished from the world. Ectoplasm was a milky emission which gave life to spirit forms. It emanated from the medium's nose and mouth and from the area of darkness within her clothes, and took on semi-solid form, with features that the willing onlooker could recognise. One witness to a performance by Hellish Nell described it as 'a liquid spurting from the nipples of her breasts'. In giving birth to the dead, the medium is both male and female; ectoplasm is both semen and breast-milk. From time to time sitters attempted to snip or wrench or tug pieces of it away, in order to submit it to laboratory analysis. Tests were often inconclusive: it was cloth, or paper fibres bound with egg white – or it was a substance unknown. In its most detectable form it consisted of yards of fine muslin packed within the medium's capacious undergarments, or possibly within the medium's capacious body cavities. It was often suggested that the muslin was regurgitated, and it was seriously maintained that some mediums had two stomachs. Ectoplasm smelled like old cloth; or, some said, like death.

Another feature of a medium's performance was a 'spirit guide', in whose voice the medium would often speak. Nell's guide was called Albert. He was tall, and rather superior, and his favourite song was 'South of the Border'. He spoke in a strangulated drawl, his accent veering between RP and Strine. When photographed, he looked like a rolled-up newspaper. He often ridiculed Henry Duncan and showed a degree of contempt for the audience. Helen had a second guide, Peggy, who was a mischievous child-spirit made out of a stockinette vest. Her party-piece was 'Baa-Baa Black Sheep', though she could also produce a verse of 'Loch Lomond'.

This was the practice of mediumship, as carried out by Helen Duncan in a career which spanned some twenty years, and engrossed thousands; it was a joke, a fiction that a child could see through. But the body of theory that Henry assimilated during his long sickly days was created by some of the finest minds of the late 19th and early 20th centuries. The Society for Psychical Research was founded in 1882 by a selection of eminent Victorians. It seems strange to us now that some of the best scientific brains of an era could have been employed on ghost hunts. But these men were not fools. They were asking reasonable questions about the natural world, and trying to establish an investigative framework for a new branch of science. They tried to maintain a healthy scepticism while not rejecting evidence because it came in unorthodox ways, and to formulate an experimental protocol which would be equal in rigour to that employed by practitioners in the more established branches of scientific knowledge. Their intellectual efforts were constantly sabotaged by the antics of some of the mediums themselves: so that spiritualism began to seem shoddy, trivial and childish. And if the showmen made problems for the scientists, so did the scientists make problems for the toiling medium, tied perspiring to her chair, tussling with the outrageous demands of her own unconscious. The events with which parapsychology concerns itself are irregular, spontaneous and ambivalent, but in order to prove that parapsychology was a science, researchers needed to analyse and quantify events which were repeatable, regular and unequivocal. The business of cheating is therefore not hard to understand. Once a medium had achieved results among her family and friends, the pressure was on to perform in public, and then obtain credentials by performing before investigative bodies. Mediums resorted to magicians' tricks, often as much out of a desire to please as a desire to make money; their suggestible personalities and sometimes low status made them vulnerable to flattery and afraid of losing their reputations if they did not get consistent results. Exposure might be shaming, but was not necessarily, or even usually, the end of a career. True believers hit back hard at anyone who challenged them; and there was always a small percentage of phenomena that no one could explain away without resorting to mental contortions that were greater than those required to accept, simply, that the dead were walking nightly through the land.

When Duncan began to practise as a medium, some of her early 'manifestations' were terrifying in their violence and hostility. Her first séances brought her no profit, but around 1930 she began to glimpse commercial possibilities. Soon afterwards she agreed to her first London season, making a contract for sittings with the London Spiritualist Alliance, and decamping to a rented house in Thornton Heath. These sittings attracted genteel society, but they were also test séances, and proved a challenge for Henry Duncan when he had to explain why his wife extruded surgical gauze and fragments of a sanitary towel. Henry, more in sorrow than in anger, admitted that an hour or two before her sittings Helen would pass into a dissociated state in which she would secrete various articles about her person, not knowing what she did. Helen was, then, out of his control: and out of her own. If she cheated, she couldn't help it. Accused of theatrical feats of regurgitation, Helen said ingenuously: 'they give me credit for more than I can do.'

Her great mistake was her involvement with Harry Price, a ghost-hunter, professional journalist and professional sceptic. Price liked to present himself as in pursuit of know-ledge but was really, like so many in the spirit game, in pursuit of profit. In 1923 he had split off from the Society for Psychical Research – ghost-hunters are sectarian and quarrel a lot – and founded the National Laboratory of Psychical Research. The first time Helen saw him, at the headquarters of the LSA, she sensed 'malevolent vibrations'. Nevertheless she agreed to give sittings for him. It was easy to get her into his power, because she always wanted money; her trade was anything but secure. Gaskill does not try to work out how much money Duncan made, but is certain that the various bodies and soc-ieties who exhibited her took a much greater share of the pro-ceeds of her work. By the evidence he gives of changes in her family's circumstances, she made enough to lift them out of poverty; this was achieved by a tough schedule and constant travelling, and by submitting herself to physical indignities at which a prostitute might baulk.

Harry Price set about Duncan's humiliation with sadistic relish. He drafted in two doctors to examine her. 'They brought a bag of tools with them,' he wrote, 'took off their coats to the job and really got down to it. But they found nothing. Every orifice and crack where an instrument or hand would go was thoroughly explored; every nook and cranny was examined; but at each fresh place they drew a blank.' This blankness did not exonerate Helen. At her next séance the doctors pounced on her 'ectoplasm' with surgical scissors, and roused her from a trance by shouting into her face. She was in such bad physical shape that she was admitted to St Thomas's, where she swigged a bottle of disinfectant and had her stomach pumped. When she recovered, the LSA packed her off home.

In 1933, at a séance in Scotland, she was surprised by a sitter who made a grab at her, turned on the lights and found her rapidly concealing 'Peggy' under her clothes. 'I'll brain you, you bloody bugger,' Helen shouted; she was prosecuted for fraud and fined ten pounds. But this setback, and Price's debunking report, hardly affected the esteem in which she was held in the world of spiritualist churches and societies. She flourished, especially when World War Two brought new separations and griefs to which she could cater. Once again, belief was not confined to the uneducated, but was widespread among dons, clergymen and officers in the armed forces; bereavement affected all classes. Gaskill estimates that the creed had a million adherents by 1944; there were a thousand churches and some fifty thousand home circles. In 1941 the royal navy recognised spiritualism as a religion and sailors were allowed to hold spiritualist services at sea. Helen pulled in huge audiences – until she attracted the attention of the authorities, and her antics at the Master Temple Psychic Centre in Portsmouth brought her to court under the Witchcraft Act.

Gaskill leaves it till rather late in the book to ask what might have been going on in Duncan's head through her many years as empress and chief freak of the psychic world. As a historian of popular beliefs, he is more interested in her audiences than in Duncan herself, and his description of the heartless tricks practised by her colleagues and forebears is thorough to the point of tedium. This is not his fault; most books about spiritualism are more or less dull, because once the gross, unsophisticated nature of the frauds has been laid bare, there is no entertainment value in multiplying examples. The 'inner' history of mediumship is far more interesting, but it would necessarily comprehend a history of 'hysteria', in its various incarnations through the centuries: for since the end of the 19th century mediumship has been viewed as a ritualised form of hysteria, which converts weakness to strength and empowers the powerless. (To say this is to adopt the term, neutrally, for the purpose of discussion, and to leave aside the question of whether hysteria exists, or ever did exist, as a definable disease entity; the term may change, but the complex of behaviour once described as 'hysterical' can still be observed.) Gaskill recognises that, when shares in Helen's body are allocated, feminist and also psychoanalytical theories have a claim, but it is beyond the scope of his book to map their territory and patrol the borders. As he observes, it is not difficult to see how mediumship liberated its more genteel female practitioners. They could flirt with their audience and mock them; in deep trance, they could behave aggressively and with an overt sexuality.

With Hellish Nell, the case is rather different. One senses a powerful personality trapped in a sick and disabled body which others despised for its ugliness. Swoons and faints were not the least of it for Nell; her flesh was marked with circular burns from 'returning ectoplasm' (or her own cigarettes) and she often ended sessions as if she had been in a fight, 'dazed in the corner, blood and slime dripping from her chin'. In the world in which she grew up, there was a vast and perhaps damaging disjunction between middle-class ideals of femininity and the reality of working women's lives. Hysteria is empowering but it is also a punishable offence. For Helen, such fame and prosperity as she attained came at a high cost in physical and mental degradation: she was a performer in the pornography of her age. One of Harry Price's allies, a woman who examined Helen, told him she possessed 'enormous depths of pelvis', and assured him that 'pelvic concealment of articles is one of the commonest acts of insane females, especially if there is any taint of immorality in them. One, two and three large bath towels, secreted in the pelvis, is of common occurrence in any Female Lunatic Asylum.'

This is the late-night gossip of ward orderlies, redolent of cocoa and gaslight; it is the chatter of the freak show, from that Hogarthian London which Gaskill evokes early in the book; it is at the frontier of what one can say of a human being, without confiscating their humanity entirely. It would have been good to find Gaskill a little keener to nail it as mythmaking and stigmatisation. But of course, it is not his job to defend Nell or pity her, slumped and bleeding in her corner, the corpses of the Western Front packed into her knickers, the drowned mariners of the *Barham* leaking from her ears. Sympathy is left to Nell herself, who like an infant can only speak of herself in the third person, and speak through the disdainful Albert: 'Thank goodness I love her, she is a poor beggar.'

Gaskill gives a detailed account of the trial of Hellish Nell, but her subsequent history, and the history of her profession, can be summarised briefly. Emerging from Holloway, she was soon back at work, but she had to dodge the spiritualist authorities, and never quite recovered her former glory. In 1956 a séance in Nottingham was raided by the police; subsequently she was taken ill, and died five weeks later, aged 59. By then, the statute which had trapped her at the Old Bailey had been superseded. The Fraudulent Mediums Act of 1951 stated that no prosecutions were to be undertaken without the involvement of the DPP; where money had changed hands, spiritualists could be fined or imprisoned for fraud, but there was an exemption for 'anything done solely for the purposes of entertainment'. This Act, friendly to the trade, drew its teeth. The occult was degraded to an amusement, and television soon offered a better one. During the 1950s, interest in spiritualism fell away; communities fractured; credulity invested itself in flying saucers, and later in crop circles, reincarnation, alien pregnancies, millennial cults. Simple death – except to the rawly bereaved – was no longer interesting enough.

Helen Duncan has successors, though she might despise them. Every weekend – in the South-East of England, at least – the newspapers advertise a selection of 'Psychic Fayres', as an alternative to the usual pursuits of DIY and out-of-town shopping. They are held in the banqueting annexes of steak-houses and the hospitality suites of non-league football clubs, and the mediums – who often themselves practise a variety of psychic arts – are mixed promiscuously with the tarot card readers and the palmists. Here they sit on fringed cushions behind trestle tables draped in sleazy silks and nylon velvets, stacked with an array of crystals and charms: carefully conforming to stereotype, just as if they were in a film about themselves. They have name cards which identify them as 'Tanya' or 'Lilia'; there are no Nells these days. There are male fortune-tellers, but it's hard to see how they make a living: unsavoury, sallow, they slump in their chairs and watch the milling customers with dead eyes; if you touch palms with them, they feel damp and desperate. But the female psychics are smart, sharp-eyed, avid, hungry to work; they buzz with goodwill. If anything, they are too busy; they smudge their lipstick by snatching burgers between clients. They are all of Russian descent, they say, mixed with Romany; in psychic terms, Russian is the new Irish. It is true their accents often suggest an eastern derivation: Essex.

Sometimes mediums give solo demonstrations, to audiences of a hundred or more. They operate in daylight, or in the glare of spotlights; there is no ectoplasm, no materialisation, nothing in the way of apports, no music and no dogma. True professionals, they know how to work a room; they are unnaturally sharp, intuitive and knowing, expert in making the trivial seem profound, or the general particular. Finger hovering over a group of middle-aged women, they will diagnose headaches, or a need to see the optician; they are not above fixing a row with their gaze, and declaring 'someone here needs to see the dentist,' zooming in without error on the traces of childish guilt they have elicited. These observations come to them courtesy of your dead relatives, and it is impossible not to shudder at the banal concerns of the spirits. 'Your mum likes your new kitchen units,' they will tell some hapless woman, who will shift and bleat on her stacking chair, and often shed a tear.

Their reasoning is this: if Mum gave messages of an ethereal nature, pronouncing on the harmony of the spheres, we'd be no further forward, would we? But if she says, that's a very nice double sink, and your mixer tap is beyond reproach, and if she compliments you on your choice of dishwasher, we're in business: it's simple enough – have you a new kitchen, or haven't you?

The suburbanisation of the psychic world was underway before Hellish Nell ceased her trade. Fitted kitchens aside, it has not moved on from the 1950s; to judge by accounts of what the dead get up to, the other world is still observing a British Sunday, old-style, with birdsong, and a picnic in the park. The weather is always fine; no one is in pain; no one ever dies, they 'pass'. In 'spirit world', everyone is at their own 'best age'. The concept of being 'differently abled' has not been introduced there. Torn-off limbs are restored, and amputated breasts. No one is blind or lame. Miscarried babies, of whatever gestation, are thriving in the arms of their great-grandmothers. Those who were aborted are never mentioned.

The psychics draw out information as skilfully as the mediums of Nell's day, and they coax assent from their public by a sort of sweet bullying. It is fair to say that most members of their audience are scared witless; they have paid their money for prophecy and supernatural advice, but if fingered they sit staring like demented cod, struck speechless, and probably unable to take in what is being said to them, let alone process it and make a sensible reply. It looks like the most naked, risible form of public exploitation: but it is possible, even now, to feel pity for the practitioners of this desperate art. It is a sad thing to see a medium hyperventilating, trembling, running with sweat, gasping out messages from the ancestors to the gormless deracinated teenagers of the Thames Valley, who are too ignorant to know their grandparents' names or where they came from. The dead are all around us, they insist, hovering, taking care, taking an interest; but brokering them to the living is a wretched trade. What is the use of the dead talking, if no one has the skill to listen?

From: ▮▮▮▮▮▮▮▮▮▮
Sent: 17 September 2003 01:25
To: edit@lrb.co.uk
Subject: Re:

I think really it would be a bad prospect, because I find the phenomenon a
little coy, cloying; as it happens I've just written a piece for the NYRB about
Norman Rush, saying - well, many things - but how narrow his view of the
country is, and saying how by setting his novel back just a few years, he has
evaded the one, single, crucial Botswana story, which is AIDS - So to be
consistent, I'd have to get on my high horse and denounce the triviality of this
perfectly harmless little set of novels, and I'd end up sounding like Savonarola. I
think it might be over-kill.
An astonishing thing has happened, just this morning, which you will like to
know about. I had a letter concerning my real father, Henry, whom I last saw
in 1963. It was a fair bet that the memoir would make something happen, but of
course you can't be prepared for it. He is dead, it seems. In 1971 (the year
in which he and my mother were finally divorced) he married again - a widow
with daughters. It is one of the daughters who writes to me. Henry and this
second wife got divorced, and then re-married. They knew he had a daughter called
Hilary, and he once saw me on TV and remarked that I was the very image of his
first wife - which is rather flattering to me, in fact, but perhaps I had some
very good make-up. The writer invites me to be in touch if I want to know
more. I do, of course. It is a beautifully-judged and very sensitive letter,
which heartens me. I am surprised he is dead. He would be 77, but I had imagined,
because he was so lean and fit, that he would make old bones.
I will tell you more when I know it. It's been such an odd day! I picked up
the mail five minutes before I left to come up to town, to CBC, to do a long,
searching interview with Eleonor Wachtel. (She had booked an hour and a half of
studio time, to talk right through the memoir.) And of course there came the
moment when she said 'You last saw your father in 1963, and you have never
heard of him since?' And I was able to reply, 'Not till three hours ago.'

Much love, Hilary

Email from Hilary Mantel to the editors,
2003

Diary
Meeting My Stepfather
2003

L ET US SAY, life changes at a glance. Let us say you're walking forward, you turn your head to look over your shoulder, and behind you the landscape has changed. One life, a life you might have led, is snatched back into the shadows. A different life begins.

This is the day I meet my stepfather; it is the day he meets me. I must not take for granted that you know the topography. You have not seen with your own eyes the long snaking road, nor the hedge on one side, behind which the land rises, nor the wall on the other side, beyond which the land falls away. I am four now. I don't go to school yet. I am small. I wear a bonnet. And everything about me is as sweet as sweety-pie. My head is slightly too big for my body. The inside of it is bulging with knowledge.

The hedge looks dusty, grey masking green, as if a deposit of ash has fallen, from some distant perpetual fire. The waste ground behind it, steep and tussocky, seems to fade to monochrome. On the other side of the road the wall is made of blackened stone. Beyond it is the cannery. We are walking uphill towards home.

This is the geography I have purchase on. I don't know

left or right. This is a steep village and so I just know up from down. I just know there and back, what's before me and what's behind. St Charles Borromeo, behind me, is called 'our church'. The school of St Charles Borromeo is called 'our school'. Up ahead is Bankbottom, that is called 'home': I am slow with the word 'home', because no one says it, they say 'our house'.

I am forging towards the crossroads, Station Road cross Woolley Bridge Road cross Tintwistle Road, Tintwistle pronounced (except by my mother) Tinsel. If you leave the door open when you come into our house, people say: 'Do you come from Tinsel?' And indeed, at the very crossroads, you may see the first front door standing open, in the Tinsel manner: not open wide, just fifteen inches or so, just enough to take the effort out of being nosy.

At this age I have to decode the streets before they are safe to walk. It's a snag that I can't read, but I am having all signboards read to me, also the covers of drains and manholes, and those square yellow plates bolted to walls with numbers on them. If you take care to be observant you will see that the roads teem with spoors and tracks, the tracks left for each other by one trade or another, by the companies of men about their business. This plate affixed to the wall, my grandad says, denotes the presence of a hydrant, so many yards that way and so many this. He does not point, but uses his whole hand to indicate: to the forward, to the swerve. Beneath the pavements are pipes and drains, culverts and sewers, and above ground are words to the wise, if you know how to find them. We have just walked on to the toffee shop, at the top of Woolley Bridge Road. If you care to be observant, Grandad, I say, look into this crack in the wall and you will see a big spider. He faces the craggy stonework, bending his back but not his knees. It is low, for a grown man. He presses his hands into his back as he rises. Ee, love, he says, I take my hat off to you. He is a big 'un.

I say yes, he is always there.

Let us say, life changes at a glance. Let us say you are still moving towards home, towards Bankbottom, confident and purposive. Let us say it is still five minutes before you will turn and look back over your shoulder and your prospects will be transformed. Coming up now, just before the crossroads, is the Wesleyan chapel.

One day, previous to this, you are coming home from Sunday Mass at our church. For some time now you have been able to take your eyes off your own feet without the general danger of falling over; that's the stage of walking you are up to. You notice this structure looming up – a big flat frontage, a big dim window. It has some features resembling a church, but not all. Huge window, but no tower: mighty double doors, shut. You cast your eye across the road to establish how it's located for fire hydrants. You touch your mother's sleeve, the deep-cuffed sleeve of her winter coat; soft wool brushes your cheek. You say, would this be a church? The reply is soothing: no, it is a chapel. Read the sign, please. It is the Wesleyan chapel. What would be Wesleyan? Well, it is Methodist. What should be the method? No, no, no, it is a church, of sorts. It is a chapel.

I torment her for particulars. It is called pestering. Pestering about Methodists. She says, they sing different hymns. Have you been there? Oh, once, she says, once or twice, with non-Catholic friends; though strictly speaking I should not.

On higher ground, on another street, on another day but soon, you find a second chapel, the Primitive Methodists. You pull her sleeve again. You are out of breath from the climb up the steep street. Your eyes grow round.

You go about and about, seeking enlightenment. This is how the world gets wrong, this is how the wires get crossed. You should persist in questioning with each individual, not stumble about all over the place looking for answers: but you have to get definitions from whoever isn't too busy. What is primitive? Soon I am seized with mirth: baseless, I know, but I can't help it. I imagine the Methodists draped in animal skins, beating drums, and I imagine them chalking on the walls. People look around in alarm, checking over their shoulders to see who in our backyard I'm offending. 'Mrs Clayton's chapel,' someone says plaintively.

Ho, ho, is she? I run to read her door number. It's No. 60; I'm glad of it. Till now, 58 was the highest number I knew. I frolic outside her door, waiting for her to form a hunting party, or rush out and scalp me; though I know she's a small poor lady, with a piping voice and a bird's neck. Till someone explains why it's wrong, I'm sticking by my joke. I know it's ridiculous, but it's the only joke I've got.

I know everything about denominations: church, chapel, various chapels, Protestant which is St Andrews. At the top of the village is the station. I know various stations, pegs on the map of the line my grandfather draws. To other people stations are places you go to on trips, but Grandad will talk about them even when you aren't at them or on your way to them.

The whole vast train system forms an invisible mesh, drawn tight, under his railway guard's cap. For him stations are places that exist in pure thought form, and which you may represent in the form of a drawing, a drawing in the form of a double streak, a worm, a worm divided into segments, scored off by his pencil. His pencil is not painted, it is the colour of wood. I bite and gnaw the end. Don't do that. Don't worry, I want to say, I won't, it is not a fixed habit with me. I am only imitating Walter Drain.

It is Walter I sit next to, when in time I go to school. He is a penance for me – a penance before the fact, as I am not up to the Sacraments yet, not till I'm seven. Till then, Walter is a punishment for me because I am so distractible, always looking around for someone to engage in conversation. Walter gnaws his pencil so constantly that the wood dissolves into mush and the lead protrudes, fragile, snappable, and taps against his grey baby teeth. It is why Walter never speaks: his mouth is otherwise occupied, sucking, chomping. Walter's father shaves his head. It is a penance for him, perhaps.

When I am five I learn the catechism.

Who made you? God made me.

Why did God make you? God made me to know him, love him and serve him.

What is a Methodist? It is just another method.

What is a hairnet? It is a net made of hair.

At the end of the railway line is Manchester. Land of my father. Every day he travels there, wearing his trilby hat. A Manchester word is 'civil'. Oh yes, he is a very civil man. He wears a trilby and he is a very civil man.

So let us say you are on this road, and it is a year or two earlier, it is before Walter and his pencil, and let us say you are not yet five, and you are walking uphill because you've been down to our school: not for teaching, for a visit. Running ahead of your mother, you are approaching the Wesleyan chapel. You turn and look back. Your mother is pushing a heavy, shrouded object on a baby's trolley. Walking with her is a man you don't know.

Immediately, you feel you should run back and put him in the picture. Does he know what object she is pushing? Does he know this trolley is yours? Does he know you at all, your name and address?

Let's unwrap this. Let's shine a torch back into the mouth of the underworld, and take some notes in the mouth of the cavern. Let's return there, as the fabled dog to its vomit. Let it be a trotty dog with an eager curled tail.

Your mother goes to the school each day but is not a teacher, though she could have been, she could have been, she says, Father Coleman implored her, and he would have got her a grant: a grant is a payment. Father Coleman came up himself and directly implored her, describing to her the reference he would write, and a reference – what is a reference? It is praise of you written down, a recommendation, your suitability. Father Coleman would not have hesitated to put the weight of himself behind it. But an opportunity was missed, I fear, she says: once again she was denied her chance. Other people have their chances in life, but hers it would seem is never. No one would mind the baby while she went to the training college. They could not be responsible, they said, and didn't feel themselves up to it. The baby they would not mind is me.

So she is not a teacher nor a pupil, though once she sat herself, once she, in these very classrooms, these very benches. Once she herself at those desks and chairs, an exemplary, her work books shown about, reverently preserved by Mother Urban long after she had left: shown about to other pupils to discourage them, long after Margaret Mary Foster has gone to work in the mill. She is called MMCF, Margaret Mary Cecilia, Cecilia for the patron saint of music, an art in which she is perfect: her embroidery as elegant on the wrong side as on the right, chain stitch and satin stitch. Her work is unblotted, both religion and sums, and most widely praised her compositions. Her recitation: 'A host of golden daffodils'.

Now she is the school secretary. She does the books; this means enters figures in columns in a big ledger, this ledger is the books. To enter is to write in. It is to write in, *at the correct place*. She types the letters on the typewriter. Keenly she strikes the keys.

One day, we walk down the road to school pushing my trolley. The trolley is empty, as I can walk, thank you. But I remember when my feet rested on its broad running-board, and my fingers grazed its smart grey coachwork.

So this is school! This is the top class, she says, you will not be in here, this is Mother Malachy's. Of course, she says, in your grandma's day it was one great schoolroom, but now between rooms as you see there are half-glazed partitions. I think they are called petitions, but she corrects me.

The air is acrid. The floors are bare boards. I look around. Where did Grandma sit? She says she doesn't know. Did she sit there? Or there? I'll ask her, I say, when we get home, but my mother says she truly doubts I'll get much sense out of her, on that point or any other.

My grandma says all of her life she was in terror of Sister Deshonkle and Mother Desensailes; those, she swears, were their names. If you broke your needle sewing, you were in for it then! We'd to chase a horse to get a hair out of its tail, you put it on your hand and the stick doesn't hurt so much. She asked for a needle to take from home to make up for the broken one, but her mother shouted a curse and chased her out of the door throwing shoes at her. She ran to school where Sister Deshonkle was waiting, grinning and prancing, whipping her cane through the air.

One day, Grandma says, when we was going down to our school, a lass said: look in our window, you can see me mam and dad rolling drunk under the table, and beating each other.

So they peeped through the gap in the drawn curtains, and that was exactly what they saw.

Those were the olden days.

The days of yore.

My mother, because she visits the school so often, brings me red lollipops from it. These are what you can buy at playtime, she says. I realise that, though I am her only daughter (as she is my only mother), she knows how to induct a child towards the prospect of pleasure. My mouth is hardly wide enough to insert the vast red stop sign inside it, but all the same I try.

This is the office, my mother says. She opens the door. It leads off the top class's classroom, and it's really a corner of the room petitioned – no, partitioned off. It's not big, I say, she says no, really just a cubicle. Papers lie stacked on the desk. The typewriter squats among them. It is a great metal machine, gleaming and black. 'Is it steam?' I ask. My mother corrects me: *is it driven* by steam? Then says, no.

She lunges at it, and heaves it up into her arms. Its teeth tip against the front of her frock. She groans, she gasps. She drops it with a thud and a clatter into my trolley. Though delicate she is strong as any man, she says, yet the typewriter causes her to groan. She puts a hand on her back. She closes her eyes. We are pushing the typewriter home, she explains. So that she can type the letters at home, it is going in the trolley instead of me.

I peer at it. Letters lie on its flat yellow teeth. I dab at one with a finger. Don't, she says. Don't interfere with that. She masks it with a great black cloth which she says is to protect it: it is called its protective cover. I finger it; it feels wet but not like ink; I inhale it, a faint smell I can't name. I stare at my fingers, to see if the black has come off.

My mother rests her hands on the push-bar of the trolley, eases it backwards out of the cubicle. She pushes down, rocks it back on its hind wheels, makes a half-circle turn. It rumbles over the floor; we leave the classroom. A big brass bell sits on a ledge. I ask to ring it, she says it would be inadvisable. I take a final breath of the lung-scrubbing air. I see that no one else is at the school, just us. My mother explains it is the holidays; I say, oh, that's nice. We push the trolley across the whole façade of the school, then run it down the slope to the gates.

At the school gates we turn onto the track called the carriage drive. I stop to peer into the Holy Well. It is St Winifred's

Well. The proper name for it is a grotto. The ground all around it runs with damp. Rusted railings stop you from climbing in to touch the stonework, clotted with drifts of dead leaves. If you hang about there at midnight you will see the devil; my grandmother has told me so. It is also true that if you hang about there in the afternoon you will see a frog.

We have reached the main road, Woolley Bridge Road; we turn uphill. What if I am tired, I say: what will we do? I cast a piteous look at the trolley. Under its protective cover, hidden from all eyes, the machine steams gently, it puffs, it clatters at me. What if I am tired and can't walk any further?

You are not tired, she says equably. You can walk. Oh, OK. I always wait to be informed by her of what state I am in. It is a feature of mothers to understand their daughters thoroughly and speak about their states. You are hungry, no you are not hungry, you are tired, you are overtired, I am afraid you have a temperature, I think you need to go to the toilet. They can inquire, have you done anything? This is not a general inquiry, but a rather specific one. My grandmother puts it another way, have you done your business? To ensure you do your business you have Syrup of Figs. In colour like muddied water, it is poured nightly into the shining bowl of a spoon. As my mouth approaches, it foams lightly.

With beaded bubbles winking at the brim.

So we are pushing the trolley. We are pushing the laden trolley up towards Bankbottom, wheeling its important passenger up Woolley Bridge Road. I put my hands on the bar, to help. That, my mother says, is what she calls hindering. When Grandad comes off his shift I can tell him I've been to school today; Good Lord, he will exclaim, you are very advanced! I can tell him I've been hindering, been in a cubicle; I rang a great brass bell.

As it seems I am not tired, I romp ahead, ranging up and down the road, running twenty steps to every one of hers, forward and back, forward and back. I skip, I hop, I glance back to see if my frisking is appreciated; I am not tired. I cast my glance back and my mother is walking with a man I don't know. She knows him, though.

I set my eye on the chapel, looming ahead. I know it's only the Wesleyan Methodists, but it does not stop me thinking merrily about the savage sort. The building is set back from the road behind a high wall, and fronting this wall is a rampart of grass. If you are small it is irresistible to run up and across it, so a muddy path is worn, the width of a small child's shoe, and in the middle of the path is a hole down which I hope there is a rabbit: a sort of token, a town rabbit, available to any toddler who looks into this hole. I've never seen a hair of it, not a glimpse of scut, yet I will lisp, wilfully, spitefully: 'rabbit down there.' Just my little whimsical fantasy, I know. I want to be a child. I want to play my role. My family has only one child and I am it.

I look back at them walking, my mother, the man. I run along the shoe-path, wide as a child's shoe. I skid down to the pavement; I run and skid down again, so long are they taking, so long are they taking to get anywhere, so slow: so slowly, slowly, slowly are they walking.

I look back down Woolley Bridge Road. The weight of the steaming typewriter oppresses my mother, she is trailing her feet, the man is trailing his feet too, his hands are on the bar and he is hindering. They lean together as they talk. Time passes I am sure, though I don't have a watch. I loop back to catch up with them. I make remarks about Methodists: more to myself than to them, but I need my presence to be registered. The register is what they call at school. My mother brings home and checks the register. I count the ticks, she explains. The names denote the children. Zero denotes absence. Absent is missing.

I say: missing? Missing means lost! She says no, it means ill. What are they ill of? She says she can't imagine.

I frisk back towards them; the slow walkers, still hindering, his hands beside hers on the bar of the trolley. I chatter to attract their attention. The Methodists live in there, it is savage. I have seen a half-glazed petition, has he seen it, does he know what one is? I have seen a big brass bell, it is on a shelf, such a small shelf we call a ledge. The devil lives on Woolley Bridge Road, the road between our house and our church, looking for souls to snaffle, looking to catch them in a greasy leather pouch.

Snaffle means to catch up quickly. It is what you do when you are on the qui vive! When Grandma brings in a plate of cakes, Grandad says: 'That one looks good, love – I'd snaffle it, if I were you.'

Thus the devil reaches out, he takes our soul as if it were an iced bun.

When he is unoccupied he lies flat in the ditch. At midnight you will spot him; he has luminous tips to his horns, and flat on his leather paw he carries one tiny candle, the candle from a birthday cake.

The man nods; his face, which is yellow and narrow, makes a narrow smile. Small brown hair, like feathers, springs from his brow. Like my mother, he smiles without showing his teeth. He smiles in a minimal way, as a social obligation: turning up the corners of his mouth. He nods; he acknowledges me.

We are home at Bankbottom, in my grandmother's house, which is to say, our house too. My father is not at home yet. He is still in Manchester, wearing his trilby and being civil. My Auntie Margaret is there from next door perhaps, the back door is open, various people are walking freely in and out. I am in the kitchen. My mother is walking, pacing between the kitchen and the front room. Sometimes she quickens her stride as new people buzz in and out. She turns about and about, to smile at those who come in at the front door and those who come in at the back; she swivels on her heels, smiling into their faces. She is saying to everybody, guess who I saw, Jack Mantel, Jack Mantel. She indicates me and says I was embarrassing about the Methodists; she flutters that she hopes Jack Mantel was not offended, for 'they're chapel, aren't they?' She turns about and about, her hand laid to her cheek; she is performing for an audience. I am in the scene, a thing to be indicated, an accessory.

The typewriter is in the front room, just inside the door, still squatting in the trolley.

It is an appealing tale, the tale of guess-who-I-met. Yet no one stays or lingers. No one pauses in their everyday routine, which includes running in and out of each other's houses every few minutes. There seems, in general, to be a stony response to my mother's news. I met Jack Mantel, Jack Mantel, she says. Her head is thrown back, her hair rippling to her shoulders, her voice trilling with laughter. She stands with one pretty calf advanced, one foot rocking in her high-heeled shoe. Guess who I met? No one answers. Her voice rises high and hangs itself on one of the vacant cuphooks on the shelves above my grandmother's kitchen table.

Knaphill   7th September

Dear Mary-Kay,

I hope you've had a good summer. I've just about
got down to work on my novel, following 3
months of chasing around in the wake of
publication. The memoir comes out in the US
next month but I don't have any plans to go
over — I want 6 months' writing if I can get it.

I know it's been a long time, but would
you still have space for my saints, hysterics
& anorexics, if I were to write a piece

in the next 2/3 weeks? I had done a lot of
background reading, then publication
rolled over me. (There are topics you don't
easily reached the end of, though I'm trying
to keep away from Simone Weil.)

I am so much in your debt for your support
for the memoir. (Sales haven't been great — I
think they over-priced the book — but the critical
response has been more than I could have
hoped for, & the LRB primed that.

I am writing more about my stepfather,
between other things.

Love, Hilary.

LRB (editorial)

From: ███████████████

Sent: 26 November 2003 03:54

To: LRB (editorial)

Subject: Re: saints

It's actually *done* - after a fashion - I need to check the quotes and refs: I am afraid it will be far too long but you can tell me which bits you want and which you don't: you have seen my difficulty - I almost wrote a book. So - by the end of the week. You have been a patron - you know when I got critic's block, and couldn't do Weil? It was almost the same with this piece, and (via my memoir) I have been on a tourist trip via Husserl and Edith Stein, and about and about again with Weil. But I have left this out of the piece.

You are a much more generous friend and publisher than anyone has a right to expect.

mich love, Hilary

26/11/2003

_____

Email *from Hilary Mantel to the editors,*
2003

Some Girls Want Out
The Hair Shirt Sisterhood
2004

WE ARE LIVING through a great era of saint-making. Under John Paul II an industrial revolution has overtaken the Vatican, an age of mass production. Saints are fast-tracked to the top, and there are beatifications by the bucketload. It seems a shame to have all the virtues required for beatification, but not to get your full name in the *Catholic Almanac Online*. When the blessed are turned out at such a rate, the most they can hope for is a listing by nationality. In the current listings there are 103 Korean martyrs, 96 Vietnamese martyrs, 122 left over from the Spanish Civil War (with another batch of 45 in their wake), and a hundred-plus who have been hanging around since the French Revolution. And for the canonised, the site lists nine full saints for 2002 alone, though this is a considerable fallback from the glory days of 1988, when more than a hundred came marching in.

Under previous popes, they dawdled along, at the rate of one or two a year. Gemma Galgani became a saint in 1940, in the reign of Pius XII. It was a rapid promotion, by the standard of those days. After a miserable life, Gemma died of TB in 1903, when she was 25. She is an old-fashioned saint, Italian,

passive, repressed, yet given to displays of flamboyant suffering – to public and extreme fasting and self-denial, to the ex-
hibition of torn and bleeding flesh. Her behaviour recalled the
gruesome penitential practices of her medieval foremothers
and resembled that of the 'hysterics' of her own day, whose
case histories promoted the careers of Charcot, Janet, Breuer
and Freud. But we can't quite consign Gemma to history, to
the dustbin of outmoded signs and symptoms or the waste-
tip of an age of faith. When we think of young adults in the
West, driven by secular demons of unknown provenance to
starve and purge themselves, and to pierce and slash their
flesh, we wonder uneasily if she is our sister under the skin.

Gemma is far less famous than her contemporary Thérèse
of Lisieux, whose remains a short while ago went on a four-
month US tour. Thérèse also died of TB, in 1897, just short of
her 25th birthday. Her illness was excruciating and prolonged.
But popular piety preserved the romantic lie about the wasting consumptive and her gentle death; the sordid realities of
vomiting and bedsores were suppressed, and her convent's
policy of denying Thérèse pain relief was elevated into suffering gladly embraced. Kathryn Harrison's short life of Thérèse
complements Monica Furlong's 1987 study, and is in many
ways more sympathetic.* Neither biographer found the saint
easy to like. Despite her sobriquet of the 'Little Flower',
Thérèse was tough when her saintly interests were at stake.
She wanted to enter the Carmelite order at the age of 14, and
when the local convent told her to wait she took advantage of
a pilgrimage to Rome to harangue Leo XIII, clinging to his
knees until attendants carried her off.

---

* *Saint Thérèse of Lisieux* by Kathryn Harrison (Weidenfeld, 2003).

Gemma never got near the pope, never managed to get admitted to a convent at any age. They regarded her as too strange and too sick. 'They don't want me living,' she said, 'but they'll have me when I'm dead.' Both Gemma and Thérèse were quite sure they were saints. Thérèse had a fantastic imagination, suffused by fantasies of being flayed alive and boiled in oil, but the spiritual path known as the 'Little Way', expounded in her writing, is about the unheroic journey that awaits smaller souls. Thérèse lived within the convent rule, which discouraged displays of zeal, or at least kept news of them behind the grille until the would-be saint's CV had been worked over.

Rudolph Bell's book *Holy Anorexia* (1985) concentrates on Italian saints, and is especially rewarding for connoisseurs of the spiritually lurid. St Maria Maddalena de' Pazzi lay naked on thorns. Saint Catherine of Siena drank pus from a cancerous sore. One confessor ordered Veronica Giuliani to kneel while a novice of the order kicked her in the mouth. Another ordered her to clean the walls and floor of her cell with her tongue; when she swallowed the spiders and their webs, even he thought it was going too far. Scourges, chains and hair shirts were the must-have accessories in these women's lives. Eustochia of Messina stretched her arms on a DIY rack she had constructed. St Margaret of Cortona bought herself a razor and was narrowly dissuaded from slicing through her nostrils and upper lip. St Angela of Foligno drank water contaminated by the putrefying flesh of a leper. And what St Francesca Romana did, I find I am not able to write down.

Starvation was a constant in these women's lives. It melted their flesh away, so that the beating of their hearts could be seen behind the racks of their ribs. It made them one with the poor and destitute, and united them with the image of Christ on the cross. What does this holy anorexia mean? Can we find any imaginative connection with a woman like Gemma Galgani? Like her medieval predecessors, she received the stigmata, the mark of Christ's wounds. Like them, she was beaten up by devils. Like them, she performed miracles of healing after her death. When you look at her strange life, you wonder what kind of language you can use to talk about her – through which discipline will you approach her?

Born in 1878, Gemma Galgani spent almost her whole life in the Tuscan city of Lucca. She was the first daughter in her family, after four sons. Her father was a pharmacist. (This explains why she is the patron saint of Catholic pharmacists. She is also the patron of parachutists – it is hard to work out why, and whether she protects all parachutists, or only Catholic ones.) Her family were financially secure at the time of her birth, though they became poor in her late teens, after her father died. Gemma's mother gave birth to three more children, but died of TB when Gemma was seven. In losing her mother early in life, Gemma was again like Thérèse of Lisieux. But whereas Thérèse was brought up in an atmosphere of stifling religiosity, the Galgani family seem to have been only conventionally pious, and sometimes barely that; when the young Gemma entered one of her 'ecstasies', her sister Angelina brought her schoolfriends home to laugh at her, and later, when she manifested wounds on her head, body, hands and feet, her aunt Elisa complained about having to scrub bloodstains from the floor of her room.

News of Gemma's florid and discomfiting style soon leaked out, and no convent would admit her. So her agonies couldn't be concealed behind convent walls; she remained a citizen of Lucca, with a semi-public career. After her family became almost destitute, another Lucca family took her in, and when she fell into ecstasy, instead of jeering, they took notes. The priests who surrounded her in her later years, members of the Passionist order, had little regard for her privacy once they made up their minds that she was saint material. And yet much we would like to know remains hidden; and so much we need to know is hidden in the footnotes of Rudolph Bell and Cristina Mazzoni's book.[†] There is a certain scattiness, as well as scruple, in the authors' methods, and you wish that, for part of the book at least, they would adopt Harrison's straightforward and conventional narrative manner. Harrison recognises that the subject matter is strange enough that it's pointless to add to the reader's dislocation. At the centre of Bell and Mazzoni's book is Gemma's own account of her childhood and selections from her diary and her letters, but without close guidance from the authors – and we do want to know what they think – it is difficult to fill in the gaps or to make sense of Gemma's petulant and flirtatious relationship with her guardian angel.

The authors do not give us a sequential account of Gemma's life and death. They have both written about her before – the historian Bell in his book on Italian mystics, and Mazzoni, the literary scholar, in her book *Saint Hysteria* (1996), in which she tried to cast light on the relationship

---

[†] *The Voices of Gemma Galgani: The Life and Afterlife of a Modern Saint* by Rudolph Bell and Cristina Mazzoni (Chicago, 2003).

between the typical female manifestations of sanctity and the concept of hysteria, as it was understood at the turn of the 20th century – that is, around the time of Gemma's death. Here, Bell contributes the note on historical context with which the book begins, and writes on Gemma's 'afterlife' – the process of hagiography and canonisation. Mazzoni ends the book with a 'Saint's Alphabet', looking at Gemma's career through the eyes of feminist theology, cutting up the issues under headings. F is for Food, P is for Passion and X is for Extasy. The authors' intention seems to be that we construct the story for ourselves, rather than receive it ready-made from them. They want to explain Gemma without explaining her away. The danger is that her meaning slips between the lines. Gemma is the mistress of ellipsis, her sentences often petering out after a conjunction; her 'but' and 'because' conjoin us to nothing but guesswork. Q is for Question, and the reader has many.

We can understand when Gemma says that her first memory is of praying beside her dying mother. It is the kind of first memory permitted to saints, like Thérèse's sickly assertion that the first word she could read without help was 'heaven'. But we don't know how to understand a passing mention, in Gemma's autobiographical notes, of a household servant who 'used to take me into a closed room and undress me'. We don't know much about Gemma's education; her teachers' recollections of her were muddled and scanty. So we can't tell how much she had read; how far she was an original, and how far she was conscious of modelling herself on earlier saints. Her writing style was childlike, but it is possible that her mind was not. Like Thérèse, she presents a model of arrested development. Like Thérèse, she expressed herself simply, but didn't have simple thoughts.

Sometimes we can trace Gemma's efforts to fit herself into a tradition. At around eight years old, she heard in a sermon of the Venerable Bartolomea Capitanio (d. 1833) who combined the role of mystic with that of teacher, and who was known, Bell says, 'for absolutely never striking her students' – which is a good deal to say, in the context of Catholic education. Like her medieval predecessors, Bartolomea was keen on licking floors, but with this piquant variation of self-abasement: she licked the floor in a pattern of crosses, until her tongue bled. With such a role model to contemplate, it's maybe not surprising that Gemma's first confession, made at the age of nine, stretched over three days.

What did she have to confess? Like Thérèse, she describes herself as a little girl who would cry if she didn't get what she wanted; if she didn't cry, she didn't get. (But what she wanted, usually, was to spend more time hanging around with nuns, or to be allowed to give money to the poor.) She was, she says (displaying the streak of melodrama she and Thérèse share), 'a bad example to my companions and a scandal to all'. She liked to stroll out in pretty dresses. One of her teachers called her 'Miss Pride'. Behind the formulaic accusation is a bereft, needy little girl. Whereas Thérèse proudly promenaded on her father's arm, his 'little queen', Gemma pushed her father away as he tried to hug her. No one was to touch her, she said; and one thinks of the nefarious servant, in the locked room. When her one pious brother, a seminarian, died of TB, she took to wearing his clothes; and when her father died of throat cancer, she slept in the bed his corpse had vacated. There is something desperately sad about these gestures. They are quasi-suicidal, for sure, for she hoped to 'catch' their illness – she had very little investment in life – but there is also something thwarted about them, a bungled attempt at both closeness and control. Living, she won't let them touch her; when they are dead, she touches them. She tries on a man's life, a priest's life; she tries to follow her father, who had abandoned her just as her mother had done years before. Nuns at their clothing ceremonies dress as brides, so Thérèse had her wreath of orange blossom, and veil of Alençon lace: Gemma had a sheet with the sweat of death on it.

Thérèse had been the adored baby of her family, instructed every day by two elder sisters who preceded her into the Carmelite convent in Lisieux. Gemma had to beg for instruction. If she got high marks in class, a teacher rewarded her by spending an hour explaining some aspect of Christ's passion and death. After one of these sessions, at the age of eight or nine, she fell into a high fever, the first of many such illnesses. Sometimes paralysed, sometimes corpse-like, sometimes bleeding and almost always starving, Gemma, in her ecstasies, talked intimately with Christ and with his mother.

What did her ecstasies look like? They were not like the ecstasy of Teresa of Avila, sculpted by Bernini: that most passionate, fluid artefact, art's most convincing orgasm. Gemma lived in the era of photography, and her spiritual advisers provided her household with a camera. She looks demure, her hands clasped. Her eyes are raised to heaven, but she isn't doing anything dramatic, like rolling her pupils up into her lids. Jotted down, her words are broken, repetitive, a string of conventional pieties. Yet she returns from these states of self-hypnosis riven with supernatural pleasure and shot through with natural pain.

Harrison puts it very well: 'Ecstasies are unforgettable, and they are tyrannical. Those who experience them helplessly shape their lives in order to create the possibility of another encounter with the holy.' Like all mystics, Gemma is terrified that God will turn his face away. She wants to love God, but is baffled: how do you do it? Her confessor cannot help her. Jesus says to her: 'See this cross, these thorns, this blood? They are all works of love . . . Do you want to truly love me? First learn to suffer.'

What should Jesus want her to suffer? To talk about female masochism seems reductive and unhelpful. You have to look the saints in the face; say how the facts of their lives revolt and frighten you, but when you have got over being satirical and atheistical, and saying how silly it all is, the only productive way is the one the psychologist Pierre Janet recommended, early in the 20th century: first, you must respect the beliefs that underlie the phenomena. Both Gemma and Thérèse believed suffering had an effect that was not limited in time or space. They could, just for a while, share the pain of crucifixion. They could offer up their pain to buy time out for the souls suffering in purgatory. Their suffering could be an expiation for the sins of others, it could be a restitution, a substitution. Margaret of Cortona said: 'I want to die of starvation to satiate the poor.' Behind the ecstasy is a ferocious moral drive, a purpose – and no doubt a sexual drive, too. Simone Weil believed that 'sexual energy constitutes the physiological foundation' of mystical experience. Why must this be true? Because, Weil said, 'we haven't anything else with which to love.'

Such loving isn't easy. Thérèse, dying, bleeding from her intestines and unable to keep down water, was tormented by the thought of banquets. Gemma, too, dreamed of food; would it be all right, she asked her confessor, to ask Jesus to take away her sense of taste? Permission was granted. She arranged with Jesus that she should begin to expiate, through her own suffering, all the sins committed by priests: after this bargain was struck, for sixty days she vomited whenever she tried to eat. Her guardian angel was her constant attendant and is addressed in the language of the playground and the kitchen. Sometimes he brought her coffee, and when she was weak he helped her into bed. Once he manifested in the kitchen, while the servant was making meatballs. The devil showed himself, too. He was 'a . . . little man, black, very black, little, very little . . . a tiny, tiny man . . . all covered in black hair'. He would grimace and threaten at the foot of her bed; he would jump on the bed and pummel her; when she called on Jesus, he rolled around the floor, cursing. Once he came in the form of a great black dog, and put his paws on her shoulders. Gemma had the bruises to show, and the charred paper where Satan had tried to burn her writings.

In 1899, when Gemma was approaching her 21st birthday, she became paralysed and remained paralysed for some months. She was so ill she received the last rites. In prayer she appealed to the Blessed Margaret Mary Alacoque, who two centuries earlier had been confined to bed for four years by paralysis, and who had made a vow to become a nun if she was healed. The cure was instantaneous and Margaret Mary began a career of spectacular saintliness. During the long nights when Gemma prayed she was visited by a strange presence, someone who touched her with burning hands and prayed with her. After nine nights she was out of pain and able to rise from her bed.

She recovered from her paralysis in February 1899. In May she went into a convent for a retreat. She followed the nuns' strict timetable for prayer and thought it 'too easy'. All the same, she wanted to stay with them, but they wouldn't let her because of her poor health. They demanded 'four medical certificates' before she could be considered. Later she would apply to several orders, and be rebuffed. She had no money for the dowry that convents demanded, but she offered herself as a lay sister – that is, one of the nuns who performs all the heavy work of the house. Nobody was keen to take her up on this offer.

Shortly after her rejection by the first convent, Gemma suffered a crisis. In June 1899, on the eve of the Feast of the Sacred Heart, the marks of Christ's wounds appeared on her hands. She put on gloves and went to church as usual. She said nothing to her local confessor. She was in the habit of concealing things from him – though she knew she shouldn't. This confessor, Monsignor Volpi, the auxiliary bishop of Lucca, never had much time for Gemma. He seemed to regard her as a potential embarrassment. He didn't accept that her experiences were divine graces and ordered her to terminate her ecstasies as soon as she felt them beginning. Even after the proceedings for her canonisation had opened, Volpi's opinion was that 'she was a silly little thing.'

Why such hostility? Volpi was a man deeply involved with church politics. During Gemma's short lifetime, the era of 'Catholic intransigence' was giving way to a tentative accommodation between church and state. The church in Lucca was as beleaguered as in any other city, anxious to give no ammunition to liberals and free thinkers, afraid of being mocked by anti-clerical rationalists. This fear governed the way clerics responded to Gemma. They did not like excess, or passion, or guest appearances by Old Nick himself. It was the church that was most anxious to be reductionist about Gemma's experiences, to debunk them as 'hysteria'.

On the occasion of her paralysis, several doctors had been sent in. Gemma hated doctors. 'What distress . . . to have to allow myself to be undressed,' she says. Having examined her, she goes on, 'nearly all the doctors said it was spinal meningitis, only one insisted in saying it was hysteria.' Now, after Gemma had received the stigmata, Volpi brought in a local doctor who said that the wounds on her head and hands were self-inflicted. He saw marks on her skin which were easily wiped away; he saw a sewing needle on the floor by her feet. After this, Volpi told Gemma that when she saw a vision of Jesus she should regard it as diabolically inspired. She should make the horn sign to ward off evil and spit in the apparition's face. You wonder if this advice would have placated the rationalist opponents of whom the church was so afraid – would they have found the auxiliary bishop even funnier than the would-be saint?

To Gemma it sometimes seemed the local clergy were doing everything they could to obstruct her passage to heaven. At every turn they sought to control and limit her experience.

Her heart told her that the local priests were sometimes wrong, and yet she knew she would commit a sin if she was not obedient to the men who were set over her as spiritual authorities. They told her not to trust her imagination; to stop imagining. Yet her imagination was what connected her to Jesus. Her greatest trial was the emptiness she experienced when she didn't see him face to face. She solved this problem neatly. In one of her ecstasies she dedicated her imagination to the Virgin Mary. The Virgin Mary accepted it – which meant that from that day onwards heaven would work through Gemma's imagination. Imagination, in her view, was the essence of reality. Dreams and visions allowed her to see the true nature of events, discern motivation, penetrate disguises. The devil, satirical as always, assumed the form of Monsignor Volpi and followed her through the town. Just so she didn't miss him, he wore a mitre.

Then to her rescue came a professional saint-maker, Father Germano, a member of the Passionist order – a missionary order, founded in 1741, which shared with Gemma a devotion to the emblem of the Sacred Heart. Germano boasted that he could bring even Garibaldi to 'the honours of the altar'. He talent-spotted Gemma on a brief visit to Lucca, and asked Volpi if he could take over primary responsibility for her spiritual development. He would publish her biography four years after her death and it was in his interest that during her lifetime she should feed him material by putting on paper as much as he could persuade her to confide about her life and her thoughts. In the same way, Thérèse was ordered to write her life-story – but by her own elder sister, who was at that time superior of her convent. Thérèse took to the business with flair and verve, her mind flooded by recollections of her childhood. Gemma, on the other hand, was not particularly co-operative. Germano asked her to write him a 'general confession'. 'All the sins of the world, I have done them all,' she replied. Yet she began to set down the scant record of her life to date.

When the Passionists looked at Gemma they did not see a hysteric or a fake. Where Volpi's doctor had seen blood that could be wiped away, and that suspicious sewing needle on the floor, the Passionists saw eloquent wounds. In *Julius Caesar*, Antony promises to 'put a tongue in every wound of Caesar'. Father Germano undertook a similar duty for Gemma. Meanwhile, his advice to the people around her was to keep her busy – plenty of manual labour – and away from doctors. Catholic doctors could be just as bad as 'unbelievers and freemasons'. Gemma continued fainting, convulsing, vomiting blood and showing the stigmata; Germano advised her to pray for the cessation of these physical manifestations and to ask for spiritual graces instead.

Spiritual graces were safer; even Germano didn't want the girl making a holy show of herself. Bell and Mazzoni demonstrate how potentially subversive Gemma's physical eloquence was. The saint first affected by the stigmata was Francis of Assisi, but it has afflicted many more women than men. It insists on the likeness of the believer's body to that of Christ. It argues that the gender of the redemptive body does not matter. It undermines the notion of a masculine God. It shows that Christ can represent women and women can represent Christ – no wonder it makes the church nervous. There is a trap the church has created for itself – it wants Jesus to have a gender but not sexuality. Under the loincloth of the crucified Christ, what would you find? Only a smooth groin of wood or plaster. His ability to love has to centre on some other organ.

Throughout her life Gemma suffered from palpitations and pains in her chest. Sometimes the beating of her heart was so violent that everyone around could observe it; at autopsy it was seen (by a devout doctor) to be engorged with fresh blood. For Gemma, the heart is the place her pain is centred, the place where metaphors converge. She calls Jesus 'the powerful King of Hearts'. Hélène Cixous has pointed out that the heart is the place where male and female metaphors become one. Both sexes agree it is there that love is bred and contained. The heart beats faster when you see your lover, or in the sexual act. It is the place where Gemma's identity collapses into that of Jesus. She insists that her heart wants to enlarge; she uses an expression that also means, 'to take comfort'. In *Saint Hysteria*, Mazzoni shows how the woman mystic pushes language to do what it can, and abandons it when it reaches its limit. When telling is insufficient, she shows.

This was the church's great problem: men's language, frozen in liturgy and protocol, and women's language, plastic, elastic, expressed in the heaving bosom and the arched spine – the flicky tongue of hysteria, juicy with unspoken words. The church had got itself embroiled in competing systems of metaphor, parallel discourses which it was too intellectually cowardly or inept to try to reconcile; it could only shuffle into shady alliances with the kind of science that suited it. We can see, as 'Catholic neurologists' of the time did, that Gemma's symptoms are a representational strategy. They are an art form and a highly successful one; they are also (possibly) the product of mental pain and distress turned into physical symptoms. We must say 'possibly' because we don't know enough about Gemma's illnesses – at least, Bell and Mazzoni don't give us enough detail to judge whether they were functional or organic. It seems that her doctors were more interested in ascribing meaning to her illnesses than in recording their physical features. If you want to look at Gemma's life as Freud and Josef Breuer might have looked at it (*Studies in Hysteria* was published in 1895) you can collude with the church in describing Gemma as a hysteric. But where does that get us? Holiness and psychopathology can coexist, and perhaps by the time Gemma was making her career you couldn't have the first without what looked like the second. The state of virginity itself was pathologised, and part of the definition of psychological health was an ability to defer to men and accept penetrative sex. Gemma thought she could be both a hysteric and a saint. She clearly understood that the diagnosis was pejorative, and regarded it as just another of the humiliations that God had lined up for her.

At the heart of Bell and Mazzoni's endeavour is an understanding that a phenomenon may retain spiritual value, even after its biological and psychological roots have been uncovered. To describe the physical basis of an experience is not to negate the experience, as William James pointed out long ago. But now that neuroscience has such excellent tools for envisaging and describing the brain, we are tempted to accept descriptions of physiological processes as a complete account of experience. We then go further, and make value judgments about certain experiences, and deny their value if they don't fit a consensus; we medicate the mysterious, and in relieving suffering, take its meaning away. This won't do; there is always more suffering, and a pain is never generic, but particular and personal. We denigrate the female saints as masochists; noting that anorexic girls have contempt for their own flesh, we hospitalise them and force-feed them, taking away their liberties as if they were criminals or infants, treating them as if they have lost the right to self-determination. But we don't extend the same contempt to pub brawlers or career soldiers. Men own their bodies, but women's bodies are owned by the wider society; this observation is far from original, but perhaps bears restatement.

In the 'Saint's Alphabet' which concludes the Bell-Mazzoni book, Cristina Mazzoni works hard at making Gemma's story one of the triumph of the disempowered. It is true that the reckless intensity of her self-belief, combined with her passionate lack of self-regard, make her seem very modern: a Simone Weil by other means. But very unlike Weil, she speaks in the language of the nursery. She calls her confessor 'Dad'. She calls him 'Mum' as well, if she feels like it. She calls Jesus her brother and her lover and her mother. If she obeys Jesus – deferring to him as to one who has suffered and been humiliated – it can be argued that she took on his pain not in a spirit of masochism or passivity but in a spirit of solidarity.

When Gemma was canonised, the church made a weasely accommodation with her career history, recognising the sanctity of her life but not the supernatural manifestations which surrounded her: manifestations which are so dangerously impressive to lay people, who are always looking for a sign they can understand – even an illiterate woman could have read the marks on Gemma's body. So Gemma got her reward for being downtrodden, humble, abject – not for being a living testimony to Christ's passion. Her bodily sufferings and her visions were not part of her claim to sainthood. The church recognised that Gemma had actually felt certain pains and sincerely believed that heaven had sent them; but they were consigned to the subjective realm. Within the church, pain can become productive, suffering can be put to work. But outside the church suffering loses its meaning, degenerates into physical squalor. It only has the meaning we ascribe to it; but now we lack a context in which to understand the consent to suffering that the saints gave.

Anorexia nervosa is said to be a modern epidemic. If you skimmed the press in any one week it would be hard to see what is perceived as more threatening to society: the flabby, rolling mass of couch-potato kids, or their teenage sisters with thighs like gnawed chicken-bones, sunken cheeks and putrid breath. Are we threatened by flesh or its opposite? Though the temporarily thin find it easy to preach against the fat, we are much more interested by anorexia than by obesity. We all understand self-indulgence but are afraid that self-denial might be beyond us. We are fascinated by anyone who will embrace it – especially if there's no money in it for them.

Bell emphasises in his introduction that what Gemma experienced was 'holy anorexia' and that it is different from anorexia nervosa. But what may strike the reader of a secular orientation is how similar they are. Starvation, as Bell shows in *Holy Anorexia*, was not an extension of convent practice, but a defiance of it. A fast is a controlled penitential practice.

Most nuns fasted to keep the rule: the anorexics fasted to break it. Most nuns fasted to conform to their community: the starvation artists aimed to be extraordinary, exemplary. The secular slimming diet is also conformist and self-limiting. Dieting is culturally approved, associative behaviour, almost ritualistic. Restaurants adapt their menus to the Dr Atkins faddists; in a thousand church halls every week, less fashionable dieters discuss their 'points' and 'sins', their little liberties and their permitted lapses. Diets are prescriptive, like convent fasts – so much of this, so little of that. The anorexic, holy or otherwise, makes her own laws. Every normal diet ends when the dieter's will fails, or the 'target weight' is reached, at which point the dieter will celebrate, the deprived body will take its revenge, and the whole cycle will begin again – next Monday, or next Lent. Diets are meant to fail, fasts to end in a feast day. Anorexia succeeds, and ends in death more frequently than any other psychiatric disorder.

Should we be comfortable in regarding it as a psychiatric disorder? Is it not a social construct? If the fashion industry were responsible for modern anorexia, it would be true that we are dealing with a very different condition from holy anorexia. But the phenomenon of starving girls predates any kind of fashion industry. In *The Disease of Virgins: Green Sickness, Chlorosis and the Problems of Puberty*, Helen King has amassed a huge number of references to a disease entity that was recognised from classical times to the 1920s.[‡] Greensick virgins went about looking moony, and didn't menstruate, possibly because they didn't weigh enough; in all eras, food refusal

---

[‡] *The Disease of Virgins: Green Sickness, Chlorosis and the Problems of Puberty* by Helen King (Routledge, 2003).

was part of the condition. The cure was a good seeing to – within marriage, of course. The snag was that men weren't keen to marry women of unproven fertility. They must show, by bleeding, how worthy they were. If green sickness was a protest against fate, it was a horribly conflicted and fraught protest. The cloister is the logical destination for those who protest too much. But in or out of the nunnery, how much should a good girl bleed? Should she settle for the natural orifice, or bleed from novelty ones – palms, eyes?

Sometimes the starving saints broke their fasts, were found at midnight raiding the convent larder. How did their communities accommodate this embarrassment? They simply said that, while Sister X snoozed celestially in her cell, the devil assumed her form and shape, tucked his tail under a habit, crept downstairs and ate all the pies. Starvation can be, must be, sustained by pride. Siân Busby's book 'A *Wonderful Little Girl*' introduces us to this pride in a secular context.§ In 1869, a 12-year-old called Sarah Jacob starved to death in a Welsh farmhouse, under the eye of doctors and nurses who were watching her around the clock. Sarah had been a sickly little girl whose parents didn't want to force food on her. She became a local phenomenon; visitors came to look at her not eating, and left useful donations. It is likely she was fed, minimally and secretly, by her siblings. But when the medical vigil began, this source of supply was cut off, and Sarah was too polite to say she needed anything – even water. Politely, proudly and quietly, she slipped away while the doctors and nurses watched.

---

§ 'A *Wonderful Little Girl*': *The True Story of Sarah Jacob, the Welsh Fasting Girl* by Siân Busby (Short Books, 2004).

It is a grim story of social hypocrisy, deprivation and bone-headed stupidity, but it is also a shadowy story with a meaning that is difficult to penetrate. This is true of the whole phenomenon of anorexia. The anorexics are always, you feel, politely losing the game. When the fashionable and enviable shape was stick-thin, a sly duplicity was at work. One girl, considered photogenic, could earn a living from thinness; another girl, with the same famine proportions but less poster-appeal, would be a suitable case for treatment. The deciding factor seemed to be economic: could she earn a living by anorexia? If so, make her a cover girl; if not, hospitalise her. The case is now altered. The ideal body is attainable only by plastic surgery. The ideal woman has the earning powers of a CEO, breasts like an inflatable doll, no hips at all and the tidy, hairless labia of an unviolated six-year-old. The world gets harder and harder. There's no pleasing it. No wonder some girls want out.

The young women who survive anorexia do not like themselves. Their memoirs burn with self-hatred, expressed in terms which often seem anachronistic. In *My Hungry Hell* (2002), Kate Chisholm says: 'Pride is the besetting sin of the anorexic: pride in her self-denial, in her thin body, in her superiority.' Survivors are reluctant to admit that anorexia, which in the end leads to invalidity and death, is along the way a path of pleasure and power: it is the power that confers pleasure, however freakish and fragile the gratification may seem. When you are isolated, back to the social wall, control over your own ingestion and excretion is all you have left; this is why professional torturers make sure to remove it. Why would women feel so hounded, when feminism is a done deal? Think about it. What are the choices on offer? First, the promise of equality was extended to educated professional women. You can be like men, occupy the same positions, earn the same salary. Then equal opportunities were extended to uneducated girls; you, too, can get drunk, and fight in the streets on pay-night. You'll fit in childcare somehow, around the practice of constant self-assertion – a practice now as obligatory as self-abasement used to be. Self-assertion means acting; it means denying your nature; it means embracing superficiality and coarseness. Girls may not be girls; they may be gross and sexually primed, like adolescent boys.

Not every young woman wants to take the world up on this offer. It is possible that there is a certain personality structure which has always been problematical for women, and which is as difficult to live with today as it ever was – a type which is withdrawn, thoughtful, reserved, self-contained and judgmental, naturally more cerebral than emotional. Adolescence is difficult for such people; peer pressure and hormonal disruption whips them into forced emotion, sends them spinning like that Victorian toy called a whipping-top. Suddenly self-containment becomes difficult. Emotions become labile. Why do some children cut themselves, stud themselves and arrange for bodily modifications that turn passers-by sick in the streets, while others merely dwindle quietly? Is it a class issue? Is it to do with educational level? The subject is complex and intractable. The cutters have chosen a form of display that even the great secular hysterics of the 19th century would have found unsubtle, while the starvers defy all the ingenuities of modern medicine; the bulimics borrow the tricks of both, and are perhaps the true heirs of those spider-swallowers. Anorexia itself seems like mad behaviour, but I don't think it is madness. It is a way of shrinking back, of reserving, preserving the self, fighting free of sexual and emotional entanglements. It says, like Christ, 'noli me tangere.' Touch me not and take yourself off. For a year or two, it may be a valid strategy; to be greensick, to be out of the game; to die just a little; to nourish the inner being while starving the outer being; to buy time. Most anorexics do recover, after all: somehow, and despite the violence visited on them in the name of therapy, the physical and psychological invasion, they recover, fatten, compromise. Anorexia can be an accommodation, a strategy for survival. In *Holy Anorexia*, Bell remarks how often, once recovered, notorious starvers became leaders of their communities, serene young mothers superior who were noticeably wise and moderate in setting the rules for their own convents. Such career opportunities are not available these days. I don't think holy anorexia is very different from secular anorexia. I wish it were. It ought to be possible to live and thrive, without conforming, complying, giving in, but also without imitating a man, even Christ: it should be possible to live without constant falsification. It should be possible for a woman to live – without feeling that she is starving on the doorstep of plenty – as light, remarkable, strong and free. As an evolved fish: in her element, and without scales.

Neal Ascherson in Saakashvili's Georgia

London Review
OF BOOKS

VOLUME 26 NUMBER 5   4 MARCH 2004   £2.99 US & CANADA $3.95

James Lasdun: Losing in Las Vegas

Frank Kermode: Winnicott

Adam Phillips: Dylan Thomas

Andrew O'Hagan: Morrissey

Jenny Diski: Goffman

Hilary Mantel on the Hair Shirt Sisterhood

Covers from the 4 March 2004 and
20 April 2006 issues of the 'LRB'

178

Hilary Mantel: The People's Robespierre

London Review
OF BOOKS

VOLUME 28 NUMBER 8   20 APRIL 2006   £2.99 US & CANADA $3.95

Jacqueline Rose: On Being Nadine Gordimer
Thomas Lynch: MacSwiggan's Ashes

Dinah Birch: Anglicising the Holy Land
Sherry Turkle: Tamagotchi Love
Amit Chaudhuri: Tagore's Modernism
Steven Shapin: A Wakefull and Civill Drink

If You'd Seen His Green Eyes
The People's Robespierre
2006

H E EXPECTED it to end badly, and it did: a bullet from a pistol which shattered his jaw, a night of unspeaking agony, death without trial. During that night – ninth Thermidor, or 27 July 1794 – he made signs that he wanted a pen and paper. What would he have written? We cannot hope that it would have helped us understand him. He'd had his chance, you'd think: five years in politics. The historian George Rudé estimates that Robespierre made some nine hundred speeches. He had spoken, of course; but had he been heard?

Literally speaking, perhaps not. The halls of most revolutionary assemblies had poor acoustics. Then there was the matter of his timidity. When he first emerged on the French political scene, in the spring of 1789, he said that he 'trembled like a child' before each intervention. Many would have felt the fear, but few would have admitted to it. He was easy to shout down. His accent was provincial, his person – he was short and slight and pale – designed to be overlooked. But if he was not a gifted orator, he was a persistent one. By the autumn of 1789, journalists had learned to spell his name.

Most of his speeches survive, if at all, in short newspaper reports. When you read those that were printed at the time, and have been preserved whole, what you find is a pervasive sentimentality, a strong self-referential tendency, a structure of iron logic. The Incorruptible was also the unpredictable. He was a fissiparous bundle of contradictions. He idealised 'the people' and profoundly distrusted anyone who claimed to speak for them. He distrusted the very structures of representation that he helped to put in place. He sought power, and he despised it. He was a pacifist, and helped run a war. In the middle of the most detailed and quotidian debate, he was thinking about posterity; and while he was planning for success he was hymning the purity of failure. He was blessed or cursed with foresight. In the ordinary sense, his vision was defective. Even with the help of spectacles, he didn't see very well, and was, Ruth Scurr suggests, both short-sighted and long-sighted.* His perspectives were strange; the lines between himself and the outside world were blurred. Diffident, rather gauche, he should have kept himself apart from the world; instead, he seems to merge hazily with the times he lived through. He thought he was the revolution, and he thought the revolution was him.

Scurr approaches his complicated story with brisk but sympathetic efficiency. Robespierre was born a nobody, but he is not undocumented. Unhappy childhoods always leave something behind – if only death certificates. Born in Arras in 1758, Robespierre was the eldest in his family; his mother died when he was six, giving birth to a fifth child. She was a brewer's daughter, and had been five months pregnant when

---

* *Fatal Purity: Robespierre and the French Revolution* by Ruth Scurr (Chatto, 2006).

François de Robespierre, a lawyer, got around to marrying her. The de Robespierres were a 'good' family with no money. His mother's death was followed by his father's desertion. François left debts and, no doubt, gossip behind him. The children were split up and cared for by aunts and grandparents.

Later, Rousseau would assure him that people were naturally good, that nature could be trusted, that he was free from original sin. Did he feel he was good, that he was free? His touchiness, his vulnerability, his tendency to flinch from people, suggest an active sense of shame. Later he would champion the rights of illegitimate children. He insisted, at an early stage in his career as a legislator, that the age-old concept of 'bad blood' should be abandoned. Children were not responsible for what their parents did, what their parents were. You get a fresh start in this life; the ideal Robespierrist state would have guaranteed it, educating you and keeping you from want. In a democracy, an individual would be judged by his merits, not by the accident of his birth.

The life of Maximilien is conventionally divided into 31 years that don't matter and five that do. It's like the life of Christ: private obscurity followed by public ministry and agonising and public death. (The parallels were not lost on those who were inclined to adore him or satirise him.) We do not know how the break-up of his family affected him, because he never talked about his early life. But to make sense of him we probably do need to think about what he was like as a child. How has Scurr engaged with her subject? 'I have tried to be his friend,' she says. If you had met him when he was ten you would probably have thought: he needs one.

Robespierre had a scholarship to the prestigious Louis-le-Grand, formerly a Jesuit institution, which operated under the auspices of the University of Paris. His strength of character, his seriousness, were thought remarkable. One of the priests, Father Hérivaux, called him 'my Roman'. Later, a disaffected former schoolfellow, the journalist Camille Desmoulins, would compare the reign of Robespierre to the reign of the Emperor Tiberius. That wasn't what Father Hérivaux had meant at the time.

At 23, Robespierre returned to Arras to make a career as a lawyer, and look after his brother Augustin and his sister Charlotte. Augustin would follow him into revolutionary politics and die with him. Charlotte, who lived to be an old woman, left ghostwritten memoirs; she was gushingly fond of her brothers, though when they were alive she complained incessantly that she didn't get enough of their attention. She gives us the domestic detail; records of the Artois courts give us a little more. Like many educated young men of the time, Robespierre cultivated his sensibilities. He wrote a little light verse. He was sociable, up to a point. He had women friends. He could easily have married. Except for his spectacular absent-mindedness – he once served the soup onto the tablecloth, not noticing the absence of a bowl – he was like other people. Reform was in the air; liberal opinions were the fashionable ones. Usually they didn't hamper the individual in his pursuit of a place within the system. But Robespierre was a poor-man's lawyer. He put principles ahead of profit, and ahead of friendship. He was ready to take offence, and ready to give it. In an early poem he says that the worst thing that can happen to a just man is to know, at the point of his death, 'the hate of those for whom he gives his life'.

Robespierre thought about pain and death with an un-flinching intensity which would have destabilised lesser be-ings. It's a mistake to think he possessed an awful prescience, or that he had a power, quite unsuspected by those about him, to organise the next decade on a pattern he had pre-determined. Perhaps his dreams were different in intensity, though not in kind, from the dreams of those around him. It was an era for the young, clutching their copies of *La Nouvelle Héloïse*, to look for something interesting to die of: love, or something else. The young dream of transcending their circumstances, of shaming the mediocrities around them; of saving lives, of being martyrs. When you have so much future before you, life seems cheap; perhaps you cannot fully imag-ine, as older people can, being extinguished, simply coming to nothing.

For most people, the era of selfless risk-taking is a phase. It irritates their elders while it lasts; though sometimes, in pol-itical movements, those elders find a way to exploit it. But then, if young persons survive their ideals, something hap-pens which surprises them: they learn a trade, they develop ambitions, they fall in love, they get a stake in life. Or simply time passes, and middle age beckons, with its shoddy com-promises. But for the Incorruptible, idealism was not a phase. He kept his vision carefully in his head through his twenties and carried it carefully to Versailles, where he arrived a few days before his 31st birthday. Because he was perfectly at-tuned to the times he lived in, because there was a real cause to be served, his wishfulness hardened into conviction, his dreams set in stone. Still, he sounds more like a priest, a saint-in-training, than the seasoned political operator he would become. 'My life's task,' he said, according to his sister, 'will be to help those who suffer.'

We must deduce that he was suffering too. His whole-hearted identification was with the poor, the deprived, the hopeless, and it was this identification which later made him violently reject the atheism of certain strands of revolutionary thought. Given that you couldn't create a perfect society – at least not overnight – you had to leave people with the consolations of belief. It was too cruel to try to convince them that the universe was ethically blind. They had to know that their persecutors were going to be punished – in the next world if not in this. And if you could not abolish poverty, you could at least take away its stigma. You could make poverty honourable, while you were working – through a system of universal education – to help lift people out of it. And you could take away the powerlessness of the poor man; you could give him a vote.

First, of course, you had to give him an election. The poor did not have votes in the election that sent Robespierre to Versailles, for France's first meeting of the Estates General since 1614. He arrived with no polish, no grace and, as Scurr says, 'completely devoid of ironic distance from the events on which he was staking his life'. But he was realistic and clear-sighted when it came to predicting the flow of events. 'Unexpectedly, fragile, bookish Robespierre turned out far more talented at the practice than the theory of politics.'

Just as Scurr understands the powerful religious impulse behind Robespierre's thought, she also understands revolution. It may seem an odd claim to make, but so many of the people who have written about Robespierre, and about the revolution in general, don't seem to understand why the people of '89 didn't stay quietly at home waiting for evolutionary change. Scurr reminds us that Arthur Young, the agriculturalist who travelled through France on the eve of the revolution, was shocked by the landless, the shoeless, the hopeless; he thought the French peasants were as poor and hungry as the Irish. She sees precisely why, to some people, the promise of amelioration didn't seem enough; she understands the need to be out on the streets getting direct results. It's wise, though, to be careful with certain loaded terms: 'mob' is not the collective noun for Parisians, and should not be applied to the curious spectators who came, in 1790, to stare at the royal family when they took the air in the gardens of the Tuileries.

The impetus for popular revolution came, of course, from the towns: from Paris especially. Townspeople were always at risk of bread shortages, of wage cuts, and they were scared of being swamped by even hungrier refugees from the countryside. Small riots were almost routine in those years; they were suppressed, more or less efficiently, more or less humanely. The revolution was given its intellectual justification by educated professionals and by the more liberal-minded clergymen and nobility, but Scurr does not allow us to forget the groundswell of popular desire – the transformative, unifying power of the events of 1789. To anyone with a political consciousness, it must have seemed as if history had speeded up. The slow centuries had dragged by, punctuated by oddly regressive peasants' revolts; then there was the summer of 1789.

The Estates General turned into the National Assembly. The Third Estate had a voice. The king surrounded Paris with troops, and Paris erupted in protest. The crowds attacked the Bastille for good practical reasons – they wanted the gunpowder shut up inside – but when the fortress fell, something fundamental seemed to have shifted in the historical process, perhaps in human nature itself. Camille Desmoulins wrote: 'Old men cease, for the first time, to regret the past; now they blush for it.'

As soon as Robespierre had any direct experience of politics, he understood what type of thought and language a revolutionary needed. When the minister Foulon was killed in the post-Bastille lynchings, he wrote: 'M. Foulon was hanged yesterday by the people's decree.' He grasped at once what was needed – speed, resolution, and a willingness to tear up the law books. Robespierre didn't operate within the conventional power structure, even the one that the early revolution had set in place. He sat in the first National Assembly, but was excluded from its successor by the self-denying ordinance that he himself had proposed. He was never a government minister. His power base was within the Jacobin club, which had branches all over France; he was one of the first to grasp the potential of its cellular organisation. He climbed to power through the insurrectionary commune of 1792, and through a National Convention, which was elected on a basis of universal manhood suffrage – though admittedly, a large percentage of the potential electorate were too confused or too frightened to vote. Finally, the instrument of his power was the Committee of Public Safety. It is the Robespierre of these latter days who haunts our imagination: implacable, remote, his hair immaculately powdered, his well-shaven jaw set, his thin shoulders stiff with rectitude inside his well-brushed coat.

As Norman Hampson wrote in *The Life and Opinions of Maximilien Robespierre*, 'there's nothing the facts can do to change the myth.' Still, one must keep trying: stating the facts as we have them, living with the myth while scrutinising it. Robespierre was keen on scrutiny: he wanted a parliament building with room for ten thousand spectators. His opponents were often dismayed, when he was under attack in one public forum or another, to find the public galleries packed with his female fans. So it is time that a woman wrote his biography. Scurr says that 'throughout his short life, women loved Robespierre: his combination of strength and vulnerability, ambition and scruples, compassion and refinement attracted women with strong defences against obviously vulgar men, but none against the seemingly sensitive.' She herself is defended well enough. 'By all accounts,' she says, 'he was remarkably odd.' In this book, he is singular, but not unrecognisable to us. We may not find his adamant moral purpose among our friends and neighbours; but we listen fearfully to the news, and we know it does exist, elsewhere in the world.

Like all biographers, Scurr hopes to give her subject a private life. She possibly makes too much of Pierre Villiers, a man who claimed, much later, that he was Robespierre's unpaid secretary in 1790. He is the only witness who tells us Robespierre had a love affair. Scurr knows Villiers is a suspect source, but can hardly resist him. (It's as if you can't have a Frenchman without a mistress.) From 1791, Robespierre lived quietly with the family of a master carpenter, whose daughter may or may not have been his fiancée, and probably, Scurr thinks, wasn't his lover. It's not much to go on. The writer, and the reader, knows that an unrecorded private life doesn't mean there was none. It just means that it's private.

Scurr keeps her promise to be Robespierre's friend; at this distance, a critical friend can get close without the risk of a falling-out leading to rapid decapitation. Her book is a straightforward narrative history, and she is a steady guide through complex events. It is judicious, balanced, and admirably clear at every point. Her explanations are economical and precise, her examples well chosen and imaginative, and her quotations from original sources pointed and apt. It is quite the calmest and least abusive history of the revolution you will ever read. It works well as a general history of the years 1789-94, besides being a succinct guide to one of its dominant figures. She doesn't go in for denunciation or character assassination, of the kind favoured by many historians and by the revolutionaries themselves. After a certain point one begins to miss the vituperation: one wonders if she has plumbed the depth of Danton's crookedness, Mirabeau's treachery, St Just's psychopathology. But there's a word that everyone uses when talking about Robespierre, and Scurr is quite free with it: the word is 'paranoia'. Did he have delusions of persecution? No: he had enemies, and they went armed. 'Share my fear,' he would exhort his listeners. They had enemies too; and they were not always the obvious ones, the hostile troops massed on the borders.

Among certain revolutionaries, by 1791, there was a strong suspicion that the glorious Bastille days were not as glorious as they had seemed at the time. How far had events been stage-managed by the Duke of Orléans, who wished to be king, and by foreign powers – the English particularly – who had an interest in undermining Louis? Robespierre suspected that his colleagues were 'masked', that the meaning of events was 'veiled', and he was right. He had once thought Louis a well-disposed king; he had come to learn that he was prepared to betray his own country. Lafayette, the hero of the early revolution, crossed the Austrian lines; so did General Dumouriez, who had led the French armies to their first victory at Valmy. Robespierre had believed in the purity of heart of his colleague Pétion, who had sat in the Estates General with him; he had seen Pétion turn into a pompous, self-serving windbag who thought the king's sister had fallen in love with him. Others – and they were numerous – simply fooled him, from the actor-poet Fabre d'Eglantine to Danton himself. The East India Company fraud, which came to light in late 1793, and which implicated both Fabre and Danton, was a business of such farcical complexity that nobody could see the end of it, or plumb its depths. One can see how threatening it must have seemed – the idea that the war effort and the whole economy was being undermined by crooked army contractors, in alliance with sinister foreign interests. It is perfectly sane to feel threatened by what you cannot see clearly and don't understand. The things that Robespierre didn't understand were multifarious, and ranged from the workings of international finance to the human capacity for duplicity.

Was he duplicitous himself? He was not consistent, and Scurr sees why. He made a sharp distinction between what was possible in a country at peace and a country under threat from external aggression and civil war. In ordinary times, he thought, there was no need for capital punishment, because the state had enough power to constrain the criminal and render him harmless. But in a time of war, when the state was subject to sabotage, it could not necessarily protect itself; you could not ask the soldier to kill enemies on the battlefield if the state did not have similar sanctions for its internal enemies. Similarly, he was anti-censorship, taking the principle of freedom of expression so seriously that he would have carried it to a logical conclusion and permitted pornography. But once again, the principle must give way before the greater necessity of national defence: a government at war cannot, he thought, allow its journalists to be the enemy within.

What Scurr shows very ably is how liberal instincts succumbed to circumstance. By the middle of 1792, King Louis was expecting imminent rescue by foreign troops. In July, the commander of the enemy allies threatened to raze Paris to the ground. The *journée* of 10 August was the response – the mass invasion of the palace of the Tuileries. If the first revolution had been conditional, flawed, and had ended in the creation of a new elite, this republican revolution was a chance to start again. But under the terrible pressure of events there was no chance to turn ideals into solid fact. The Duke of Brunswick's troops crossed the border on 19 August and the prison massacres of September took place in an atmosphere of mass panic. When the butchers went to work, they killed imprisoned prostitutes, and young people in a reformatory, as well as those who could be seen as the enemy within. Robespierre took the opportunity to try to get his opponent Brissot placed under arrest. If he had actually been arrested – Danton blocked the warrant – there is a strong possibility that Brissot would have been caught up in the slaughter.

In Robespierre's terms, this would have been an economical bit of blood-letting. He blamed the Brissot faction for the war, and he did not think they had been misled, but that they were actively conspiring against the revolution. He never extended to his opponents the courtesy of believing them merely mistaken, or misinformed, or even stupid. In an emergency, such a courtesy is meaningless. He knew them by their deeds and he knew them to be malicious. With the enemy only days away, malice equalled treason. So he thought, anyway. He had to wait another year for Brissot to be 'unmasked' before the Revolutionary Tribunal, and guillotined with his supporters. Robespierre deplored needless violence, but could persuade himself rather readily to see the need. Due process was too slow for his fast-moving instincts.

Certainly the war was not of his making, and Scurr emphasises how during 1792 he struggled for peace, standing out against the drift of public opinion and losing in the process any personal popularity he had amassed. He did not agree either with Danton's war of territorial expansion, or with Brissot's war of ideological expansion; he didn't think you could export the revolution's ideals by force of arms. It was a no-win situation, as he was aware. If France lost, the revolution would be over; if she began to win, she would have to thank her generals, whose commitment to democracy was always suspect. The Bourbons would be back, vengeful and furious; or a power vacuum would let in a military dictator. However it worked out, Robespierre foresaw 'a gaping chasm filled with victims'. If you look at the subsequent Napoleonic years, you can see that he was not wrong.

But once the war was a fact, it could be used to justify the instruments of internal repression – the Revolutionary Tribunal, the internment of suspects, and then the infamous law of 22 Prairial, which denied the accused a defence. The Committee of Public Safety – which was originally, like the Tribunal, a Dantonist invention – accreted power after Robespierre joined it, and became in effect a provisional revolutionary government, overseeing the Terror. Robespierre checked the excesses of Fouché and Tallien, who, on mission in the provinces, had committed atrocities in the name of the revolution; and he intervened to save individuals. But his part in the Terror cannot be wished away. Was he a good man who deteriorated under the pressure of events, or was it only in the extreme situations thrown up by the war that he was able to show what was latent in him, for better or worse? How far was he responsible for the bloodshed of 1794? If you take away his responsibility, you take away his claim to greatness. He saw the problem himself: 'Obliging persons have been found to attribute to me more good than I have done in order to impute to me mischief in which I had no hand.' The people's salvation was, he said, 'a task beyond any single man's powers – certainly beyond mine, exhausted as I am by four years of revolution'. In 1794, when the king's sister Mme Elisabeth was guillotined, he was blamed for it by people in the street, even though he had opposed it: 'You see,' he said, 'it is always me.' But he had asked for this intense identification with the revolution, and couldn't now complain.

Why was his purity fatal? Because it seemed to be absolute. You couldn't buy him. You couldn't impress him. You couldn't frighten him. You couldn't lay claim to him – he wasn't a man without human affection, but he didn't let it get in the way of the guillotine's blade when he thought old friends were blocking the revolutionary path. In the end you couldn't even negotiate with him, because he was afraid of getting his hands dirty. For such a pure soul, death was the only logical outcome. You would be martyred, or you would be compromised. You would be the people's enemy, or – as Marat called himself – the people's friend, or you would simply be 'the people', which is how Robespierre thought of himself: the sum of their hopes, the sum of their fears. But could the people ever triumph? Was it even possible to state their case, since history was written by the winners? By the summer of 1794 a revolutionary pessimism had taken hold of him. He was depressed, and physically ill. He was tired; he could well have said, with Marat, 'I haven't taken a quarter of an hour's recreation for more than three years.' He began to stay away from the Committee and the Convention. Who would the public blame, when he wasn't there, if events took an unfortunate turn? The answer was: we blame you.

In the Convention, Robespierre sat on a high tier of seats, which people called the Mountain. His voice was no louder, he'd grown no bigger; but now people listened and they looked. They scrutinised every gesture, they weighed every word. What did he say? What did he mean? Who does he mean? Does he mean me? What brought Robespierre down finally was not a further access of fanaticism, or a proposal to intensify the Terror, but a proposal to moderate it. His mistake, in his last speech to the Convention, was to threaten his opponents without naming names. Every member of the assembly felt himself close to the guillotine, and men with disparate interests acted in concert to destroy him. Many years later, when he was an old man, Merlin de Thionville was asked how he could have brought himself to turn against Robespierre. 'Ah,' he said, 'if you had seen *his green eyes* . . .'

It seems doubtful whether Merlin or many others ever got close enough to see his green eyes. Scurr seems to have got closer than most. In 1865, the writer Edgar Quinet said of the actors of the revolution: 'However dead they are . . . they are still in the fray. They go on fighting and hating.' And hoping, one might add; even now they are two centuries away, we should still be looking to see what we can learn from their hopes and their violent expression. The revolution is not over, any more than history is at an end. Whenever Robespierre was interrupted, something is missing still. Whenever he was silenced, we are listening to the silences. Whatever else he was, he was a man of conviction and a man of principle. We are not now attuned to principle or conviction, but to the trivia of politics and the politics of trivia. This is why we cannot understand the Islamic world, or the conviction of its militants, their rage for purity, their willingness to die. What they have, the heirs to the liberal tradition have let slip away; we're ironical, comfortable, self-absorbed and fatally smug. We think justice has been done; good enough justice, anyway – and we hope that charity will fill the gaps. Robespierre had no holy book, but he had a militant faith, not in a Christian god, but in a good revolutionary god who had made men equal. He did not see his 'Supreme Being' as a figure who offered consolation alone, but as an active force for change. Revolutionaries were to enjoy an afterlife; death, he said, was 'their safe and precious asylum'. His ferocity of intent, his fierce demand for martyrdom, are suddenly familiar to us; he appears to be our contemporary.

When the Abbé Sieyès was old, and the past and present had got jumbled in his head, he used to say: 'If M. Robespierre comes to call, tell him I'm not at home.' Today we must sympathise with the abbé. But however much we don't want to see him, we can hear his light tread on the stair.

LRB (editorial)

From: ▮▮▮▮▮▮▮▮▮▮▮▮

Sent: 18 November 2005 11:39

To: LRB (editorial)

Subject: message for Mary-kay

Dear Mary-Kay,

Just an idea. If you mean to review John Burnside's memoir, *A Lie about My Father*, will you think of me? It comes out in March from Cape.. I've just read it and found it very thought-provoking - it's complex and nuanced and the pleasantly admiring adjectives one sticks on to most memoirs just don't apply. It has a lot to say about fathers and sons and old-fashioned working-class masculinity, but it is also very good on myth-making through the generations and on the imaginative writer's grim underworld - it almost says the unsayable, about the more gruesome parts of one's imagination. And some beautiful prose.

Will you let me know?

How are you? I am as happy as it's possible to be with my new book - I mean, happy in writing it, though it will be a long time - 3 years at least - before I have a finished product to judge. I started writing *The Complete Stranger*, my novel set in Africa, and left it off because it was frightening me - I hope that means it will be good, ultimately - and decided to have a go at *Wolf Hall*, my novel about Thomas Cromwell. Oh, the joy of having a main character who's not neurotic! I wish I'd thought of it before. The only trouble is I have to kill off Cardinal Wolsey soon, and I'm going to miss him so much. The outfits, my dear! I wonder why we bother wearing anything but scarlet.

much love, Hilary

18/11/2003

Email from Hilary Mantel to
Mary-Kay Wilmers, 2005

Frocks and Shocks
On Jane Boleyn
2008

YOU MAY FEAR, from the title of this book, that they've found yet another 'Boleyn girl'.* The subject of this biography has already been fearlessly minced into fiction by the energetic Philippa Gregory. But there is no sign so far that another inert and vacuous feature film will be clogging up the multiplexes. In reworkings of the Tudor soap opera, Jane Boleyn is more often known as Jane Rochford, wife of George Boleyn, sister-in-law to Anne the queen. There are some lives we read backwards, from bloody exit to obscure entrance, and Jane's is one of them. She was beheaded in 1542, with Henry VIII's fifth queen, Katherine Howard. She was one of Katherine's ladies, and for reasons which remain inaccessible to us, she had helped the dizzy little person carry on a love affair with a courtier, Thomas Culpepper. She passed on letters and misled and misdirected Katherine's other attendants; while the lovers got down to business, she snoozed in a chair. Whatever emotion she felt when she found herself sentenced to death, it can't have been surprise. Why did she do it? Stupidity? Perversity? For some voyeuristic thrill? Historians and novelists have enjoyed speculating.

---

* *Jane Boleyn: The Infamous Lady Rochford* by Julia Fox (Phoenix, 2008).

Her black reputation dates from an earlier episode. When George Boleyn was executed in 1536 with his sister the queen, the allegations against him included incest with Anne, and his own wife is suspected of laying the accusation against him. Fox has set out to find the traces of Jane, and to see if her role can be reworked. Is she maligned, misunderstood? Biography must surely begin with an act of imagination. Julia Fox says: 'I'm not sure quite how Jane Boleyn came into my life. She simply did. One moment I was considering a book on Henry VIII's queens and the next those beguiling ladies were totally sidelined in favour of this woman, a pariah of Tudor history, whom no one had really considered before.'

Fox's first chapter is carefully crafted around an absence of fact; she describes, in a generic way, the upbringing of a young gentlewoman with a future at the Tudor court. Born Jane Parker, around 1505, she grew up, probably, on her father's estates in Essex. Jane's mother was Alice St John, daughter of a Bedfordshire landowner. Her father was Henry, Lord Morley, the scholarly translator of Petrarch and Plutarch. David Starkey begins an essay on Lord Morley by wondering whether we should class him like Prufrock as an 'attendant lord': 'one that will do/To swell a progress, start a scene or two,/Advise the prince.' Lord Morley never did become a royal adviser, which meant he was not in Henry's firing line. But he was a loyal servant, impeccably connected, who always voted in Parliament the way the king would have wished and who was wheeled out to dignify state occasions. He gave his translations as New Year gifts to Henry, to the Princess Mary, to Thomas Cromwell. In religious matters he moved, like the king, from orthodoxy to an anti-papalist position, without departing from doctrinal conservatism. In 1537 he sent Cromwell copies of Machiavelli's *The History of Florence* and *The Prince*, 'to pass the time with all in the Italian tongue'. He asked Cromwell to show certain anti-clerical passages to the king: 'In such places as the Author touches anything concerning the Bishop of Rome, I have noted it with a hand or words in the margin to the intent it should be in a readiness to you at all times in the reading.' There is something of the wistful armchair traveller about Lord Morley, an Italophile who had never made it to Florence or Venice: 'Your Lordship I have oftentimes heard you say has been conversant among them,' he wrote to Cromwell. 'Seen their factions and manners. And so was I never.' But he had been abroad, serving as a diplomat in Germany. In 1523, when he was in his forties, Dürer made a beautiful portrait of him; he has a bad haircut and a lean, handsome face, sensitive, alert and still young.

There is no portrait of his daughter Jane. The beringed hands that decorate the book's cover belong to Jane Seymour. No one seems to have noted what Jane looked like, or if they did no description survives. There is a drawing by Holbein labelled 'Lady Parker', and if this delicate wide-eyed child were really Jane, we would never entertain an evil thought about her. But it is almost certainly her brother's wife, the heiress Grace Newport. How does a biographer work, without a single image to hold in mind? Fox's imagination clings to a Holbein fashion sketch, featuring an unknown woman, 'elegant, poised and animated. It is not Jane, but it is how she really was.' To me, Holbein's model looks bossy, sly and smug. That's how far the eye of imagination gets you. Jane made her debut in the historical record in 1522, when she danced in a masque at York Place, Cardinal Wolsey's London house. The ladies were dressed as Virtues. Jane Parker was Constancy. Mary Boleyn was Kindness. Her sister, Anne, was Perseverance. If the cardinal had known how persevering Anne Boleyn would prove, he would probably have stopped the show.

Jane married George Boleyn about 1525. There is no portrait of him either. But we know him as a clever, cultured young man, sympathetic like his sister to the evangelical cause and the vernacular Bible. He was said to be a womaniser, said to be proud. Like his father, Thomas Boleyn, he served Henry in France on many diplomatic missions. He and Jane spent long stretches apart. We have no idea whether they were happy. Their marriage seems to have produced no children. We can suppose that George was displeased to have no heir. On the other hand, it is possible that Jane's childlessness made her a more restful companion for Anne Boleyn than her own fecund sister, Mary; Mary Boleyn was widowed in 1528, and the children born within her first marriage may or may not have been the king's, but she was gloriously pregnant in 1534, when her sister threw her out of the court after her secret marriage to a Mr Nobody called William Stafford. Grumble all you like about the feminisation of history, at Henry's court you can't avoid it; the politics of sex and procreation dominate, so chatter of caudles and possets and babies' caps drowns out the masculine drone of tunnage and poundage and signets and seals. We can assume that Jane was at Anne Boleyn's side on the cross-Channel trip of 1532, when the English and French courts met, and when, detained in Calais by storms at sea, Anne eventually went to bed with Henry. Jane may have been with the queen when Elizabeth was born, and when she suffered two miscarriages, but we don't know what Jane thought about any of it. There is a dubious story that has her involved in an incident in 1535, when a group of London women gathered outside the palace at Greenwich, hoping to see the princess Mary. Henry's elder daughter had by this stage been barred from the succession and downgraded to 'Lady Mary the king's daughter', and there was considerable sympathy for her among women in the country at large, as there was for her discarded mother, Katherine of Aragon. Fox discounts this story; why would Jane have acted against the interests of the family she had married into?

The Boleyn marriage was a good one for her. George ascended from royal page to gentleman of the privy chamber. He was one of Henry's sporting set, a gambler, and like his father he became a rich and powerful man as a result of the sexual favours granted to the king by his two sisters and, if contemporary gossip is to be believed, by his mother before them; even the most fevered bodice-ripping novelist has trouble keeping up with what these people said and thought about each other. When Jane married him, her jointure was £1300, a very large sum to which the king contributed. Her settlement decided what Jane would receive should her husband die before her and was later to become the subject of interesting negotiations. Fox is thorough in her exploration of Jane's financial position at every stage of her life. It is often the only clue as to her more general fortunes. The figures are there on paper; for the rest, it's like chasing a ghost. Perhaps it's Jane's very centrality that reduces her to a vanishing dot on the page. She's always where the action is, if never precisely part of it. No one writes to tell her what's going on, because she already knows. She sees and hears everything, and keeps no diary.

In 1534 Jane crops up in the despatches of the imperial ambassador, Eustace Chapuys. It seems that Henry has been paying attention to one of the court ladies, and Jane has joined her sister-in-law the queen in a plot to drive the young woman from court; the king has found out, he is displeased, and Jane is rusticated. It is understandable that Fox seizes on the ambassador's remarks. No other source offers such personalities, such gossip. But how good was Chapuys's information? He couldn't even put a name to Henry's passing love interest, and he was always looking hopefully for signs of cracks in the Boleyn marriage. The ambassador didn't speak English, and the court was not so obliging as to tittle-tattle in Latin. Possibly the queen's circle gossiped in French, but Chapuys had no entrée there.

If Jane did leave the court, we don't know where she went or how long she was away. Inevitably, her story gets subsumed into Anne's, which in turn is subsumed into the story of the break with Rome. Fox is inclined to make Henry's state sound more despotic, more successful in its absolutism, than it really was. In the 1530s, she says, 'Henry would not countenance rebellion, disobedience, protest or even the mildest and most tentative disagreement.' No state, of course, will countenance rebellion, or it would soon cease to be a state. But there was plenty of protest and disagreement, and Henry and his advisers existed in a ferment of debate. Where did a king get his power from? What made the law into the law? Parliament frequently resisted and amended government bills, and in 1534 the government 'lost' a treason trial. William Tyndale had fled England to escape Thomas More and his heresy hunters, but Anne Boleyn put Tyndale's work into Henry's hands. Henry detested Luther, but listened to preachers who were near Lutheran. He detested the notion of married priests, but his own archbishop of Canterbury was married; either Henry knew this and tolerated it, or his system of surveillance was less efficient than is sometimes claimed. Perhaps Henry would have liked to be an autocrat. But he didn't have the mechanisms of the modern state to help him achieve it. Determined, vigilant and ruthless as your advisers may be, you can't have a police state till you've invented the police. If Henry had possessed the means to stifle dissent in the way Fox suggests, his reign would be much less interesting and easier to understand. She pays little attention to the international situation, though she tries to fill in the domestic one. Her difficulty is obvious. The larger the story becomes, the more Jane Boleyn dwindles and fades. But you can't understand Henry's fiercer proceedings unless you take on board the fact that he was under threat of excommunication, and that once outside the Christian community he was fair game for any assassin or claimant to the throne. At the time of which Fox is writing, the early 1530s, England was on the fringe of being an outlaw state, isolated in Europe. If this does not excuse internal repression, it explains it. It sprang from realpolitik, not from some personal pathology of the monarch.

By the spring of 1536, the best days of the Boleyns were behind them. There is no consensus among historians on how the plot to bring them down was orchestrated, or how far ahead and how tightly it was organised. Possible co-conspirators include Thomas Cromwell, the Seymour family, the conservative 'Aragonese' faction at court, Mary the ex-princess and Anne Boleyn's uncle, the Duke of Norfolk. Arrests took place in the first week of May: of Mark Smeaton, a court musician, and a number of gentlemen close to the king. George Boleyn was one of them. Along with the queen, the suspects were sent to the Tower, and a trial process set in motion. In the end, five men, including George, were charged with adultery with the queen. Smeaton confessed: possibly tortured, possibly just very scared and hoping for mercy. Like the other ladies around the queen, Jane was questioned by Thomas Cromwell. Her vilifiers believe that at this point she lodged an accusation of incest against George, in return for a promise of good treatment after his death. Is this likely? Fox points out how much Jane had to lose: status, wealth. If George were guilty of treason his estates and possessions would be forfeit. It is possible, of course, that something Jane said, unwittingly and without malice, provided ammunition against her husband. But to demonstrate her total innocence is hard. It is true that she wrote to her husband in the Tower, saying she would plead for him with the king. But she could hardly have been seen to do less, and there was no prospect of her meeting Henry face to face. Cromwell was turning away all petitioners, and letting Henry out only by night, to visit the incoming queen, Jane Seymour.

At the trial, George Boleyn was handed a piece of paper, and asked to answer yes or no to the question written on it. Defiantly, he read it aloud: had the queen told his wife, Jane, that Henry was useless in bed, that 'le Roy n'estait habile en cas de soy copuler avec femme, et qu'il n'avait ni vertu ni puissance?' George didn't deny it, and the next question followed naturally: had he spread the rumour that Henry was not Elizabeth's father? In Anne's circle, gossip had become a fatal activity. Did Jane do more than pass on rumours? The records of George's trial are patchy and dubious, but one source has him saying this: 'On the evidence of only one woman you are willing to believe this great evil of me, and on the basis of her allegations you are deciding my judgment.'

But the 'one woman' need not have been Jane. Other companions of Anne's had given statements to Cromwell, and it seems one of them spoke from beyond the grave. Some years before she became queen, Anne had written a strange letter to Bridget, Lady Wingfield, who had grown up in Kent, a neighbour of the Boleyn family at Hever. It is impossible to work out the circumstances behind the letter, but Anne sounds like a woman trying to placate a possible blackmailer. What did Bridget Wingfield know about the queen's early life? One of the witnesses to the trial believed that on her deathbed in 1534, Bridget Wingfield had made a dying declaration to clear her conscience of matters concerning the queen. Perhaps she was George's 'one woman'. Fox points out that Anne's letter to Bridget Wingfield has ended up among Cromwell's papers, and it would not be there if he had not thought it important.

In excusing Jane a role in her husband's downfall, Fox is making her story less sensational, not more; it's good history, but it gives her a problem in holding the general reader. Alternative theories about Anne's downfall are mentioned in the notes, which are therefore more exciting than the text. Sometimes the reader is reminded of Wilde's Miss Prism: 'The chapter on the fall of the Rupee you may omit. It is somewhat too sensational.' The difficulty with Fox's book is this: who is it for? She knows more about Jane Boleyn than anyone else. Her painstaking research would make a handsome academic paper. Her publisher has dressed it up as popular history, and she has provided the padding to go with it; but her credentials as a judicious and restrained historian make her unwilling to set out to entertain, and her uncertainty about who her reader is and what her reader wants makes her unwilling to air conflicting theories in the body of the book. The historian Retha Warnicke, author of *The Rise and Fall of Anne Boleyn*, also finds Jane Rochford blameless, but her view of the last days of the Boleyns is quite different from Fox's. She suggests that the foetus Anne miscarried in 1536 was deformed, and that this deformity, which became known, opened the queen and her circle to accusations of witchcraft. Witchcraft, Warnicke points out, was associated with deviant sexuality; she also believes that Mark Smeaton was George Boleyn's lover. Warnicke's arguments, though dense, are circular. It's likely, though, the readers of Fox's book would find them gruesomely fascinating.

After George's death, his possessions were inventoried, and so were Jane's. We can dress her, if not see her face: her satins, damasks and velvets are laid out for our inspection. The original document detailing her marriage settlement is lost but Fox has reconstructed it from other references, to see what she had to live on. It was a competence, no more; her father-in-law, Thomas Boleyn, didn't exactly cheat Jane, but he was hardly helpful to her. He was hanging onto his assets as hard as he could; his family was disgraced, and he had lost his job as Lord Privy Seal to Thomas Cromwell. Her father, Lord Morley, didn't seem inclined to intervene. He was, though, always on excellent terms with Cromwell, and Jane now wrote to the minister. Her letter, Fox points out, might well have been written from a template. There is no evidence of a special deal. The minister helped her sort out her affairs, but that was part of his job. Thomas Boleyn was unwilling to part with land, but came up with some more money for her. It would take a private Act of Parliament to settle Jane's entitlements, but eventually she would become a wealthy woman. In the meantime, she was soon back at court as a lady-in-waiting to Jane Seymour. We don't know what she did during that queen's short reign. Fox is reduced to: 'With her weeping ladies clustered at her side, one of them almost certainly Jane, the queen had died.'

Along with the young Katherine Howard, the Duke of Norfolk's niece, Jane then attended the fourth queen, Anne of Cleves. During Anne's divorce, Jane was one of the ladies who gave testimony that, to the best of their belief, the marriage had not been consummated; their conversations with Anne suggested that not only was she still a virgin but she was a sexual innocent who saw nothing amiss with her situation. The fifth queen was far from innocent, in the sexual sense. A neglected little girl with no particular prospects, the tenth child of a Howard with no money, Katherine had grown up in the household of the dowager Duchess of Norfolk, where after dark in the 'maidens' chamber' young men brought in apples, strawberries and wine and lay on the beds with the young girls: 'puffing and blowing' followed. Katherine's first lover was a music master called Henry Mannox, a charmer who would later boast: 'I have had her by the cunt and know it amongst a hundred.' She moved on to Francis Dereham, whose activities caused one of the other 'maidens', who must have been trying to get some sleep, to plead: 'I pray you, Mr Dereham, lie still.' Katherine is usually reckoned to have been about 18 when she was married to the besotted Henry, though her recent biographer Joanna Denny thinks she may have been as young as 15. Henry was nearly fifty, obese, unpredictable, increasingly irrational. The marriage took place on the day of Cromwell's execution. Fox says of Jane that 'with the death of Cromwell, she had lost her protector' – which is rather odd if there was no special relationship to be considered. Whatever drove the next part of Jane Boleyn's career, it wasn't the fact that she didn't have a man around who would tell her what to do.

She had now amassed years of court experience. She had been caught up in one huge, death-dealing scandal. She knew of Henry's emotional volatility. Yet she stepped straight out of the role of 'attendant lady' and onto the scaffold. Whatever possessed her, when the little queen fell in love with Henry's favourite Tom Culpepper, to facilitate their meetings? Why did she spy and lie for the queen, help her seek out unlocked doors and back stairs when the court went on progress to the north? 'Come when my lady Rochford is here,' Katherine wrote to him, 'for then I shall be best at leisure to be at your commandment.' Katherine wasn't a good picker. Once she became queen, Dereham turned up at court and pressured her into taking him on as a secretary. Culpepper had a rape and a homicide in his past – the kinds of boyish prank you could get away with, if you were close to Henry. But he was handsome, and the queen's feelings about him were easily apparent to one of her women, Margaret Morton, who 'first suspected the queen at Hatfield when the queen looked out at her privy chamber window at Mr Culpepper'. We all know those looks. Katherine was a poor risk for this sort of game. Culpepper was a little thug to whom Jane owed nothing. So why did she risk her life for them? Again, Fox leaves discussion to the back of the book: 'I think the most plausible explanation for Jane's foolish behaviour is simply that she became involved because Catherine gave her a direct order.' Warnicke suggests that Jane was 'probably bribed' and was 'financially straitened'. Fox's research strikes down this theory; Jane was her own woman, wealthy in her own right, in no financial need of a position at court. But then, Warnicke thinks that Katherine didn't have an affair with Culpepper. While Jane dozed in the chair, they were just talking: Culpepper knew about the queen's past, and she was stringing him along, hoping to placate him somehow, keep him quiet.

It's good to remember, as every page of Tudor history is turned, the misogyny of the age, and the unconscious misogyny involved in repeating uncritically the age's judgments. Jane's villainy may come out of the same deep drawer as Anne Boleyn's deformity – the extra finger, the one that no one saw during her lifetime. That said, it takes a great stretch of the feminist imagination to make Culpepper a blackmailer and not a lover, and Jane Boleyn a woman who was just obeying orders. Jane's personality unravelled with Katherine Howard's fortunes, and one historian, Lacey Baldwin Smith, thinks perhaps she was mad in a covert way all along; this theory has not found many takers. Still, for a short time, she acted suicidally. She was a woman in her mid-thirties, a courtier bred in the bone. She was familiar with the vicious faction-fighting of the court, and must have known that people hostile to the Howard family had an eye on Katherine. Eventual discovery was almost certain. While the court was in the north, the king's councillors back in London were unravelling the queen's past.

It was in the wake of her arrest that Jane 'went mad'. It is the invaluable Chapuys who tells us so. She was released from the Tower, cosseted back to health in the custody of people she knew. Bringing into Parliament an Act of Attainder, which avoided the need for a public trial, Lord Chancellor Audley referred to 'that bawd, the lady Jane Rochford'. She was returned to the Tower three days before her execution. In her speech from the scaffold, if the reports are to be believed, she was pious and conventional, as her husband had been when he faced the executioner. There was a set form for scaffold speeches. You acknowledged you had been convicted by the operation of the law. You praised the king for being merciful; after all, you could be dying a nastier death than by the axe. You didn't have to say you were guilty, but you had to acknowledge that, in the eternal scheme of things, you were a great sinner and that you trusted to God's mercy. Anne Boleyn died like that, as did her 'lovers'. Thomas Cromwell died like that. If you tried anything else, possibly the shocked chroniclers would have taken the words out of your mouth, confiscated them, and replaced them with the usual formula. Your death, if not your life, should be edifying. Katherine Howard managed it, and so did Jane.

And how did Lord Morley mark the occasion? He made a translation from Boccaccio's *De claris mulieribus*, and presented it to the king at New Year 1543. Always scribble, scribble, scribble, Lord Morley: another exquisite velvet-bound book. It contained the story of 46 female figures, some goddesses and others drawn from the Bible and classical history. In his essay on it, James Simpson detected an interpolation in Morley's translation of the story of Polyxena, who was sacrificed by Pyrrhus at Troy to obtain a favourable wind for the homebound Greeks. Departing from the original, Morley writes that it was 'against all good order . . . that so sweet a maiden should be devoured by the hands of Pyrrhus for to satisfy for another woman's offence'. Fox has looked again at the translation and found that Boccaccio's original reference to the 'throat' of the sacrificed woman has been turned into 'neck'. It can be taken as a reference to Jane, and Fox describes it as 'a veiled obituary', though calling Jane a 'maiden' seems to be stretching a point – unless Lord Morley was telling us a surprising truth about the Boleyn marriage. Most of the women in the stories come in for censure, as they did in the original. Europa, when she was raped by the bull, was asking for it; if she had been dutifully minding her flock, it wouldn't have happened. Women have a propensity to disgrace their menfolk, and the only safe way is not even to look at them: 'If then men were wise . . . they would look up with their eyes to heaven, or else shut them and look downwards to the earth; betwixt both is none too sure way.'

Katherine had blamed Jane for entangling her with Culpepper. Jane had blamed Katherine, saying she was only doing as the queen told her. The whole sad and sordid story is distinctively of its time and place. Fox's publisher misrepresents her book by suggesting in the cover copy that Jane was 'a rather modern woman'. Do they think we wouldn't be interested, otherwise? The claim belies Fox's careful method and the sincerity of her intentions. In the end, Jane, like many of her contemporaries, is hardly a fit subject for biography. Her inner life is lost to us. We know more about what she wore than what she thought. We know the company she kept. We know about her grim fate. We don't know why she agreed to walk towards it. It's no surprise that the era has generated so much fiction. If writers are driven, in part, by the frocks and the shocks, they may also be driven by a need to know, and if knowing is impossible, to imagine. It would be improper for a historian to do this, and Julia Fox has not. She has put the factual case for Jane as neatly as anyone could. There is still, though, a gap in our understanding. Too much has been erased. Whatever dangerous knowledge Jane Boleyn carried, it's lost; whatever secrets she knew, she's not going to tell us now.

LRB (editorial)

From: ▮▮▮▮▮▮▮▮▮▮

Sent: 02 February 2006 18:14

To: LRB (editorial)

Subject: Re: (no subject)

That's fine, I'll aim to have it to you in a fortnight. Just opened the new issue, and looking forward to reading the piece on The Tyrannicide Brief - it's such and interesting book - I read it early and put it in all my Christmas selections. Not that I know much about the period, but as you know I have a penchant for regicides - speaking of which, Robespierre has arrived safely. Thomas Cromwell didn't kill the king, but I suspect it may have been a near thing at times. I spend most my time gradgrinding facts at this stage, but I can't help feel a psychopathological bubbling and seething below the surface. They were all so determined on incest or quasi-incest, like people enthralled by their own nightmares. Cromwell was the same age as Henry's dead elder brother, Arthur the shadow-king. He - Cromwell - made two attempts to get related to Henry, and succeeded in marrying his son to Jane Seymour's sister, which was not bad going, since Cromwell's own father was a violent and drunken blacksmith from Putney. Then (as a prelude to executing him) Henry accused Cromwell of plotting to marry his daughter, Princess Mary, and overthrow him. So there is an alternative history of England in which Cromwells are king.
I just thought you might like to know that.
much love, Hilary

03/02/2006

Email from Hilary Mantel to the editors, 2006

Hilary Mantel: The Virgin and I

London Review
OF BOOKS

VOLUME 31 NUMBER 7   9 APRIL 2009   £3.20 US & CANADA $4.95

Michael Wood: G.K. Chesterton
Graham Usher: India in Afghanistan
Marina Warner: Dear Old Khayyám   Rosemary Hill: Bowen in Love
J. Hoberman: Red Chagall   Christopher Clark: Nazi Toffs

Cover from the 9 April 2009 issue of the
'LRB'

The Virgin and I
Marian Devotion
2009

I N MY CATHOLIC GIRLHOOD she was everywhere, perched up on ledges and in niches like a CCTV camera, with her painted mouth and her painted eyes of policeman blue. She was, her litany stated, Mirror of Justice, Cause of Our Joy, Spiritual Vessel, Mystical Rose, Tower of David, House of Gold, Ark of the Covenant, Gate of Heaven and Morning Star. Not a woman I liked, on the whole. She was the improbability at the heart of spiritual life; a paradox, unpollinated but fruitful, above nature yet also against nature. She could have been a benign second mother, and on your side, but she always seemed to be in cahoots with authority; she knew your every move, and had a low opinion of it. It was because of her purity that you had to guard your darker thoughts; each of your little sins was, you were assured, a sword piercing her heart. She was the example you were urged to follow, while knowing that you would fail. Pray all you like, you are not going to be both a virgin and a mother; this was a one-off by the deity, a singular chance for sullied female flesh to make itself acceptable to the celibate males who were in charge of whether or not we got to heaven. It always seemed odd and distasteful to hear priests speak reverently of the Virgin Mary, when you knew they despised women or feared them or regarded them as being as strange as talking fish.

To outsiders, the cult of Mary can seem quaint and charming; but it introduced into the life of every small Catholic girl a terrifying bind, and into the mind of every small Catholic boy a standard impossible for women to meet. By adolescence they had perhaps given up praying to statues, but they carried into manhood a frozen concept of femininity, which they modernised only in so far as they held in mind more current models of abnegation. The adulation of God's mother does not place any necessary limit on misogyny, because she is no ordinary woman, and indeed shows up their frailties, their faults and their follies; she is a standing reproach, best emulated not through spiritual exercises but through hard work and humility. In the Catholic world in which I grew up, men were ministers of grace, and women mopped the church floor on a Friday night with big soggy string mops.

Perhaps the worship of Mary would have been easier to live with if we had understood its deep cultural roots and appreciated how they bound us, schoolgirls with our garden bouquets wilting before plaster images, to the history and prehistory of Europe. I would have liked it if I had known that the 'Regina coeli', droned and muttered through my childhood, was a 12th-century prayer: 'Queen of heaven rejoice, alleluia: for He whom you merited to bear, alleluia, Has risen as he said, alleluia. Pray for us to God, alleluia.' Mary existed in eternity; we were not encouraged to think of her as having a history. Instead we were urged to ponder the practical use to which she could be put. If we didn't sign up to some

Marian sodality, and say our rosary diligently, the world would be taken over by communists. The Russians would be marching down our high streets, and instead of May processions in the Virgin's honour, there would be exhibitions of Cossack dancing.

Miri Rubin's excellent and learned book explores how the meaning of Mary was constructed and directed, how its possibilities blossomed out through two millennia and were negotiated between clergy and faithful, between one culture and another, between Christians, Muslims and Jews.* She shows how a symbol is fleshed out, and layers of meaning are accreted. She surveys Mary's story roughly as it unfolded, whereas Marina Warner's book, *Alone of All Her Sex* (1976), is organised thematically; the two books share a fascinating readability and cross-cultural ease. There is little about Mary in the gospels – she is mentioned more often in the Quran. Giving substance to the Mother of God therefore became a great exercise in Christian creativity. Rubin traces how the specifics of Mary's life were sorted out, with confidence but not without fierce argument, by centuries of theologians and teachers, drawing on folklore and the gospel apocrypha. She describes Syriac Mary and Byzantine Mary as well as Rome's Mary. She shows how Mary became part of the court ceremonial of the Eastern Empire, no longer just a young Jewish girl but a queen, the patron of Constantinople, her milk-stained dress serving as the city's protective relic.

From the east, the image and worship of Mary spread through the Mediterranean. Black Madonnas were worshipped in the groves once sacred to Roman fertility goddesses.

* *Mother of God: A History of the Virgin Mary* by Miri Rubin (Allen Lane, 2009).

Egyptian Mary borrowed from the cult of Isis, a life-giving beneficent goddess, and was painted with 'large dark eyes set under strong eyebrows'. Court painters in the 15th century showed Mary as a fashionable beauty, with a high plucked forehead, tight bodice and silk veil. It is dismaying at first sight that a statue at Ely Cathedral, commissioned for the millennium, still shows Mary as a Barbie blonde. No doubt it's true to how she's been imagined, the projections she's carried. Centuries rolled by when she was an excuse for painting a woman, her breasts exposed and a smirk of gratification on her pretty face.

Rubin is a fluent and stylish writer whose recent book *The Hollow Crown*, a history of Britain in the late Middle Ages, showed her skill in keeping together a vast and many-layered narrative. She writes with sensitivity and delicate expertise of how, through art, music and Marian poetry, the Virgin's life story became elaborated. She was valued as an intercessor, a high-level negotiator between erring humans and the heavenly judge; her son could refuse her nothing. Blathmac, Irish monk and martyr of the ninth century, wheedles: 'Let me have from you my three petitions, beautiful Mary, little bright-necked one; get them, sun of women, from your son who has them in his power.'

Her worship has taken many forms, not just artistic and liturgical but acrobatic: a lay brother at the monastery of Clairvaux, who had joined not knowing the liturgy, offered his praises to Mary by walking about on his hands at night, while his brethren were asleep. Every aspect of her miraculous career was dwelled on, reimagined. Sometimes these imaginings have great sweetness. The eighth-century preacher

Andrew of Crete pictured the Angel Gabriel hesitating on the brink of annunciation, wondering how to enter the Virgin's room: 'Shall I knock on the door? And how? For this is not customary for angels.' Neither woman nor girl, Mary hovers on the threshold of experience, rapt in a domestic interior swarming with symbols, like a house but a heavenly house; she is baffled by the angel's message and enthralled by the glitter of gilded wings. The German theologian Uta Ranke-Heinemann, in her book *Putting Away Childish Things* (1994), calls it 'stork theology', but what it really reminds us of is Zeus impregnating Leda. As Yeats describes it, she is 'mastered by the brute blood of the air'. Then she is left with the consequences, human and divine.

It's easy to imagine the figure of Mary as ubiquitous and always present, but Rubin shows that the early church preferred martyrs, missionaries, local saints. The monastic orders founded in the 11th and 12th centuries were the cheerleaders for Mary, and pilgrims to sites throughout Europe took home news of cures and miracles and carried her devotion far and wide. Between 1000 and 1200, as the parish structure was set into place throughout the continent, statues of Mary appeared in almost every church. Over the next two centuries she was made 'local and vernacular'. A 15th-century commonplace book kept by a Norfolk alderman had the facts of her life all sorted out:

> The Virgin parent Mary lived 63 years.
> She was 14 at the blessed birth,
> She lived 33 [years] with her son,
> And 16, she suffered alone, like the stars.

She becomes an icon of tenderness; the plates here include a carving from Poitiers, where the rapt interlocked gaze of mother and child seems drawn from life. For generations of monks and celibates, absorbed into all-male communities as children, Mary was the only mother they knew. The orders of friars incorporated Mary into their myths of origin. She consoled female celibates too: St Clare assured the women who followed her that they could always carry Jesus 'spiritually in a chaste and virginal body'. The German Dominican nun Christina Ebner, born in 1277, dreamed she was pregnant with Jesus, and that she held his baby form in her arms. Sometimes Mary allowed these lonely women to nurse her child, filling their virginal bodies with the satisfaction of the breast-feeding mother. In the 14th century, St Birgitta of Sweden felt one Christmas Eve as if 'a living child were in her heart turning itself around and around'.

Mary's body was a battleground from the beginning. Who was she before the angel called? Why was she chosen, why not some other good girl? Did she suffer pain in childbirth? What was her afterlife? Did she have more children? What happened to her body when she died? There's something about Rubin's respectful, soothing, even-handed tone that makes you want to raise all the old embarrassing questions, as if you were some sniggering medieval novice in the first week of your induction to the convent. When Jesus was delivered, what happened to Mary's hymen? The scholar Jovinian in the fourth century thought her virginity came to an end in childbirth. He was excommunicated for his error. Body-loathing Manicheans did not believe that a divine person could be born in the messy human way. For Syriac scholars, and later for the Cathars, Mary conceived through the ear when the Holy Spirit whispered to her, and she was pregnant for only two months. In the Quran, where she is an ordinary woman, she gives birth to a prophet, a talking baby, but she delivers alone and suffers an agony which 'drove her to the trunk of a palm tree. She said: "Would that I had died before this and become a forgotten thing."' But in Christian legend Christ's birth is painless, even ecstatic, and his mother is surrounded by signs and wonders.

St Ambrose stressed her purity: her sealed womb, her intact state, her substance unmingled with the alien substance of the body of the opposite sex. The tension between her divine and her human nature is troubling and exquisite. Augustine said that Mary and Joseph were really married, but without 'intercourse of the flesh'. If Jesus was divine, every aspect of his story had to accord with his divinity, and Mary's life had to be worthy of him. Was she conceived without original sin, or did she receive a special grace in the womb that made her sinless? The dispute ran for centuries. Rubin traces, as it evolves, the notion of Mary's Immaculate Conception: the idea that she herself was conceived without the stain of original sin, which has been the heritage of humanity since the sin of Eve. It was impossible that such a temple of purity should die and rot in the ordinary way. Scholars reassured the faithful that gusts of perfume, not the whiff of putrefaction, issued from her corpse; she did not so much die as fall asleep, and was 'assumed' to heaven.

This did not mean nothing of her was left on earth. Her relics were drops of milk, hairs from her head, threads from her robes. A medieval serf called Boso was less than respectful of the Virgin's slipper, and Mary our vindictive Mother twisted his face into a painful rictus; he had to go back to church in Soissons and adore the slipper before she put him right and he looked like himself again. Miracles proliferated: Mary's house flew from the Holy Land and rebuilt itself in Loreto in Italy. Medieval Mary was a luxury object, cast in silver and gold, draped in velvet and silks. Her lineage had become aristocratic; sometimes in paintings she is seated in a rose garden in the grounds of a castle. Eve's garden is the garden of death, Mary's of life.

What had the universal mother to teach her mortal followers? Athanasius, patriarch of Alexandria, born at the end of the third century, established Mary as an exemplar of the ascetic life, but also, one can't help notice, as an example of feminine compliance; she did not have 'an eagerness to leave her house, nor was she at all acquainted with the streets; rather, she remained in her house being calm, imitating the fly in honey . . . And she did not permit anyone near her body unless it was covered, and she controlled her anger and extinguished her wrath in her inmost thoughts.' Centuries later her life was still being turned to exemplary account. A Paris bourgeois writes a handbook of instruction for his young wife, suggesting she model herself on Mary who, when she was called by Gabriel to mother the saviour, didn't say: 'It is not reasonable . . . I will not suffer it.' Fingered by the angel, she jumped to, obedient as every good wife and daughter should be. Medieval Mary cooks and spins, she knits, she weaves Christ's seamless tunic herself. A whole extended family is constructed around her: the life stories of her cousin Elizabeth and her mother St Anne (and her three husbands) embellish the legend. Mary's image becomes intimate, even banal. Joseph, squeezed out of the nativity scene by magi, shepherds and livestock, makes himself useful at the periphery of religious paintings, mending shoes or working away at his carpenter's trade.

But childhood ends; the blithe figure of the mother with babe in arms gives way to Mary at the foot of the Cross. Artists portray her 'fainting, leaning, falling, sometimes pulling at her son's body'. The image of the Pietà – Mary with Christ's bleeding body draped across her knees – emerges in the 13th century, the era of plague, war, famine. Here, as in her book *Corpus Christi* (1992), about the Eucharist, Rubin fights shy of psychological exploration. It is a good idea, in dealing with the medieval mind, to be aware of its impenetrability. But it is hard not to think that, during years of vast premature mortality, the worshippers of Mary were sublimating their own grief and loss, finding purpose for short and blighted lives in their belief in redemption through suffering; for did not the Virgin suffer? God placed her in shame and peril; 33 years on, he left her childless, broken with grief. God's reasons for tormenting us may, after all, be revealed somewhere; if we don't know why he does it, perhaps Mother Mary knows why. For the charismatic 15th-century Franciscan preacher Bernardino of Siena, Mary was queen of knowledge about God's creation: 'There is not a star of the starry sky whose course Mary would not know.' Chosen herself for a singular hard destiny, she must understand adversity, rejection and scorn; for what did her neighbours say when Gabriel had gone, and her belly filled with her inexplicable conception?

Rubin's book contains and illustrates a chilling history of antisemitism. Christians borrowed their learning from Jewish scholars, using Old Testament exegesis to justify themselves, dignifying both Christ and Mary as living fulfilment of Old Testament prophecies. The central text is in Isaiah: 'Behold a virgin shall conceive and bear a son and shall call his name Emmanuel.' The word used is *alma*, which means a young girl rather than a virgin, but early Christian thinkers were keen to tell the Jews that they didn't understand their own scriptures. Jewish scholars familiar with the Greek world were uncomfortably aware that Christian claims about virgin birth echoed pagan legends. Jewish polemicists continued through the centuries to dissent, and struck back against Christian myth, sometimes ferociously: Mary was an infertile woman, who had intercourse not with Joseph, but with an enemy of Joseph who tricked her; and to make matters worse, this trickster had sex with her during menstruation, when she was unclean. A Jewish text of the early 13th century asked shrewdly why Jesus was born to a 13-year-old, not a three or four-year-old; now, that would have been what you call a miracle. In the 13th century the rabbi David Kimhi of Provence (1160-1235) asked:

> [How can I believe] in a living God who is born of a woman, a child without knowledge and sense, an innocent who cannot tell his right from his left, who defecates, urinates and sucks from his mother's breast out of hunger and thirst, and cries when he is thirsty and whom his mother pities; and if she would not he would die of hunger as other people do?

The smug unanswerable Christian argument to all logical objections, to all historical and philological objections, was simple: God knows best. He makes the words that frame experience, he makes human anatomy, he is Lord of impossibilities; he can break his own universal laws at a whim. Denying Christ's divine nature, Jews were seen, by the Middle Ages, as not just ignorant but malevolent, active enemies of Mary and those whom she protected. In an essay in *Framing Medieval Bodies* (1994) Rubin explored medieval horror stories in which Jews cut out the wombs of Christian women. In 1240 Louis IX staged a mock trial in which the Talmud was tried for blasphemies against Mary. As the blood libel took hold of Europe, Mary's miracles served to bring the murderous misdeeds of Jews to light, and to resuscitate their innocent victims, who sang the Virgin's praises even with their throats cut. Marian chapels were built on the razed sites of synagogues and Jewish houses.

On the cusp of the Reformation, Rubin shows, Marian devotion was still developing. The process of disenchantment was slow. The late 15th century saw a resurgence in devotion grounded in scripture rather than legend. Bejewelled (and sometimes bleeding) statues of the Virgin became objects of suspicion. Erasmus, visiting the shrines of Walsingham and Canterbury, wrote satirically about the greed and credulity he encountered. Though Luther rejected much accreted Marian lore, he still saw her value for keeping women in their place: 'She seeks not any glory, but goes about her meals and her usual household duties, milking the cows, cooking the meals, washing pots and kettles, sweeping out the rooms.' And the years of the Reformation were also the years in which Mary's cult was carried to the New World, where its power was reinforced.

Rubin ends her story at the Counter-Reformation, but she points out how Mary's image survived into the Protestant world, and beyond, into the world of the Enlightenment. Elizabeth I converted herself into an icon of a ruling virgin, and the French republic created the image of Marianne. In the 19th century the Catholic Church found it necessary to re-inforce the theories of the Immaculate Conception and the Assumption, codifying as doctrine two beliefs which had been debated for centuries. It would have been interesting to have Rubin explain at greater length why this happened and why it happened when it did, just as it would have been interesting to read her on Mary in Salazar's Portugal and Franco's Spain, and to have her thoughts on modern Marian visions and pil-grim sites: on Lourdes, Fatima, Knock. There is an intriguing pattern here: Mary, as patron of the meek and the marginal, sometimes chooses scruffy peasant children, not bishops, as recipients of her message. The Church frowns on parish cults and yokel enthusiasts, then embraces the commercial bene-fits; as before the Reformation, oases of superstition become blessed if they are lucrative. Pilgrim towns are built, or, as at Knock, an airport; Mary becomes a patron of economic re-generation. The Mother of God makes herself useful after all.

Will we always need Mary? Is she in some way innate, an archetype we can't escape? In the closing pages of her book Rubin says that 'Mary is a conduit towards the exploration of female subjectivity,' but she is aware that mostly the explor-ation has been performed by men, who colonised what was most intimate in feminine experience, laying claim to what nature had decreed they could not share. For modern day 'consumers of Mary' she remains an ambivalent figure. 'Mary has been truly rediscovered through a feminist sensibility,' Rubin says, but admits that 'scholars and activists see the Mary tradition so closely linked with a history of subjugation and subordination as to make it unfit as a vehicle for the successful integration of women into contemporary Catholicism.' Marina Warner's view was that Mary's legend is now 'emptied of moral significance'. But Rubin has only a brief afterword in which to reflect on Mary in the modern world. We may wish she would write other books. This one does what it sets out to do, gracefully and enticingly, and it is at its most elegant, mysterious and touching when it leads us into the heart and mind of the medieval world and its wondering, emotional, awe-struck believers, finding the heavens patterned in the earth, and earth in heaven:

> The dew of Averil, id est gracia et bonitas Spiritus Sancti; Haveth y-maked the grene lef to spryng, id est Beatam Virginem . . . My sorrow is gon . . . My joye is comen . . . Ich herde a foul synge, id est angelum . . . Ave Maria.

He Roared
On Danton
2009

'GIVE ME A PLACE to stand,' said Archimedes, 'and I will move the earth.' In the spring of 1789, your place to stand was a huddle of streets on Paris's left bank. If you put your head out of the window of the café Procope, almost everyone you needed to overthrow the regime was within shouting distance. The revolution was dreamed here before it was enacted, beneath the dark towers of Saint-Sulpice. Georges-Jacques Danton lived here, and Camille Desmoulins, Jean-Paul Marat, Legendre the master butcher, Fabre d'Eglantine the political playwright, and a dozen others who would make their names through the fall of the old order. In the year the revolution began, this area was known as the Cordeliers district, taking its name from the monastery of the Cordeliers, the Franciscan friars. It was not a working- class area like Saint-Antoine, but respectable with a bohemian fringe, bankers and civil servants ensconced on first floors, garrets stuffed with malcontent actors; its agitators garnished their invective with classical allusions. From 1789 onwards, this district, with Danton as ward boss, became notorious for hair-trigger revolutionary reflexes. 'Spontaneous' street protests could erupt there in an instant, and radical journalists hid their presses and their persons in the warren of houses. When a reorganisation of the city's divisions threatened the identity of the district, the citizens turned themselves into a political club, and colonised the disused monastery for a meeting place. With Danton in the chair, the Cordeliers were a formidably disruptive force, noisier and cheaper to join than the Jacobin club on the right bank. The Cordeliers had an opinion on everything, from the parish to the world; you would think they owned the revolution.

You would disagree, of course, if you were across the river at City Hall, and struggling to impose good order on the populace. In the months after the fall of the Bastille, Mayor Bailly thought he owned the revolution, along with Lafayette, commander of the National Guard. The National Assembly thought they owned it; the Duc d'Orléans, who hoped to replace his cousin Louis as king, thought that if he did not own it he had certainly paid for it. Mirabeau, the renegade aristocrat who was a hero both to parliamentarians and to the crowd, thought he had a right to it – was this not his hour to save his country, and at the same time get his debts paid? And perhaps Mr Pitt, plotting in London, thought it was Whitehall's revolution; the opportunity to destabilise, embarrass and disable the old enemy could not be let slip, and if a bribe here and there could do it, he would be glad to have some revolutionaries in England's pocket. Later, in 1793, the journalist Desmoulins would denounce the revolution of 1789 as a false revolution, bought and paid for, sold and resold, a put-up job, a fix. As a republican from the start, he could claim his hands were clean and his motives were pure; but where did that leave Danton, his old revolutionary comrade? Ambiguity hangs over his life and over his conduct as a leader of the revolution, and what is soon evident about David Lawday's spirited and highly readable biography is that he stands Danton in a flattering light and pays insufficient attention to movements in the shadows.* 'The Gentle Giant of Terror', the subtitle calls him: which suggests, along with revolutionary *vertu*, a certain daft innocence. Lawday's Danton is the Danton that Gérard Depardieu enacted for Andrzej Wajda in his 1983 film about the great man's trial and death. He is a passionate defender of instinct and truth against the cold formulations of Robespierre: he is a peasant in a lawyer's coat, a son of the soil, one of nature's patriots; he is, in himself, a force of nature.

Such men are not often successful lawyers. Before the revolution, Danton was doing well; he was not one of the people with nothing to lose. He had a wife, a comfortable home, and an established legal practice; many of the men who were his future comrades had nothing but sheaves of unpublished poems, unsung operas and unapplauded plays. But he was restless and perhaps, as Büchner suggested in his play *Dantons Tod*, he was easily bored. Revolution offered him five years of diversion and aggrandisement, and amplified his voice to the whole of Europe; in quieter times, thirty years of plodding application, bowing and scraping to his intellectual inferiors, would perhaps have taken him into the lower ranks of the establishment. Danton's origins were one generation removed from the peasantry. He was born in 1759 in Arcis-sur-Aube in the Champagne region, the fifth child of a petty lawyer, who died when his only son was three. Georges-

* Danton: The Gentle Giant of Terror by David Lawday (Cape, 2009).

Jacques's father had been married before; his mother would marry again; he had a network of relatives through the region. The family structure was stable, cohesive; his uncles and cousins were farmers, merchants, priests. His childhood was rural but eventful. Encounters with livestock left him broken-nosed, with a gash from a bull's horn across his lips; smallpox left him scarred; he was tall, and grew burly if not obese. His ugliness was not of the craggy kind: 'His bulbous cheeks,' Lawday says, 'gave him the look of an enormous cherub.' To his political opponent Vadier, during the Terror, he was a *turbot farci*, a huge fish to be gutted. Danton's riposte embodied all his smooth elegance: 'I'll eat his brains and use his skull to shit in.'

In Troyes, Danton was given the best of modern educations by the Oratorian order. Later, he built up an extensive library, and he spoke, or at least read, both English and Italian. He was twenty when he went to try his luck in Paris. He clerked for a Maître Vinot on the Ile Saint-Louis. Rather than sit the Parisian bar exams, he took a pragmatic trip to Reims, where the diploma could be picked up for a fee on proof of a few days' residence. In 1787, in one of those arrangements so French that they almost defy translation, he bought the legal office of avocat au Conseil du Roi from a man called Huet de Paisy, who was engaged to marry his long-time mistress, Françoise Duhauttoir; Françoise herself lent Danton some of the purchase price. A 1964 biographer, Robert Christophe, speculated that Françoise may have had a child by Danton, and that he paid an inflated price to settle his obligations. He certainly drew on the dowry for his upcoming marriage to Gabrielle Charpentier, whose father was a tax official and the owner of a popular café near the law courts. As France slid towards bankruptcy and political turmoil, Danton had assets and prospects, but he also had entangling debts, obligations.

The Dantons had a son within a year of marriage. He did not survive babyhood, but two more boys followed. The household made an ambitious move to an apartment in one of the recently built townhouses near the Théâtre Français. There was an entrance on the cour du Commerce; his front door, it is thought, opened approximately where his statue stands now, in the carrefour de l'Odéon. He would live there for the rest of his short life. At this time, Danton may have talked of 'revolution', as he did – in Latin, and in typically ambivalent terms – at his reception into his new association of advocates. But he clearly thought the upheaval would be of a limited nature, for he chose to adopt the particle of nobility, calling himself d'Anton. It's unlikely that anyone laughed; the manoeuvre was too familiar a stage in the progress of a social climber.

In May 1789 the Estates General met in Versailles. In Paris, there was sporadic rioting throughout the spring, the price of bread shot up, and Louis ringed the capital with troops. When the Bastille fell, Danton was not there; he was often elsewhere on days of revolutionary action, as he had a canny regard for his own skin. But within days a citizen militia, which would become the National Guard, was formed to keep the peace on the streets. This was Danton's chance to put on a paramilitary uniform and strut about impressively. People were looking for leaders, and he – with the big presence and the big voice – was a natural leader. He was hospitable, a generous host, the glad-handing focus of the neighbourhood. He had also joined a Freemasons' lodge; probably that was how he met the liberal, anglophile Philippe d'Orléans. In the duke's circles, money changed hands, Lawday says, 'and Danton was aware of it. Who wasn't? But the giant from Arcis was not there out of greed, he was there riding the tide.' At this time, it seemed a change of monarch, with the new one limited by constitution, might be enough to satisfy reformers; Orléans, the obvious candidate, functioned as a walking chequebook for Danton's friends. Was Danton the fastidious exception? So many future leaders of the revolution were scooped into the golden net of Orléanist pretentions, that they could hardly hold it against each other in the days of brutal accounting that came in with the Terror. Danton – devoted to Cicero, but fluent in street language – was just the sort of investment Orléans liked.

Nothing can be proved, though Danton's finances are worth more scrutiny than they receive here. Allegations that he was an agent in English pay had surfaced as early as the autumn of 1789. We don't know where his money came from, but we can be fairly sure it wasn't from his legal practice. We know where it went – he was buying up land in Arcis. The evidence was marshalled in Norman Hampson's 1978 biography, a wry, spare and careful assessment. Where others see a calculating opportunism running through Danton's revolution, Lawday sees a man free from 'demon ideals' and driven by 'impetuosity and heart'. At any rate, he was led by his heart when he chose his friends. Two men he was close to at the beginning went straight through his political career with him, and died on the same scaffold. Fabre d'Eglantine was an actor and playwright, interior designer and prize-winning poet, or so he said; he was a charming con-man, and his stock market scams, uncovered during the winter of 1793, would start the Dantonist faction on the slide to oblivion. Camille Desmoulins was a freakishly brilliant failure till the Bastille days. He was a timid boy with a stammer, but the revolution, he claimed, had made him brave; he made his name as a street orator, then launched one of the era's most successful newspapers. His politics were republican before the revolution; as he was ahead of everyone else, racing through a private revolution on his own speeded-up plan, it was only a matter of time before he collided messily with the rock-like Terrorist convictions of his childhood friend, Robespierre.

The company he kept, and his talents as a demagogue, made Danton suspect to the right bank grandees trying to steer the revolution on a moderate and constitutional course. He was always adaptable, always approachable, and yet he seems to have scared them. It was the second wave of revolution in the late summer of 1792 that carried him to power: the attack on the Tuileries, the fall of the monarchy, the institution of the republic and the summoning of the National Convention. At a time of national emergency, with the troops of the enemy allies just ninety miles from Paris, Danton seized a position as de facto head of a provisional government. Lafayette, the commander of the French forces, defected to the Austrians, and at the same time rebels were on the march in the Vendée under the slogan 'Death to Parisians'. The Duke of Brunswick, commander of the allied Prussian and Austrian forces, had threatened Paris itself with 'exemplary vengeance'. The leaders of the revolution were dead men walking, and the danger was that the capital would freeze with fear. Danton put the city on the march; he organised a giant recruiting drive and the seizure of all weapons in private hands. House-to-house searches picked up three thousand suspected royalists, many more than the prisons could securely hold. On 2 September 1792 Danton delivered his finest speech, 'the charge against the enemies of the *patrie*', who must be met with 'l'audace, encore de l'audace, toujours de l'audace'. This was happy and forceful phrase-making; like much revolutionary rhetoric, it loses some impact in translation, but all the same it is helpful that Lawday translates everything, and does it easily and idiomatically. That day of boldness was, Lawday says, the best and worst of Danton; his speech had a galvanising effect, but it acted as a call for direct action among the citizens, as well as a strike against the external enemy.

Danton's style as leader of the government was a simple one. 'Why do I do what he wants?' the navy minister asked. 'Because he scares the hell out of me and he'd give my head to the people otherwise.' Danton's official position was minister of justice, and he took Fabre and Desmoulins to the place Vendôme with him. Justice was in scant supply in early September, when the mobs broke into the prisons and massacred 1600 people. Some of them were prostitutes and others, detainees in a reformatory, were little more than children. Danton did nothing to stop the killing. In his 1899 biography, Hilaire Belloc said 'he might have saved his reputation by protesting, though perhaps his protest would not have saved a single life.' Danton roared on more than one occasion that he did not care about his reputation. A brutal realism prevailed: 'No power on earth,' he said, 'could have stopped the national vengeance from spilling over.' There could not be a revolution without blood, and no single man could hold up his hand and say 'Enough.' It was Danton who, the following spring, proposed to the Convention the establishment of a Revolutionary Tribunal: for which, he would later say, 'I ask the pardon of God and of humanity.' His reasoning at the time was that only swift, visible justice would stop the mobs taking the law into their own hands. But the Tribunal would become the instrument the revolutionaries used to slaughter each other.

The pressure of that terrible summer eased, though the republic's victory at Valmy in September was less a military triumph than a propaganda coup. The allied commander withdrew, and Danton's opponents claimed that he had bribed him with the French crown jewels, which had recently gone missing. If so, it was an ingenious use of them. Once the immediate panic was over, Danton left office and went home to the cour du Commerce, because as a member of the new National Convention he was not permitted to hold a ministry. Jean-Marie Roland, however, hung on to his post at the interior ministry, and mounted a relentless attack on Danton's probity, demanding he account for the large sums he had disbursed during the days of emergency. Danton could not do it, and his failure would be a thorn in his side in the months ahead. Lawday makes much of Madame Roland's animosity towards Danton, which (like generations of male historians) he takes to be a backhanded compliment to what he calls Danton's 'blatant bull-maleness'. Perhaps it's time to revisit this condescending nonsense and give Manon Roland the benefit of the doubt; maybe, when she said she disliked and distrusted Danton, she meant what she said and no more.

Readers of her memoirs may see her as an irritating and self-regarding woman, but they will also remember her frankness about her early sexual experiences; she was not a fool, and not someone who lacked self-awareness. It's questionable, anyway, if her personal feelings mattered as much as Lawday thinks. She had influence, but no power. Lawday uses the word 'party' often in relation to the Rolandins and the Girondins, though they were the loosest of groupings. In revolutionary politics, to represent your opponents as a 'party' was to defame and endanger them; it was to represent them as self-interested to the point of lacking patriotism. First you made them a 'party', and then, as they went to the guillotine, a 'batch'. At the time, the men whom later historians call Girondins were more often referred to as 'Brissotins', as so many of them were friends of Jean-Pierre Brissot, a deputy, journalist and veteran of liberal causes. Brissot had been around long enough to be compromised; Marat and Desmoulins claimed he had been a police spy before the revolution. They had been around too, so they knew. They held secret files on each other, or so they said.

What did mark out the Girondins, Rolandins and Brissotins was their federalist impulses; they distrusted Paris, and in a moment of panic in the autumn of 1792 they proposed taking the government out of the capital, an idea Danton dismissed with contempt. They favoured a policy which the left wing of the Convention saw as suicidal; unless united, how could France possibly withstand a grand European alliance dedicated to the crushing of the revolution? It was not a big step, later, for the left to represent federalist sympathies as traitorous. Robespierre blamed Brissot's friends for taking

France into what they advertised as a 'cleansing' war. He regarded it as immoral, unwinnable and likely to end in military dictatorship. Danton would have avoided war too, and worked busily behind the scenes to negotiate a cessation of hostilities, while pumping out nationalist, expansionist rhetoric: 'The boundaries of France are drawn by nature. We shall attain them on their four sides – the ocean, the Rhine, the Alps and the Pyrenees.'

Danton was with the armies in Belgium when his wife, Gabrielle, died giving birth to her fourth child. When he arrived in Paris, a grieving, howling wreck of a man who had been too long on the road, it was to find that the child was lost too and that Gabrielle had already been buried. She had been dead for a week when Danton had her exhumed so that a sculptor could take a mould for a bust; this gruesome proceeding, carried out by night, suggested that he was a man who, goaded to the edge of exhaustion, had tipped into emotional breakdown. At the king's trial, he had voted for death, and death was what he had got. Perhaps it began here, the strange numbness that overtook him when he was most required to act. His political judgment was no longer secure, his lucky touch had gone. Until almost the last moment, when he deserted to the Austrians like Lafayette before him, Danton backed the army's supreme commander, General Dumouriez. He had to explain that misjudgment to the National Convention; all the same, his domination of that body, in debate after debate, became clear in the spring of 1793. With the republic once more on the brink of being invaded, and threatening to break up internally, he launched another round of recruitment and requisitioning, declaring that Paris would have to save the country. When the Committee of Public Safety was first formed, in April 1793, it was known as the Danton Committee.

The idea was to fill a power vacuum; as the men seen to matter in France were deputies to the Convention, and so debarred from ministerial office, the old structure had lost status and the force of the executive arm had diminished. The Committee contained no Girondins, Brissotins or Rolandins. By June they were in prison or had fled. At this point, so many battles behind him, Danton faltered; he thought of his private life; he married again, Louise Gély, the 16-year-old daughter of a neighbour. To meet her family's wishes, he married her secretly, before a renegade priest who had not taken the oath to the Constitution. His secret was soon out. 'I can't live without women,' he pleaded. He took to spending time with his bride in a country house he had rented outside Paris. In July, he was dropped from the Committee. Two weeks later, Robespierre was elected. Till this point he had avoided government posts, but his time had come. He did not need women or relaxation, and did not have secrets. He often threatened to 'unmask' his opponents. For a long time he avoided thinking about what lay beneath Danton's mask.

In October 1793, pleading illness, Danton took himself off to Arcis, to seal himself up in his much renovated ancestral home and try to ignore the Paris newspapers. That autumn the city of Lyon was razed by republican troops; Marie-Antoinette and Manon Roland went to the guillotine, so did the former Duc d'Orléans, so did Bailly, Paris's first revolutionary mayor. Desmoulins and Fabre begged Danton to come back and reassert his authority. When he reappeared in Paris, he found he was living in the Year II. The old calendar had ceased to exist, and so had his old address; he was now at home in the rue Marat. The political landscape was changing as fast as the street names. As the year closed – the old-style year, 1793 – Desmoulins launched a press campaign to end the executions and release the thousands of interned suspects held throughout the country. In its first weeks, the campaign for clemency was wildly popular. Robespierre gave cautious approval; then he pulled back, becoming aware that, of all those who needed clemency, the Dantonists perhaps needed it most. A fulminating stock market scandal, in which Fabre was deeply implicated, seemed in the climate of the times to have political ramifications. Perhaps it did: forgery was involved, and insider trading, and a dubious and cosmopolitan bunch of disparate individuals suspected of being enemy agents. Perhaps wisely, Lawday doesn't attempt to unravel this affair, but he confuses his account of these crucial weeks by persistently referring to Danton's friends as 'the Cordeliers'. The club had long since been taken over by a populist faction, led by the journalist René Hébert. That was why Desmoulins's newspaper, which led the clemency campaign, was called the *Old Cordelier*. Hébert was Desmoulins's first target. Camille's notion of mercy was qualified: he would first eliminate the immediate opponent, whom he hated like poison, and then all revolutionaries would be perfect friends.

Hébert had been a nuisance to the Committee of Public Safety, and when these new Cordeliers went to the guillotine, the ground was suddenly cleared, the revolutionary atmosphere bright, the light searching: an abyss opened beneath the feet of the Dantonist faction their opponents now called the Indulgents. Danton could perhaps have escaped. He had a warning, an hour or two before his arrest. But as he said, 'You can't take the patrie with you on the soles of your shoes.' Danton lived by the word, but not the written word. He never wrote his speeches; he grew them extempore, and fed them on the emotion of his audience. All his life he was at the mercy of patchy note-takers. Alphonse Aulard, who held the first chair in revolutionary studies at the Sorbonne, invest-igated the problem in 1922: are Danton's famous phrases real, or are they later inventions, are they what historians think he ought to have said? 'It is probable that he said them. One hopes that he said them. Historically speaking, one cannot be sure. Perhaps they are more true than authentic.' In any event, and however he phrased it, Danton disdained the chance of last-minute flight. In 1791, fleeing a backlash against the rad-icals, he had spent six weeks in England. He was not welcome then, he would be less welcome now. There was nowhere to go: now, March to April 1794, it was time for Danton's many selves to meet each other.

A stormy session of two committees – the Committee of Public Safety and the Committee of General Defence, usually called the Police Committee – had resulted in two members refusing to sign the arrest warrants. Robespierre's signature appeared, very small, very faint, at the foot of the page. Leav-ing his house in the small hours, under arrest, Danton told his little wife to expect him back. A few days later he faced his accusers with great courage, but he could not face them down. By this stage, the Committee did not 'lose' a trial. Danton, Desmoulins and other deputies found themselves tried alongside men who were strangers to them – Fabre's shady cronies. Before the Convention, Saint-Just's rhetorical deconstruction of Danton's career seemed to show that every patriotic action had its ugly, shadow side. The trial process was truncated and farcical. Like the trial of the king, it was a political coup, not a forensic process; it was an assassination. Danton had hoarded a phrase for the scaffold: 'Show my head to the people. It is worth a look.' The Convention did not rally to him, the people did not rise up to save their old hero. Less than four months later, Robespierre himself stood at bay before the Convention, his voice faltering, dying in his throat. A deputy shouted: 'It is the blood of Danton that chokes you!'

'Is it Danton you regret?' he snapped back. 'Cowards! Why didn't you defend him?'

It's a good question. Historians have been doing it energetically ever since, though his contemporaries were slower to exculpate him. After Robespierre's fall, the Convention decreed that flowers should be placed on Desmoulins's presumed grave; no one had a bouquet for Danton. He divides people: those who value heart and flair, against those who are good at adding up on their fingers, sucking their teeth and shaking their heads. If you condemn him you are, like Robespierre, more in sorrow than in anger. Lawday takes Danton at his own valuation, which at all times was high. He was never reluctant to bellow out a testimonial to himself. 'I have created what I am on my own . . . I know how to marry cool reason with a burning soul and a steadfast character.' We know much more about his tactics than about his beliefs. He was a skilled, pragmatic political operator who, like Mirabeau before him, was expert in covering his tracks, and he has covered them from posterity. He had a brilliant oral memory, but avoided even writing letters, and Lawday speculates that nowadays we would have called him dyslexic. When he went to Paris, the lawyer who took him on as a clerk remarked that his handwriting was indecipherable; ça ne fait rien, Danton said haughtily, as he didn't mean to make his living as a copyist. He preferred other people to put his thoughts on paper for him; then, of course, he could always repudiate them. Perhaps Lawday is right and there was some neurological glitch; the more jaundiced explanation is that he was secretive, and with good reason.

David Lawday lives in Paris and he is not one of those tepid Englishpersons who does not understand why these desperados wanted a revolution in the first place. He takes them on their own terms, these young men who threw off their powdered wigs, sought liberation from a lifetime of stifling politesse, and ended up wading through blood. On the other hand, he has a wholly English distrust of political theory. He makes Danton a man who often reacted to events rather than trying to shape them, and that seems a shrewd assessment. When things were going his way Danton took advantage of the moment, and when they were not he cleared off to Arcis till he could see improvement. Lawday writes as if Robespierre, by contrast, was in possession all along of an unshakeable plan, which included the destruction of Danton. He sets up the Danton/Robespierre contest early in the book. At his first appearance on the page, Robespierre has a 'feline aspect' and 'joyless eyes'. This is better as drama than history. It is easy to imagine their first meeting was not a success; Danton traded in first impressions and Robespierre was very hard to impress. But for most of the revolution they worked together amicably enough, if on opposite sides of the river; and they worked in political agreement. Lawday can't stretch his imagination to see Danton as Robespierre must have seen him: a blustering windbag, with his faux heartiness, his distractibility and his unreliability. To revolution, Robespierre had a vocation; he expected to follow it, and he expected it to kill him. It may have seemed to him that Danton saw revolution as a second career; he expected it to make him rich. Until the end, Robespierre decided to believe, or at least said he believed, that the gossip against Danton was slander. He took him for a patriot, with all his faults and flaws, and Lawday persuades his reader to do the same.

His book is not searching, contains little new, and for facts it would not be first choice. It is a romantic view of the revolution; Lawday's July crowds are pulled towards the Bastille 'by some great intuitive magnet'; in fact, the fortress, almost emptied of prisoners by the authorities who had anticipated the attack, was a pre-selected target because of the explosives stored there. But Lawday creates some great set pieces and striking turning points. At Danton's first meeting with Mirabeau: 'The two men had sat inspecting each other in silence for some minutes, impressed by each other's ugliness.' He is able to capture the atmosphere of the early revolution: its inflammable mix of devilment and righteousness, reckless selflessness and flagrant self-promotion. He sees that Danton was more than the sum of his crimes, the sum of his secrets; he celebrates him, 'large heart and violent impulses in irresolvable conflict'. He understands that much of his public aggression was a pose; Danton was by nature a negotiator, even if his negotiations sometimes looked more like an offer from a prostitute. One evening at his apartment in the cour du Commerce, Danton entertained Henry Holland, Fox's nephew. 'You can pay Danton 80,000 livres,' he claimed, 'but you can't buy Danton for 80,000.' Lawday assures us: 'Gabrielle would have understood that he was talking of the compensation he had received for his legal practice.' Only a wife or the fondest of biographers could believe that. He was simply raising the stakes.

Diary
Meeting the Devil
2010

THREE OR FOUR NIGHTS after surgery – when, in the words of the staff, I have 'mobilised' – I come out of the bathroom and spot a circus strongman squatting on my bed. He sees me too; from beneath his shaggy brow he rolls a liquid eye. Brown-skinned, naked except for the tattered hide of some endangered species, he is bouncing on his heels and smoking furiously without taking the cigarette from his lips: puff, bounce, puff, bounce. What rubbish, I think, actually shouting at myself, but silently. This is a no-smoking hospital. It is impossible this man would be allowed in, to behave as he does. Therefore he's not real, and if he's not real I can take his space. As I get into bed beside him, the strongman vanishes. I pick up my diary and record him: was there, isn't any more.

This happened in early July. I had surgery on the first of the month, and was scheduled to stay in hospital for about nine days. The last thing the surgeon said to me, on the afternoon of the procedure: 'For you, this is a big thing, but remember, to us it is routine.' But when I woke up, many hours later, he was standing at the end of the trolley in the recovery room, grey and shrunken as if a decade had passed. He had expected to be home for dinner. And now look!

Hospital talk is short and exclamatory. Oops! Careful! Nice and slow! Oh dear! Did that hurt? But the night after the surgery, I felt no pain. Flighted by morphine, I thought that my bed had grown as wide as the world, and throughout the short hours of darkness I made up stories. I seemed to solve, that night, problems that had bedevilled me for years. Take just one example: the unwritten story called 'The Assassination of Margaret Thatcher'. I had seen it all, years ago: the date and place, the gunman, the bedroom behind him, the window, the light, the angle of the shot. But my problem had always been, how did the ArmaLite get in the wardrobe?

Now I saw that it just grew there. It was planted by fantasy. If a whole story is a fantasy, why must logic operate within it? The word 'planted' started another story, called 'Chlorophyll'. By morning, I had the best part of a collection. But when I sat up and tried to write them down, my handwriting fell off the lines. I kept trying to fish it up again, untangle the loops and whorls and get them back to the right of the margin, and when I think of my efforts then, I think of them in the present tense, because pain is a present-tense business. Illness involves such busywork! Remembering to breathe. Studying how to do it. Plotting to get your feet on the floor, inching a pillow to a bearable position. First move your left foot. Then your other foot, whatever they call it . . . any other foot you've got. Let us say you're swaying on your feet and sweating, you think you might fall down or throw up – you have to rivet your attention to the next ten seconds. After the crisis is over, time still behaves oddly. It takes a while for the hour to stretch out in its usual luxurious fashion, like unravelling wool. Until you are cool, settled and your vital signs good, time snaps and sings like an elastic band.

When I write my diaries I talk to myself with an inward voice. For the next week I am conscious that my brain is working oddly. Imagine you were creating all your experience by writing it into being, but were forced to write with the wrong hand; you would make up for the slow awkwardness by condensing phrases, like a poet. In the same way, my life compresses into metaphor. When I sit up and see the wound in my abdomen, I am pleased to see that it has a spiral binding, like a manuscript. On the whole I would rather be an item of stationery than be me. It is as if my thoughts are happening not inside my head but outside me in the room. A film with a soundtrack is running to my right. It keeps me busy with queries based on false premises. 'Is it safe if I drink this orange juice?' But I blink and the orange juice isn't there. Therefore I study reality carefully, the bits of it within reach. For a while I think I have grown a new line on one of my hands, a line unknown to palmistry. I think perhaps I have a new fate. But it proves to be a medical artefact, a puckering of the skin produced by one of the tubes sewn into my wrist. We call those 'lines', too. The iambic pentameter of the saline stand, the alexandrine of the blood drain, the epidural's sweet sonnet form.

Within a few days, the staff are tampering with my spiral binding when the whole wound splits open. Blood clots bubble up from inside me. Over the next hours, days, nurses speak to each other in swift acronyms, or else form sentences you might have heard in Haworth: 'Her lungs are filling up.'

But I have undentable faith in my own body. When I am told I need a blood transfusion, I plead: 'Let's give it 24 hours and see.' I have never been accepted as a blood donor, and I don't like the idea of a debt. When the blood comes, the stranger's precious blood, it leaks everywhere from the cannula on my neck, which needs to be taken out and resewn. The night sister looks meaningfully at the vampire's kiss and says: 'Another two of those wounds would do it.' Finish me off, she means. She is real but I accept her words are not. A hallucination has to be gross before I can pick it out.

My internal monologue is performed by many people – nurses and bank managers to the fore. There is a breathless void inside me, and it needs to be filled. I should put money in it, I think. Like a cash machine in reverse, notes slotting between my ribs. Certain items are taken away – the drain that takes blood from my side, a bridle that feeds me oxygen – but they are never taken far enough away, they easily come back. I clamp a smile on my face and drift. I have a switch I can press for 'patient-controlled analgesia'. But the staff seem uneasy about giving up control over my pain. Some say I am pressing the button too often, some say too seldom. I want to please them so I try and make my pain to their requirements.

Illness strips you back to an authentic self, but not one you need to meet. Too much is claimed for authenticity. Painfully we learn to live in the world, and to be false. Then all our defences are knocked down in one sweep. In sickness we can't avoid knowing about our body and what it does, its animal aspect, its demands. We see things that never should be seen; our inside is outside, the body's sewer pipes and vaults exposed to view, as if in a woodcut of our own martyrdom. The whole of life – the business of moving an inch – requires calc-ulation. The suffering body must shape itself around the iron dawn routine, which exists for the very sick as well as the con-valescent: the injection in the abdomen, pain relief, blood tests, then the long haul out of bed, the shaking progress to the bathroom, the awesome challenge of washcloth and soap.

This is a small private hospital, clean and unfancy, set in the sprawling campus of a vast public hospital of which I have experience, and have reason to distrust and detest. I feel guilty, God knows, about all sorts of things, but not about buying myself a private room. The staff looking after me are the same people who would be working at the larger instit-ution, but they are less rushed and so more considerate. It's usual in talking about the health service to say that the system needs all sorts of reforms but the workers are wonderful. I think that the workers are as apt to fail as the system is. Some people, on a hospital ward or anywhere else, always do what they say they'll do, and others just don't; to them, promises are just negotiating ploys, and the time on the clock is second-ary to some schedule of their own. Some can imagine being in pain, and some don't want to. A single extra minute to settle a patient comfortably can mean the difference between a neutral experience and an experience of slowly building misery. Some take the human body to be made of flesh, some of jointed metal. A polite radiographer bends my arm back over the side of a trolley so that it feels as if he's trying to break it. And I too think of my body as consisting of some substance that I can split apart from myself, and hand over to the professionals, while I take an informed interest in what they do to it. Far from being isolating, my experience is collaborative. The staff are there to reassure me, and I am there to reassure them; in this way we shield each other from an experience of darkness. One day soon after the surgery I vomit green gunk. 'Don't worry!' I exclaim as I retch. 'It will be fine! It's just like *The Exorcist*,' I say, before anyone else can.

And so I spin away, back into the 1970s; I am easily parted from the present day. I remember the cinema queues and the evangelicals working their way along the jeering lines, trying to dissuade us from going in. I wish I had been dissuaded. 'What were those flickering skulls about?' I asked as we filed out. (Apart from those, I thought the film quite true to life.) No one else I knew saw the skulls, not then, though by now it seems everybody did. If you have a million years to spare, you can follow the internet discussions on what 'quasi-subliminal' images may or may not have been embedded by the filmmakers, but when I was young I would always reliably see what was almost not there; when I was a student, earning a little money by being an experimental subject for trainee psychologists, I did many dull routines involving word association and memory tricks, but what I remember best is the flicker of screens with letters I could just read, and being asked, disapprovingly: 'How do you *do* that?' This was not a professional question, but an aggrieved, human one; people suspect you are sneaking some mean advantage. No doubt I have lost this ability now, if ability is what you call it. It's something you'd think age would wither. But given my record with the vaporous, I am not as surprised as some would be when in the hospital I blink and life flits sideways. The second world, the whirl of activity on my right-hand side, wakes up just after the first world, so that for a moment, as I push back the bedcovers, I am united, I speak with one voice. A second later, reality has fallen into halves. In my notebook, hour by hour, I record the hallucinations and my own scathing comments on them. But the footnotes are no more sensible than the main text, since while criticising and revising I am still hallucinating. What is this preposterous stuff, I demand of myself, about getting the nave of the church measured? 'As if,' I write, 'this were not a hospital, but a Jane Austen novel with a wedding at the summit?'

A voice from the secondary world rebukes me for thinking so little of my real father, whom I never saw after I was 11. 'Why, he sold tickets to make brickets from granite. He collected clothes and kit for historical re-enactments.' I do not mention my two worlds to the staff, as they have enough to do and it seems tactless. Most of my preoccupations are literary or religious, so they seem an elitist pursuit, and for many of my nurses, English is not their first language, or Christianity their religion. 'The existing vicar,' a voice tells me, 'will go to a smaller parish somewhere.' At once the existing vicar bobs into view, followed by an anguished Muslim father, who pleads to know: 'What are the chances of her losing her honour?' The vicar explains loftily that he and his clerical colleagues do not exist to answer that sort of question. 'They do not believe that honour lies in fearful nasties.' Sorry, I write, I misheard: that should read 'fearful chastity'. A hooded youth approaches me on the street, holding up a plucked chicken. 'You give me this bird,' he complains, 'and this bird were gay.'

There is no obvious reason for voices and visions. My temperature is near normal and my pain relief is the usual moderate regime. Later the hallies, as I think of them, become less threatening, but more childish and conspiratorial. I close my eyes and they begin to pack my belongings into a pillowcase, whispering and grinning. One sharp-faced dwarfish hally pulls at my right arm, and I drive her off with an elbow in her eye. After this they are more wary of me, intimidated. I see them slinking around the doorframe, trying to insinuate themselves. The staff are concerned that I don't cough, then that I cough too much. In soothing nurse-talk they smooth symptoms away. 'I have a raging thirst,' I say. 'Ah, you are a lit-tul bit thirsty,' says the nurse. I wonder if they laugh at the patients, who come in so brave and ignorant. None of us thinks that the complication rate applies to us.

The visitor's idea of hospital is different from the patient's idea. Visitors imagine themselves trapped in that ward, in that bed, in their present state of assertive wellbeing. They imagine being bored, but boredom occurs when your consciousness ranges about looking for somewhere to settle. It's a superfluity of unused attention. But the patient's concentration is distilled, moment by moment: breathing, not being sick, not coughing or else coughing in the right way, producing bodily secretions in the vessels provided and not on the floor. The visitor sees the hospital as needles and knives, metal teeth, metal bars; sees the foggy meeting between the damp summer air outside and the overheated exhalations of the sickroom. But the patient sees no such contrast. She cannot imagine the street, the motorway. To her the hospital is this squashed pillow, this water glass: this bell pull, and the nice judgment required to know when to use it. For the visitor everything points outwards, to the release at the end of the visiting hour, and to the patient everything points inwards, and the furthest extension of her consciousness is not the rattle of car keys, the road home, the first drink of the evening, but the beep and plip-plop of monitors and drips, the flashing of figures on screens; these are how you register your existence, these are the way you matter.

For the month of July, my world is the size of the room that, as an undergraduate, I shared with a medical student, who kept a box of bones under her bed and a skull on our shelf. I think of the long wards of the hospitals I visited as a child, fiercely disinfected but with walls too high to be cleaned properly: those walls receding, vanishing into grey mist, like clouds over a cathedral. Wheezing and fluttering, or slumped into stupor, my great-aunts and uncles died in wards like those. Wrapping and muffling themselves, gazing at the long windows streaming rain, visitors would tell the patient: 'You're in the best place.' And as the last visitor was ushered out on the dot, doors were closed, curtains pulled, and the inner drama of the ward was free to begin again: the drama enacted without spectators, within each curtained arena a private play, and written within the confines of the body a still more secret drama. Death stays when the visitors have gone, and the nurses turn a blind eye; he leans back on his portable throne, he crosses his legs, he says: 'Entertain me.'

A few days after the surgery I take a turn for the worse. No human dignity is left; in a red dawn, I stagger across the room, held by a tiny Filipina nurse, my heart hammering, unspeakable fluids pouring from me. Hours later, when my heart has subsided and I am propped up and reading the *Observer*, I think this moment is still happening, still being enacted; I live in two simultaneous realities, one serene and one ghastly beyond bearing. When my dressings are stripped off I bob up my head to look at my abdomen. My flesh is swollen, green with bruising, and the shocking, gaping wound shows a fresh pink inside; I look like a watermelon with a great slice hacked out. I say to myself, it's just another border post on the frontier between medicine and greengrocery; growths and tumours seem always to be described as 'the size of a plum' or 'the size of a grapefruit'. Later a nurse calls it 'a wound you could put your fist into'. I think, a wound the size of a double-decker bus. A wound the size of Wales. It doesn't seem possible that a person can have a wound like that and live, let alone walk about and crack jokes.

On 12 July I am attached to a small, heavy black box, which will vacuum out the cavity and gradually close its walls. A clear tube leads from beneath my dressings into the box, and the box is plugged into the wall. It snorts like an elderly pug, and bloody substances whisk along the tube. Through August, as the weather warms up, it will smell like a wastebin in a butchery, and flies will take an interest in it. I can unplug myself for a few minutes, but reconnecting is painful. There is a shoulder strap, for use by the robust, those on their way to mending, but when I get out of bed I carry the box before me in both hands. Its ferocious gasping will soon start to suck the dressings inside the wound, and sometimes in the night it will whistle and cheep, to continue until a keeper comes with knowledge of its workings.

Until now I have been giddily optimistic, but the arrival of the black box sobers me. It takes an hour each time to dress my wound. During one session, a subdued screaming comes from another room; I hope it is from another room. I have an aversion to expressing pain, an aversion which in a hospital is maladaptive. You should squeal, flinch, object and ask for relief. But I have a rooted belief that if you admit you are hurting, someone will come along and hurt you worse. As our parents used to say, 'I'll give you something to cry for.' My brain seethes with ideas, so when my wounds are dressed I go limp as an old sheet and start novels in my head; one can always start them. My favourite story is set in the Raj and its heroine is called Milly Thoroughgood; she is somewhere between Zuleika Dobson and Becky Sharp. The beauty of a novel in the head is that you can run to stereotype: the blushing young clerk with a conscience and secret lusts, the charming military blackguard with the wrecked liver. The novel is composed in elaborate Jamesian circumlocutions, and I breathe along with the punctuation. Sometimes I smile at Milly's scathing comments to her beaux. The nurses think I'm gallant, a tractable patient; they don't know I'm in another country. My least favourite nurse huffs and puffs while he is doing the dressing, and sometimes kicks the bed, as if startled to find it there. My abstraction allows the staff to talk across me: 'Kim said that David should apologise to Jules, but I said he should apologise to Samira, and she said he should apologise to Suzanne, and Suzanne said she wasn't going to apologise to anyone, ever. But I think they should all apologise to me.'

Controlled movements still pose a problem. On Bastille Day I wake myself up by throwing a glass of water in my own face. With the black box to accommodate, every excursion needs care and precision, so I start to make a heap of my possessions on my bed on the window side, and here I hoard my books, an extra towel and a clean sheet, and tussle with anyone who offers to tidy them up. There are three things I need, apart from pain control. One is a reading light, pointing at me and not across the room; I read all the time, whether I'm in or out of my wits. The second is a fan, pointing at me also. The third is a closed door, to shut out the noise of groaning and retching, and also the cheerful rattle of cutlery and the smell of other people's dinners. It's a happy half-hour when I can secure all these three things together. It doesn't happen often and when it does I feel blessed. Hospital dramas are small, desperate, self-centred: 'I had my pill, then I fell over.' 'They said they would . . . but instead they . . .' 'The tea came three hours late and was coffee.' I have no problem with asking for something six times, because eventually I will get it. And what is time, to me, in here? The trick is to keep smiling and not refer back to the other failures. Each moment one is made new.

I reread Evelyn Waugh's *Sword of Honour* trilogy, and three Ivy Compton-Burnett novels, though later I can't remember which ones. I read a new biography of Katherine of Aragon in proof. I read *On Being Ill*, by Virginia Woolf. What schoolgirl piffle, I think. It's like one of those compositions by young ladies mocked in *Tom Sawyer*. I can't understand what she means when she complains about the 'poverty of the language' we have to describe illness. For the sufferer, she says, there is 'nothing ready made'. Then what of the whole vocabulary of singing aches, of spasms, of strictures and cramps; the gouging pain, the drilling pain, the pricking and pinching, the throbbing, burning, stinging, smarting, flaying? All good words. All old words. No one's pain is so special that the devil's dictionary of anguish has not anticipated it. There is even a scale you can use to refine it: 'Tell me,' the doctor says, 'on a scale of one to ten, how much this hurts': one being a love bite, I suppose, and ten the fiery pit of hell. Pain may pass beyond language, but it doesn't start beyond it. The torture chamber is where people 'speak'. No doubt language fails in that shuttered room called melancholia, where the floor is plush and the windowless walls are draped in black velvet: where any sound you make carries only feebly to the outside world, and can be taken for some accidental, natural sound, a creak or a sigh from doorframe or drawer. But then, mental suffering is so genteel; at least, until the dribbling sets in. Virginia only has decorous illnesses. She has faints and palpitations, fevers and headaches, though I am mindful that at one stage they tried to fix her by pulling out her teeth. But she is seemly; she does not seep, or require a dressings trolley, she does not wake at dawn to find herself smeared with contact jelly from last night's ECG. Virginia never oozes. Her secretions are ladylike: tears, not bile. She may as well not have had bowels, for all the evidence of them in her book.

When the date I should have gone home has long passed, I see that it was probably an error to have read the Katherine of Aragon biography, because the twists and turns of Reformation theology have been added to my already ecclesiastical concerns. I write: 'I feel as if someone has given me a set of Endurances, the opposite of Indulgences.' The nurses are worried that I never eat. They give me a warm croissant and it takes me five minutes to work my way through one bite. If I can't think of anything else I ask for a fruit salad, but I begin to feel I am being bullied by kiwi fruit, its jealous green eye falling on me as I poke it about with a spoon. One night I say, aghast: 'I won't *die*, will I?' But the next moment I am writing and laying plans and asking for an omelette. It is a yellow sprawl, like a window cleaner's shammy slapped on a plate; that is what an omelette looks like, but I have forgotten. I wonder if it's a joke they're playing. I list in my head all the window cleaners I have ever known. After prolonged study of my fork I apply a tine to the edge of the object. Fifteen minutes pass and I'm not much further on. If beaten eggs prove too much of a challenge, they say, I can have jelly instead. I want to say tartly that, unlike Virginia Woolf, I still have my own teeth.

I wonder, though, if there is a little saint you can apply to, if you're a person with holes in them? I can hardly expect the Trinity to care about my perforations, and I see the value of intercession by some lesser breed. Sebastian, shot full of arrows? It seems like overkill. There is a term for what is happening to St Teresa in Bernini's sculpture; it is 'transverberation'. But she was pierced suddenly by the fiery lance of God's love, whereas I was pierced by prearrangement, in a hospital just off the M25. After that initial cut, nothing went on time or to plan, and it was no one's fault. Most of July was gone before I was told I could leave the hospital, and after its clean, clear spaces, my own house seemed dimity, fringed, a patchwork of colour, full of overcrowded and complex angles. There was too much of everything and it smelled of the past – it was as if, without me to order it around, it had reverted to the character suitable for a building put up in the 1860s. I still had the black box tied to me, and for that first weekend of freedom, though the hallies were back in their holes, I needed to study, moment by moment, how to get up and lie down, how to sleep always on my back. Two days later I was back in hospital, driven along a moonlit road, 11 o'clock, a perfect summer night that I would never have seen if I had been less precarious. When we arrived at the little building the main door was locked and so, clutching a vomit bowl made in the shape of a cardboard hat, I sat on a bench, breathing in icy dew. The hospital campus has one beautiful building, a curve of shining white. As you sight it you say: 'What is that lovely thing?' It is the mortuary.

But re-entering the life I had so recently left, if not the very room then one just like it, my dreams were of birth, not death. Perhaps it was because of the weight of dressings on my abdomen that I dreamed I was carrying a child. It was born offstage as it were: at a fortnight old it talked like a philosopher. Only it would not acknowledge me as its mother. But then it offered to address me as 'Queen Mary', and everybody seemed happy with that solution. The line between hallucinations, dreams and waking nightmares had blurred, and for a time I wondered if it would ever stand firm again. Once again my concentration was on details: pens, notebook, reading glasses, watch, breathe in, breathe out, pick up that fork and show those eggs who's boss. I was discharged, returned once more, and when I went home finally, still with the wound and the vacuum machine, day to day life was complicated and onerous. I had pictured a mild and productive convalescence. Instead I found the illness had used up all my resources. I imagined every day would be better, but then things would go wrong in totally unexpected ways. For a good part of the time I felt so cowed and humiliated that I would have liked to sit in a corner with a sheet over my head, but this was not practical. I kept trying to rearrange my life so that illness was only a feature of it, and not the whole, but illness insists on its pre-eminence. Now the black box has gone, and it takes ten minutes to dress my healing wound, but I am woken in the night by the itching and burning of the process of repair. Sometimes I incorporate the sensations into nightmares and imagine, for instance, that the bed is on fire. One night in my dreams I meet the devil. He is 32, 34, that sort of age, present- able, with curly hair, and he wears a lambswool V-neck with a T-shirt underneath. We exchange heated words, and he raises a swarm of biting flies; I wake, clawing at my skin.

Just before my discharge I scribbled: 'When I go home I could write up my hospital diary. Or, you know, I could not. I could defiantly leave it unprocessed, and that way the marks of experience might fade.' The truth is that, needing more surgery, I am not sure what kind of story I am in. Perhaps a shaggy dog story, or a mangled joke with the punchline deliver- ed first. The poet Jo Shapcott used a nice phrase recently about confessional writing: 'chasing your own ambulance', she called it. I am guilty of that. In my defence I can say that I am fascinated by the line between writing and physical sur- vival. In the days after the procedure I was sometimes so ex- hausted by movement that I would wait patiently for someone to come in and give me a paper cup of pills that was almost, not quite, out of my reach. But somehow, I would always con- trive to get my pen in my hand, however far it had rolled; my mood was even, despite uprushes of shame, and the only thing that would really have upset me was running out of paper. The black ink, looping across the page, flowing easily and more like water than like blood, reassured me that I was alive and could act in the world. When Virginia Woolf's doctors forbade her to write, she obeyed them. Which makes me ask, what kind of wuss was Woolf? For a time, into September, my religious preoccupations continued, as if the operation had been on my brain and not my guts, as if the so-called 'God spot' had been stirred up by a scalpel. Even now I am content that the unconscious should continue to empty itself into waking life, like some constantly flushing lavatory. 'Are we somebodies?' the voice on my right asks. 'Yes, we are somebodies,' comes the reply. 'The church counts us all. But very few of us are saved.'

LRB (editorial)

From: ▮▮▮▮▮▮▮▮▮▮▮▮▮▮

Sent: 24 September 2012 19:05

To: LRB (editorial)

Subject: Winter lecture Feb 4th

Yes, thank you, that's fine by me. I'm going to begin by telling how when I was first invited to Buckingham Palace it all got too much for me and I had to sit on the floor behind a sofa and just notice feet.
Gerald says I can kiss goodbye to my damehood.
Love, Hilary

From: LRB (editorial) [mailto:edit@lrb.co.uk]

Sent: 24 September 2012 15:56

To: ▮▮▮▮▮▮▮▮▮▮▮▮▮▮

Subject: Winter lecture Feb 4th

It's just the BM website. As far as the paper is concerned it's absolutely fine – more than fine; as I said, perfect. Why don't we just say 'from Anne Boleyn to Kate Middleton ...' rather than your wasting your time rewriting the whole thing?

No question at all of calling her the Duchess of Cambridge. That would be awful.

Love
Mary-Kay

24/09/2012

Email from Hilary Mantel to
Mary-Kay Wilmers, 2012

Royal Bodies
From Anne Boleyn to Kate Middleton
2013

L AST SUMMER at the festival in Hay-on-Wye, I was asked to name a famous person and choose a book to give them. I hate the leaden repetitiveness of these little quizzes: who would be the guests at your ideal dinner party, what book has changed your life, which fictional character do you most resemble? I had to come up with an answer, however, so I chose Kate, the Duchess of Cambridge, and I chose to give her a book published in 2006, by the cultural historian Caroline Weber; it's called *Queen of Fashion: What Marie-Antoinette Wore to the Revolution*. It's not that I think we're heading for a revolution. It's rather that I saw Kate becoming a jointed doll on which certain rags are hung. In those days she was a shop-window mannequin, with no personality of her own, entirely defined by what she wore. These days she is a mother-to-be, and draped in another set of threadbare attributions. Once she gets over being sick, the press will find that she is radiant. They will find that this young woman's life until now was nothing, her only point and purpose being to give birth.

Marie-Antoinette was a woman eaten alive by her frocks. She was transfixed by appearances, stigmatised by her fashion choices. Politics were made personal in her. Her greed for self-gratification, her half-educated dabbling in public affairs, were adduced as a reason the French were bankrupt and miserable. It was ridiculous, of course. She was one individual with limited power and influence, who focused the rays of misogyny. She was a woman who couldn't win. If she wore fine fabrics she was said to be extravagant. If she wore simple fabrics, she was accused of plotting to ruin the Lyon silk trade. But in truth she was all body and no soul: no soul, no sense, no sensitivity. She was so wedded to her appearance that when the royal family, in disguise, made its desperate escape from Paris, dashing for the border, she not only had several trunk loads of new clothes sent on in advance, but took her hairdresser along on the trip. Despite the weight of her mountainous hairdos, she didn't feel her head wobbling on her shoulders. When she returned from that trip, to the prison Paris would become for her, it was said that her hair had turned grey overnight.

Antoinette as a royal consort was a gliding, smiling disaster, much like Diana in another time and another country. But Kate Middleton, as she was, appeared to have been designed by a committee and built by craftsmen, with a perfect plastic smile and the spindles of her limbs hand-turned and gloss-varnished. When it was announced that Diana was to join the royal family, the Duke of Edinburgh is said to have given her his approval because she would 'breed in some height'. Presumably Kate was designed to breed in some manners. She looks like a nicely brought up young lady, with 'please' and 'thank you' part of her vocabulary. But in her first official portrait by Paul Emsley, unveiled in January, her eyes are dead and she wears the strained smile of a woman who really wants to tell the painter to bugger off. One critic said perceptively that she appeared 'weary of being looked at'. Another that the portrait might pass muster as the cover of a Catherine Cookson novel: an opinion I find thought-provoking, as Cookson's simple tales of poor women extricating themselves from adverse circumstances were for twenty years, according to the Public Lending Right statistics, the nation's favourite reading. Sue Townsend said of Diana that she was 'a fatal non-reader'. She didn't know the end of her own story. She enjoyed only the romances of Barbara Cartland. I'm far too snobbish to have read one, but I assume they are stories in which a wedding takes place and they all live happily ever after. Diana didn't see the possible twists in the narrative. What does Kate read? It's a question.

Kate seems to have been selected for her role of princess because she was irreproachable: as painfully thin as anyone could wish, without quirks, without oddities, without the risk of the emergence of character. She appears precision-made, machine-made, so different from Diana whose human awkwardness and emotional incontinence showed in her every gesture. Diana was capable of transforming herself from galumphing schoolgirl to ice queen, from wraith to Amazon. Kate seems capable of going from perfect bride to perfect mother, with no messy deviation. When her pregnancy became public she had been visiting her old school, and had picked up a hockey stick and run a few paces for the camera. BBC News devoted a discussion to whether a pregnant woman could safely put on a turn of speed while wearing high heels. It is sad to think that intelligent people could devote themselves to this topic with earnest furrowings of the brow, but that's what discourse about royals comes to: a compulsion to comment, a discourse empty of content, mouthed rather than spoken. And in the same way one is compelled to look at them: to ask what they are made of, and is their substance the same as ours.

I used to think that the interesting issue was whether we should have a monarchy or not. But now I think that question is rather like, should we have pandas or not? Our current royal family doesn't have the difficulties in breeding that pandas do, but pandas and royal persons alike are expensive to conserve and ill-adapted to any modern environment. But aren't they interesting? Aren't they nice to look at? Some people find them endearing; some pity them for their precarious situation; everybody stares at them, and however airy the enclosure they inhabit, it's still a cage.

A few years ago I saw the Prince of Wales at a public award ceremony. I had never seen him before, and at once I thought: what a beautiful suit! What sublime tailoring! It's for Shakespeare to penetrate the heart of a prince, and for me to study his cuff buttons. I found it hard to see the man inside the clothes; and like Thomas Cromwell in my novels, I couldn't help winding the fabric back onto the bolt and pricing him by the yard. At this ceremony, which was formal and carefully orchestrated, the prince gave an award to a young author who came up on stage in shirtsleeves to receive his cheque. He no doubt wished to show that he was a free spirit, despite taking money from the establishment. For a moment I was ashamed of my trade. I thought, this is what the royals have to contend with today: not real, principled opposition, but self-congratulatory chippiness.

And then as we drifted away from the stage I saw something else. I glanced sideways into a room off the main hall, and saw that it was full of stacking chairs. It was a depressing, institutional, impersonal sight. I thought, Charles must see this all the time. Glance sideways, into the wings, and you see the tacky preparations for the triumphant public event. You see your beautiful suit deconstructed, the tailor's chalk lines, the unsecured seams. You see that your life is a charade, that the scenery is cardboard, that the paint is peeling, the red carpet fraying, and if you linger you will notice the oily devotion fade from the faces of your subjects, and you will see their retreating backs as they turn up their collars and button their coats and walk away into real life.

Then a little later I went to Buckingham Palace for a book trade event, a large evening party. I had expected to see people pushing themselves into the queen's path, but the opposite was true. The queen walked through the reception areas at an even pace, hoping to meet someone, and you would see a set of guests, as if swept by the tide, parting before her or welling ahead of her into the next room. They acted as if they feared excruciating embarrassment should they be caught and obliged to converse. The self-possessed became gauche and the eloquent were struck dumb. The guests studied the walls, the floor, they looked everywhere except at Her Majesty. They studied exhibits in glass cases and the paintings on the walls, which were of course worth looking at, but they studied them with great intentness, as if their eyes had been glued. Vermeer was just then 'having a moment', as they say, and the guests congregated around a small example, huddled with their backs to the room. I pushed through to see the painting along with the others but I can't remember now which Vermeer it was. It's safe to say there would have been a luminous face, round or oval, there would have been a woman gazing entranced at some household object, or perhaps reading a letter with a half-smile; there may have been a curtain, suggestive of veiled meaning; there would have been an enigma. We concentrated on it at the expense of the enigma moving among us, smiling with gallant determination.

And then the queen passed close to me and I stared at her. I am ashamed now to say it but I passed my eyes over her as a cannibal views his dinner, my gaze sharp enough to pick the meat off her bones. I felt that such was the force of my devouring curiosity that the party had dematerialised and the walls melted and there were only two of us in the vast room, and such was the hard power of my stare that Her Majesty turned and looked back at me, as if she had been jabbed in the shoulder; and for a split second her face expressed not anger but hurt bewilderment. She looked young: for a moment she had turned back from a figurehead into the young woman she was, before monarchy froze her and made her a thing, a thing which only had meaning when it was exposed, a thing that existed only to be looked at.

And I felt sorry then. I wanted to apologise. I wanted to say: it's nothing personal, it's monarchy I'm staring at. I rejoined, mentally, the rest of the guests. Now flunkeys were moving among us with trays and on them were canapés, and these snacks were the queen's revenge. They were pieces of gristly meat on skewers. Let's not put too fine a point on it: they were kebabs. It took some time to chew through one of them, and then the guests were left with the little sticks in their hands.

They tried to give them back to the flunkeys, but the flunkeys smiled and sadly shook their heads, and moved away, so the guests had to carry on the evening holding them out, like children with sparklers on Guy Fawkes night.

At this point the evening became all too much for me. It was violently interesting. I went behind a sofa and sat on the floor and enjoyed the rest of the party that way, seeking privacy as my sympathies shifted. And as the guests ebbed away and the rooms emptied, I joined them, and on the threshold I looked back, and what I saw, placed precisely at the base of every pillar, was a forest of little sticks: gnawed and abandoned. So if the queen's glance had swept the room, that is what she would have seen: what we had left in our wake. It was the stacking chairs all over again; the scaffolding of reality too nakedly displayed, the daylight let in on magic.

We can be sure the queen was not traumatised by my staring, as when next we met she gave me a medal. As I prepared to go to the palace, people would say: 'Will it be the actual queen, the queen herself?' Did they think contact with the anointed hand would change you? Was that what the guests at the palace feared: to be changed by powerful royal magic, without knowing how? The faculty of awe remains intact, for all that the royal story in recent years has taken a sordid turn. There were scandals enough in centuries past, from the sneaky little adulteries of Katherine Howard to the junketings of the Prince Regent to the modern-day mischief of Mrs Simpson. But a new world began, I think, in 1980, with the discovery that Diana, the future Princess of Wales, had legs. You will remember how the young Diana taught for a few hours a week at a kindergarten called Young England, and when it was first known that she was Charles's choice of bride, the press photographed her, infants touchingly gathered around; but they induced her to stand against the light, so in the resulting photograph the nation could see straight through her skirt. A sort of licentiousness took hold, a national lip-smacking. Those gangling limbs were artlessly exposed, without her permission. It was the first violation.

When Diana drove to St Paul's she was a blur of virginal white behind glass. The public was waiting to see the dress, but this was more than a fashion moment. An everyday sort of girl had been squashed into the coach, but a goddess came out. She didn't get out of the coach in any ordinary way: she hatched. The extraordinary dress came first, like a flow of liquid, like ectoplasm emerging from the orifices of a medium. It was a long moment before she solidified. Indeed the coach was a medium, a method of conveyance and communication between two spheres, the private and the public, the common and the royal. The dress's first effect was dismaying. I could hear a nation of women catching their breath as one, not in awe but in horror: it's creased to glory, how did they let that happen? I heard the squeak as a million ironing-boards unfolded, a sigh and shudder as a collective nightmare came true: that dream we all have, that we are incorrectly dressed or not dressed at all, that we are naked in the street. But as the dress resolved about her, the princess was born and the world breathed out.

Diana was more royal than the family she joined. That had nothing to do with family trees. Something in her personality, her receptivity, her passivity, fitted her to be the carrier of myth. She came near to claiming that she had a healing touch, the ancient attribute of royal persons. The healing touch can't be felt through white gloves. Diana walked bare-handed among the multitude, and unarmed: unfortified by irony, uninformed by history. Her tragedy was located in the gap between her human capacities and the demands of the superhuman role she was required to fulfil. When I think of Diana, I remember Stevie Smith's poem about the Lorelei:

> There, on a rock majestical,
> A girl with smile equivocal,
> Painted, young and damned and fair,
> Sits and combs her yellow hair.

Soon Diana's hairstyles were as consequential as Marie-Antoinette's, and a great deal cheaper to copy.

In the next stage of her story, she passed through trials, through ordeals at the world's hands. For a time the public refrained from demanding her blood so she shed it herself, cutting her arms and legs. Her death still makes me shudder because although I know it was an accident, it wasn't just an accident. It was fate showing her hand, fate with her twisted grin. Diana visited the most feminine of cities to meet her end as a woman: to move on, from the City of Light to the place beyond black. She went into the underpass to be reborn, but reborn this time without a physical body: the airy subject of a hundred thousand photographs, a flicker at the corner of the eye, a sigh on the breeze.

For a time it was hoped, and it was feared, that Diana had changed the nation. Her funeral was a pagan outpouring, a lawless fiesta of grief. We are bad at mourning our dead. We don't make time or space for grief. The world tugs us along, back into its harsh rhythm before we are ready for it, and for the pain of loss doctors can prescribe a pill. We are at war with our nature, and nature will win; all the bottled anguish, the grief dammed up, burst the barriers of politeness and formality and restraint, and broke down the divide between private and public, so that strangers wailed in the street, people who had never met Diana lamented her with maladjusted fervour, and we all remembered our secret pain and unleashed it in one huge carnival of mass mourning. But in the end, nothing changed. We were soon back to the prosaic: shirtsleeves, stacking chairs, little sticks. And yet none of us who lived through it will forget that dislocating time, when the skin came off the surface of the world, and our inner vision cleared, and we saw the archetypes clear and plain, and we saw the collective psyche at work, and the gods pulling our strings. To quote Stevie Smith again:

> An antique story comes to me
> And fills me with anxiety,
> I wonder why I fear so much
> What surely has no modern touch?

In looking at royalty we are always looking at what is archaic, what is mysterious by its nature, and my feeling is that it will only ever half-reveal itself. This poses a challenge to historians and to those of us who work imaginatively with the past. Royal persons are both gods and beasts. They are persons but they are supra-personal, carriers of a blood line: at the most basic, they are breeding stock, collections of organs.

This brings me to the royal bodies with whom I have been most concerned recently, those of Anne Boleyn and Henry VIII.

Long before Kate's big news was announced, the tabloids wanted to look inside her to see if she was pregnant. Historians are still trying to peer inside the Tudors. Are they healthy, are they sick, can they breed? The story of Henry and his wives is peculiar to its time and place, but also timeless and universally understood; it is highly political and also highly personal. It is about body parts, about what slots in where, and when: are they body parts fit for purpose, or are they diseased? It's no surprise that so much fiction constellates around the subject of Henry and his wives. Often, if you want to write about women in history, you have to distort history to do it, or substitute fantasy for facts; you have to pretend that individual women were more important than they were or that we know more about them than we do.

But with the reign of King Bluebeard, you don't have to pretend. Women, their bodies, their reproductive capacities, their animal nature, are central to the story. The history of the reign is so graphically gynaecological that in the past it enabled lady novelists to write about sex when they were only supposed to write about love; and readers could take an avid interest in what went on in royal bedrooms by dignifying it as history, therefore instructive, edifying. Popular fiction about the Tudors has also been a form of moral teaching about women's lives, though what is taught varies with moral fashion. It used to be that Anne Boleyn was a man-stealer who got paid out. Often, now, the lesson is that if Katherine of Aragon had been a bit more foxy, she could have hung on to her husband. Anne as opportunist and sexual predator finds herself recruited to the cause of feminism. Always, the writers point to the fact that a man who marries his mistress creates a job vacancy. 'Women beware women' is a teaching that never falls out of fashion.

Anne Boleyn, in particular, is a figure who elicits a deep response, born out of ignorance often enough but also out of empathy. The internet is abuzz with stories about her, as if everything were happening today. Her real self is hidden within the dramas into which we co-opt her. There is a prurient curiosity around her, of the kind that gathered around Wallis Simpson. Henry didn't give up the throne to marry her, but he did reshape his nation's history. So what was her particular attraction? Did she have a sexual secret? A special trick? Was she beautiful, or ugly? The six fingers with which she was credited were not seen during her lifetime, and the warts and wens and extra nipple that supposedly disfigured her were witches' marks produced by the black fantasy of Catholic propagandists. Her contemporaries didn't think she was a great beauty. 'She is of middling stature', a Venetian diplomat reported. A 'swarthy complexion, long neck, wide mouth, bosom not much raised, and in fact has nothing but the English king's great appetite, and her eyes, which are black and beautiful'. It was said, though not by unbiased observers, that after her marriage she aged rapidly and grew thin. If this is true, and we put it together with reports of a swelling in her throat, and with the description of her by one contemporary as 'a goggle-eyed whore', then we're looking, possibly, at a woman with a hyperthyroid condition, a woman of frayed temper who lives on the end of her nerves. It often surprises people that there is no attested contemporary portrait. Just because an unknown hand has written 'Anne Boleyn' on a picture, it doesn't mean it's an image from the life or even an image of Anne at all. The most familiar image, in which she wears a letter 'B' hanging from a pearl necklace, exists in many forms and variants and originates at least fifty years after Anne's death.

So much close scrutiny, and none of it much help to posterity. Anne was a mercurial woman, still shaped by the projections of those who read and write about her. Royal bodies do change after death, and not just as a consequence of the universal postmortem changes. Now we know the body in the Leicester car park is indeed that of Richard III, we have to concede the curved spine was not Tudor propaganda, but we need not believe the chronicler who claimed Richard was the product of a two-year pregnancy and was born with teeth. Why are we all so pleased about digging up a king? Perhaps because the present is paying some of the debt it owes to the past, and science has come to the aid of history. The king stripped by the victors has been reclothed in his true identity. This is the essential process of history, neatly illustrated: loss, retrieval.

To return to Henry VIII: almost the first thirty years of his reign were shaped by his need for a male heir. Religious and political activity cluster around the subject. Not all the intelligence and diligence of his ministers could give Henry what he most needed. Only a woman could: but which woman? Neither of Henry's first two wives had trouble conceiving. Royal pregnancies were not announced in those days; the news generally crept out, and public anticipation was aroused only when the child quickened. We know Katherine of Aragon had at least six pregnancies, most of them ending in late miscarriages or neonatal deaths. She had a son who survived for seven weeks, but only one child made it past early infancy, and that was a daughter, the Princess Mary. Anne's first pregnancy was successful, and produced another girl, the Princess Elizabeth. Then she miscarried at least twice. It was not until his third marriage that Henry had a son who lived. Both those daughters, Mary and Elizabeth, were women of great ability, and in their very different ways were capable of ruling; but I don't think this means that Henry was wrong in his construction of his situation. What he feared was that his bloodline would end. Elizabeth found the puzzle of whom she could marry too difficult to solve, so that her reign was dominated by succession crises, and she was indeed the last of the Tudors. The line did end: just a lot later than Henry had imagined.

Anne Boleyn wasn't royal by birth. Her family were city merchants dignified into gentlefolk, and her father had married into the powerful and noble Howard family. She became royal, exalted, at her coronation when, six months pregnant, she walked the length of Westminster Abbey on a cloth of heaven-blue. It was said she had won Henry by promising him a son. Anne was a power player, a clever and determined woman. But in the end she was valued for her body parts, not her intellect or her soul; it was her womb that was central to her story. The question is whether she could ever win the battle for an heir: or was biology against her? At his trial Anne's brother, George Boleyn, entertained the court by telling them that Henry was no good in bed. Conception was thought to be tied to female orgasm, so the implication was that what George called Henry's lack of 'skill' was the problem.

Yet clearly he was able to make his wives pregnant. Was something else wrong? The old notion that Henry had syphilis has been discarded. There never was any contemporary evidence for it. The theory was constructed in the 19th century, as part of a narrative that showed Henry as a sexual beast justly punished for his promiscuity. In fact Henry constrained his sexual appetites. He had few mistresses compared to other grandees of his time. I think it was more important to him to be good, to be seen to be good, than to be gratified in this particular way. In fact I think we can say that the old monster was a bit of a romantic. Later in life, when he married Anne of Cleves, he didn't want to have sex with a woman with whom he wasn't in love; it was a scruple that baffled his contemporaries.

Recently a new hypothesis about Henry has emerged. In 2010 a paper by Catrina Banks Whitley and Kyra Cornelius Kramer appeared in the *Historical Journal*, called 'A New Explanation of the Reproductive Woes and Midlife Decline of Henry VIII'. It suggested that Henry had a blood type called Kells positive. People who are Kells positive carry an extra antibody on the surface of their red blood cells. The blood type is rare, so we can assume Henry's wives were Kells negative, and that their lack of compatibility was the reason for the multiple reproductive failures. When a woman who is Kells negative conceives by a man who is Kells positive, she will, if the foetus itself is Kells positive, become sensitised; her immune system will try to reject the foetus. The first pregnancy will go well, other things being equal. As with rhesus incompatibility, it takes one pregnancy for the woman to develop the sensitisation. But later children will die before or just after birth.

To a certain point this fits Henry's story. He had a healthy illegitimate son by Elizabeth Blount: that was a first pregnancy. His first child with Anne Boleyn was a healthy girl, and his first child with Jane Seymour a healthy boy; Jane died soon after Edward's birth, so we don't know what would have happened thereafter. With Katherine of Aragon the pattern is more blurred. Mystery surrounds her first pregnancy, much of it made by the queen herself, who perhaps didn't want to admit that she had miscarried; so we know the pregnancy didn't work out, but we don't know what happened. One of Katherine's doctors thought it was a twin pregnancy and it may have failed for any number of reasons. So Katherine's healthy child, Mary, was not her first. But every child fathered by Henry had a chance of being Kells negative, and the paper's authors suggest that this is how Mary survived.

If this is true, it makes the history of Henry's reign a different sort of tragedy: not a moral but a biological tragedy, inscribed on the body. The efforts of the wives and the politicians and the churchmen didn't avail because a genetic lottery was in operation. What makes the hypothesis persuasive, to some minds, is Henry's later medical history. Some individuals who are Kells positive go on to develop a collection of symptoms called McLeod syndrome. In early life Henry was, by all contemporary accounts, a creature of great beauty. He excelled in every sport. We wonder, of course, did his opponents let the king win? But Henry was not a fool and though he was susceptible to flattery he didn't need flattery of that simple kind; and besides, in a dangerous pursuit like jousting, where one armoured man on an armoured horse is charging at another headlong, the outcome is difficult to control. I think we can take it that he was a star. He collected a number of injuries that stopped him jousting, and then in middle age became stout, eventually gross. He developed a weakness in his legs, and by the end of his life was virtually immobile. It also seems to some authorities that he underwent personality changes in mid-life. It was said that as a young man he was sweet-natured; though the claim would have had a hollow ring if you were Richard Empson or Edmund Dudley, ministers to his father, whom he executed as soon as he came to the throne. But it's incontrovertible that as Henry aged he became increasingly angry, irrational, wilful and out of control. He fits the picture for McLeod syndrome: progressive muscular weakness and nerve deterioration in the lower body, depression, paranoia, an erosion of personality.

Some historians see the year 1536 as a turning point for Henry, personally and politically: that was the year in which Anne Boleyn was beheaded. Certainly his later years were very sad ones for a man who had been so magnificent and imposing. Pathology is at work, but of what kind? It seems to me that there are more obvious explanations for his poor health and the deterioration of his character, and the authors of the original paper didn't really understand the external pressures on the king later in his reign. Henry had suffered accidents in the tiltyard and one of his legs was permanently ulcerated. He probably had osteomyelitis, an infection in the bone. His leg caused him chronic pain and historians – and, I'm afraid, doctors – underestimate what chronic pain can do to sour the temper and wear away both the personality and the intellect. When we call him paranoid, we must acknowledge he was right to think his enemies were everywhere, though he was increasingly bad at working out who they were.

As for depression, he had a great deal to be depressed about: not just his isolation on the world stage, but his own decay and deterioration. He had magnificent portraits created, and left them as his surrogates to stare down at his courtiers while he retreated into smaller, more intimate spaces. Yet he was quite unable to keep private what was happening to his own body. The royal body exists to be looked at. The world's focus on body parts was most acute and searching in the case of Jane Seymour, Henry's third wife. No one understood what Henry saw in Jane, who was not pretty and not young. The imperial ambassador sneered that 'no doubt she has a very fine *enigme*': which is to say, secret part. We have arrived at the crux of the matter: a royal lady is a royal vagina. Along with the reverence and awe accorded to royal persons goes the conviction that the body of the monarch is public property. We are ready at any moment to rip away the veil of respect, and treat royal persons in an inhuman way, making them not more than us but less than us, not really human at all.

Is monarchy a suitable institution for a grown-up nation? I don't know. I have described how my own sympathies were activated and my simple ideas altered. The debate is not high on our agenda. We are happy to allow monarchy to be an entertainment, in the same way that we license strip joints and lap-dancing clubs. Adulation can swing to persecution, within hours, within the same press report: this is what happened to Prince Harry recently. You can understand that anybody treated this way can be destabilised, and that Harry doesn't know which he is, a person or a prince. Diana was spared, at least, the prospect of growing old under the flash-bulbs, a crime for which the media would have made her suffer. It may be that the whole phenomenon of monarchy is irrational, but that doesn't mean that when we look at it we should behave like spectators at Bedlam. Cheerful curiosity can easily become cruelty. It can easily become fatal. We don't cut off the heads of royal ladies these days, but we do sacrifice them, and we did memorably drive one to destruction a scant generation ago. History makes fools of us, makes puppets of us, often enough. But it doesn't have to repeat itself. In the current case, much lies within our control. I'm not asking for censorship. I'm not asking for pious humbug and smarmy reverence. I'm asking us to back off and not be brutes. Get your pink frilly frocks out, zhuzh up your platinum locks. We are all Barbara Cartland now. The pen is in our hands. A happy ending is ours to write.

LRB (editorial)

From:	▆▆▆▆▆▆▆▆▆▆
Sent:	19 February 2013 10:01
To:	LRB (editorial), Bill, Patrick
Subject:	press etc re British Museum lecture

Dear Mary-Kay et al,
The Daily Express is sitting outside my house, phone ringing, etc.
My line is that there is nothing to add to the original speech. It was broadly
sympathetic to the royal family and asked the press to 'back off and not be
brutes.'
These are sad days for irony.
I don't tweet or blog etc, so have no intention of getting drawn in.
Love, Hilary

19/02/2013

Emails from Hilary Mantel to
Mary-Kay Wilmers, 2013

LRB (editorial)

Alas, no , dear Mary-Kay, because of a deep need to keep away from the Elizabethans, the Cheapside Hoard, all those potentially fascinating things, in case of imagination creep...you know, the way a rug creeps across the floor , unnoticed till you trip over it and realise it's in the wrong place entirely. It's a problem. It means in effect my eyes have to close to anything after 1540. I have learned to walk around old houses deliberately unseeing what's Elizabethan. The mental soundtrack doesn't seem to be so sensitive. A good thing or I'd have to keep away from Shakespeare. Words are easier to pick over, I suppose, but visual impressions just seep. But thank you, as always. The plays are well into rehearsal now and the TV production is kicking off. I am not as far forward with the new book as I would like, but happy enough with what I've done. The difficulty now is to stop the characters existing in real time...I could be writing about them for the rest of my life. But then oddly, the more I know, the less I know. When I sat down to write character notes for the RSC I was fine with all the characters except Thomas Cromwell, about whom I was unable to make one coherent statement. Then the NPG asked me to hand-write a 'pen portrait,' one side of A4; it's taken me most of this week.

Love from me, going slower and slower, Hilary

How to Be Tudor
On Charles Brandon
2016

O N THEIR West Country progress in the summer of 1535, Henry VIII and Anne Boleyn visited Thornbury Castle near Bristol. Thornbury is an upmarket hotel now, a popular choice for guests working through their bucket list. Now that every narrative is a 'journey', TripAdvisor is an illuminating guide to what people expect when they go in search of the past. Some guests are content to know the place was 'used by Henry and Anne, back in the day', while others like to believe it was where the king spent 'one of his many honeymoons'. Guests praise 'a brilliant, authentic experience of castle life' and the ease of finding the place, 'especially if you use a GPS', but some claim a lack of attention to their particular pleasures: 'there is an archery set there to play with, but one of the arrows is broken.' Others have grumbled about poor wifi, peeling paint, lacklustre cocktails, weddings, children and mice. One review from 2015 sums up the general feeling that the past never quite lives up to its billing: 'Somewhat lacking in luxury, service and Tudor'.

What does it mean, to be lacking in Tudor? If Tudor is terror in the name of the church and torture in the name of the state, iconoclasm, cruelty to animals and poor sanitation, the castle must fall short. If it is 'living like royalty and fine dining', as one guest puts it, it seems Thornbury makes a good effort. To be Tudor is to pose. It is to strut down a long gallery, to have a chest stiffened with gemstones, and padded shoulders that block doorways. It is to wear a codpiece, take your own gold plate when you travel, and live off the fat of the land. If Tudor is measured on a scale, and scored by size of beard, love of jousting and trouble with wives, Charles Brandon would come near the top, second only to the king he served.

The subtitle of Steven Gunn's scholarly biography describes its subject as 'Henry VIII's Closest Friend'.* What a prospect of damp-palmed horror that phrase evokes! The knocking of Tudor knees echoes down the years. Can a king have friends? Could Henry VIII have friends? The pertinent anecdote is well known: he walked affectionately with Thomas More, an arm around his neck, but More told his son-in-law: 'If my head would win him a castle in France . . . it would not fail to go.' Charles Brandon fought in showy campaigns to recover those bits of France Henry thought he owned, so he must have felt the truth of More's words in every shuddering vertebra. He was one of a group of athletic courtiers employed to serve the leisure of Hooray Henry; they overlapped with, but can be distinguished from, the machiavels who served the policy of Horrid Henry, and the poets and priests employed to flatter the intellect and ease the conscience of Holy Henry. Henry came to the throne in 1509. Charles Brandon's power as a court favourite endured till death removed him in 1545. A long run, on ground slippery with blood: how did Charles do it?

---

* *Charles Brandon: Henry VIII's Closest Friend* by Steven Gunn (Amberley, 2015).

His family had been gentleman merchants in Norfolk. They had served the dukes of Norfolk when the Mowbray family held that title. The Mowbray line came to an end in 1481, but before that Charles's grandfather had married into the powerful Wingfield family and passed into the service of Edward IV. Charles's father was William Brandon, who according to the Paston letters got himself a bad reputation, 'for that he should have by force ravished and swived an ancient gentlewoman, and yet was not therewith eased, but swived her oldest daughter, and then would have swived the other sister both'. He fought for the invading Tudor forces against Richard III. Unsubstantiated legend has him as a standard-bearer at Bosworth, cut down close to the person of the man who would soon be king. Whatever the exact truth, he died a hero with a claim on the gratitude of the new regime. He did not leave much land for Charles, but his uncle Thomas had inherited a family property in Southwark which brought privileges in the borough. Thomas married well and began to build a career at court, becoming Henry VII's master of the horse. He died early in the new reign, but left nephew Charles a network of good connections.

There is no record at all of Charles's education. He would not share his prince's intellectual interests, and his spelling is among the strangest in an era when inconsistency was the rule. Charles followed his father in becoming an enthusiastic swiver. He followed his uncle in becoming a fearless and skilled jouster, beginning his career at the age of 17 in the reign of the old king. Henry VII was not, as legend suggests, a misery who went about with his garments in holes. As the Tudor family were not really very royal at all, he placed calculated reliance on flamboyant display, asserting his regime's legitimacy through allegory and pageant. The tournament was a self-consciously medieval survival, a link with the knightly past, and was at the heart of the court's solemn and costly pleasures. Charles became a star, watched with increasing admiration by the heir to the throne, who was some six years younger than he was. The old king guarded his heir closely, having already lost one prince of Wales, and while his father was alive Henry had to confine himself to martial exercises on the practice ground. But once he was his own boss, he threw himself into the pursuit, practising every day and seeking out the best opponents. He was a prince of exuberant physical energy, and had the height and weight to succeed at a sport so expensive and dangerous that it was still thought valid preparation for the battlefield. In jousting it's only with a well-matched opponent that you can make a good score. You are dependent on him to hurtle at you with full force. But more than brutality is required. The placing, the pace and the angle are crucial. Sometimes the king and Charles Brandon dressed alike, fighting as a team. Sometimes they challenged each other. Did Charles ever let Henry win? Having paid close attention to the score sheets, Gunn suggests he did. But Charles in his gilt armour could defeat any other challenger – at least, once early death in a small war had removed some of his rivals.

Charles Brandon was part of a coterie of special favourites, with Edward Howard, Thomas Knyvett and Henry Guildford. In 1512, the young king went to war with France. Charles was given command of troops for a sea attack on Brittany, to be led by Edward Howard. With Thomas Knyvett on board, the

Regent engaged the *Cordelière*, sailing out of Brest. The *Cordelière* exploded, and one of the bravest of Henry's captains was blown to pieces. Edward Howard said he would not look the king in the face till he had revenged their friend; a year on, he launched an attack on French galleys, and was drowned. Two of the men closest to Henry had perished in a war that achieved very little in any permanent sense. Henry Guildford's power lasted until 1532 when, tired of the Boleyns, he handed Henry his resignation from the post of comptroller of the household, went off to the country and died of disgust. It was Charles who was the great survivor. His influence waxed and waned but he saw out five of Henry's queens and any number of ministers and favourites. In *Mary Rose*, his book about Brandon's third wife, David Loades says: 'He was present everywhere, but it is hard to pinpoint what he actually did.' Throughout his career Charles accumulated grand-sounding titles, which confused outsiders into overestimating his importance as a policymaker. When he became Master of the Horse in 1512, he had a real job to do – the master controlled transport for the vast, itinerant royal household, and supplied the king's horses in time of war. But on great occasions of state, he rode by the king as a squire would ride by his knight. Someone so close to the king's person must, foreign observers reasoned, be of first importance. In the war of 1513, he appeared to onlookers as a 'second king'. In that year Henry campaigned in France and took Tournai; when he handed Brandon the city keys, Italian observers deduced he was giving his prize to a bastard brother. To boost his status among Henry's commanders, he was allowed to assume the style of 'viscount', a title which belonged to his

ward. In the English ranks, there were murmurs that Charles
was overpromoted. But already his survival skills were evident. His very lack of political acumen, his absence of ambition, took him out of the front line of faction fighting. He was
not subtle, so aroused no suspicion of plotting; congenial,
and disinclined to pursue grudges, he survived men who had
far greater intelligence and cunning. A flair for display, fine
equipage, costly and elaborate clothes, a sense of theatre
– these were what made a Tudor grandee. Charles's secret
was simple: he always did what Henry wanted, promptly and
gladly, when he could work out what that was.

Gunn is now a senior figure in Tudor studies, but this book
was first published in 1988. The new edition is handsomely
produced and illustrated, but the text is of specialist interest;
it is only on painstaking work like this that narratives can
confidently be built. It results from work in the archives which
will not need to be repeated, and is devoted quite properly to
the details of the duke's labyrinthine property dealings, law-
suits and household matters, with the political backdrop
sketched in only lightly. As close work with the documents,
it's hard to see how it could be done better. Gunn points to
the gaps in the evidence and is not tempted to fill them by
speculation. The book is never picturesque. You have to bring
your own Tudor. But the driest treatment cannot conceal
Charles's violent human interest. At 19, he had become involved with Anne Browne, daughter of a prominent courtier.
They were pledged, they anticipated the marriage, and Anne
became pregnant. But Charles abandoned her and married
her aunt, Margaret Mortimer, who had more money. Having
sold off some of the aunt's property, he then returned to the

niece, who had given birth to a daughter. In 1508 he did marry her, trying to keep the fact quiet, but her family insisted on a second, public ceremony. Two years on, Anne gave birth to a second girl, and died. Later, when Charles got around to thinking about the formalities, he was able to disentangle all this, obtaining with seeming ease a dispensation from the pope freeing him from the Mortimer marriage. Margaret at some stage had an illegitimate child by a priest; Charles had three recognised illegitimate children who, confusingly, share names with his legitimate ones. The addled writers of the HBO series *The Tudors* strained every nerve to come up with sensational storylines, without rivalling the truth of these people's lives. We do not know, because there is no evidence, what Charles thought of his own conduct – we never know. But his next step was to enter into a contract of marriage with his ward, Elizabeth Lady Lisle, whose title he had taken. Elizabeth was only eight but she was an heiress and the move took her off the market till she grew up, giving Charles the use of her resources. As long as the marriage was unconsummated, Charles could free himself if he found a better prospect. In 1515 he found one in the king of England's sister.

The year before, Charles had been created duke of Suffolk, and the elderly earl of Surrey, Thomas Howard, had become duke of Norfolk. The Howard family picked the wrong side at Bosworth, and so lost their ducal status. They earned it back by Surrey's annihilation of the Scottish army at Flodden. While Henry was fighting in France, the Scots forces had come over the border, with ruinous results for their kingdom. The senior Howard was covered in glory, and so was his son Lord Thomas, who had served under him. The son would become duke of Norfolk in his turn, and for the rest of Henry's reign the two great East Anglians would vie for the king's attention. At the time of his elevation it was unclear what Brandon had done to deserve a dukedom. Erasmus in a letter compared him to a drunken stable boy. Charles had shown himself a capable leader in the French campaign, but there had been no solid opportunity to distinguish himself. And he was now a duke without a ducal income. As a man close to the king, he attracted gifts to persuade him to use his influence, and he had amassed a portfolio of offices and grants, but making them pay was harder. As a magnate in East Anglia, he would find himself working with Thomas Howard to keep the region peaceful and the king's revenues flowing. The Howard family had more resources, wider and deeper connections, and Lord Thomas – who was as lean, sinewy and irritable as Charles was stout and amenable – was an astute and busily ambitious man. But it was Charles who took the eye of a princess.

In the summer of 1514, Wolsey, the king's chief councillor, negotiated an Anglo-French treaty. Its cornerstone was a match between 18-year-old Mary Rose, the younger of Henry's two sisters, and Louis XII, who was 52, a widower in poor health. Louis sent giddily generous presents, including a fabulous diamond called the Mirror of Naples – which Henry at once sent to be valued. Louis also sent an artist to paint the princess and advise her on her new wardrobe. There was a bizarre proxy ceremony in which the princess lay down on a ceremonial bed while the chief French envoy removed his red stocking and touched his bare leg against her body; the marriage was then considered consummated. In the autumn

Charles and the cream of the English nobility escorted her to France. Much jousting was involved. The marriage lasted 82 days before Louis succumbed, possibly to over-excitement. Wearing white for mourning, Mary Rose was sequestered until it could be known if she was carrying a child. She was not, but during this period 'la reine blanche' felt vulnerable: the new king, Francis, would penetrate her seclusion and make insinuations. She thought that he was planning to ruin her good name, or marry her to a French nobleman, or both; for his part, Francis was afraid that Henry would snatch her back and marry her into the Habsburg family. So when Charles arrived to take her home, and the widow said she had chosen her new husband already, Francis did not stand in the way.

It seems that before leaving England the princess had extracted a promise from Henry: once her elderly fiancé died, she would be allowed to choose her next husband for herself. Henry knew Charles and his sister were englamoured by each other – but had told his friend that nothing must happen between them till they were back in England. Perhaps they did not trust him to keep the promise. On the ground in France, matters were urgent. I had to marry her, Charles explained; I 'newar sawe woman soo wyepe'. On their return they had to face Henry. 'Hall me trost es in you,' the duke wrote to Wolsey. It had to be, since untangling his rich bride's finances was 'past me lerneng'.

It's impossible to say how much of Henry's anger was for show. He was determined the crown should be the financial gainer, and to compensate himself he annexed a large percentage of the future income from Mary's dower lands. For the former queen, getting hold of her income was not easy. It was never a matter of collecting a bag of gold at Calais. When Anglo-French relations were under strain, the money would be cut off, and the couple had to renegotiate their debt to the king. Sometimes their payments were suspended and Henry charged interest. In any year the dowry income formed a large proportion of Charles's total assets. Charles had already been in debt to the king when the marriage took place. Mary would always be called 'the French queen', and maintain royal style. She also kept up French fashions and introduced French architecture and garden design in their various properties. Though the marriage hugely enhanced Charles's prestige, it also created an embarrassing and potentially dangerous situation. The French treated him as being in their pocket, which he was, and expected him to serve their interests.

In 1522, when the Emperor Charles visited England, the Duke of Suffolk was in the king's suite at his reception, and both king and emperor dined at Suffolk Place and hunted in the park. Charles, with his deep knowledge of heraldic and chivalric matters, was useful for entertaining ambassadors and leading parades; as Gunn says, he 'combined status and amiability'. The emperor saw the point of him, and offered him a pension. Like other councillors, he was now in receipt of money from both great European powers, and the two commitments might be seen as balancing out. England was a small nation, punching above its weight because it had a brilliant chief minister. Wolsey's strategy was to maintain a balance of power, and his chief weapon was flattery and the foresight to make swift and nimble adjustments. He could promise English friendship, money, troops, first to France, then to the emperor – try to keep them hostile to each other openly or covertly, and hope he wouldn't have to cost out his promises and to go to war.

In 1523 Henry allied with the emperor and made another incursion to France, despite the fact that an obscure member of the Commons called Thomas Cromwell advised him that if he were captured and had to be ransomed, England couldn't afford him; the war was likely to use up all England's gold, and reduce the country to exchanging leather tokens for money. Brandon was put in charge of an army of ten thousand men. The English came within reach of Paris, but a combination of cold weather and lukewarm allies made the campaign, unpopular at home, pointless in the end. But it did Charles no harm, and when Henry planned – there was more planning than actual fighting – Charles always figured as a senior commander. Charles's interest, as a member of a warrior caste, was war; his personal interest was in peace, at least with the French, because then his income flowed freely. With his wife, he necessarily spent time in his own territories, but there was always the danger of being supplanted by new favourites, and the king tended to seek the company of younger men, the new tournament stars. A courtier had to be vigilant and he had to be present; access and proximity were everything; secret business, one must suppose, was transacted face to face and left no trace on the records. Documents preserve the duke for us in facts and figures, and Gunn extracts every scrap of evidence from them. States of mind are harder to assess. But it is not difficult to imagine his horror when in 1524 he came near to killing the king. Henry was running against Charles in new armour of his own design. For some reason he failed to put down his visor. Charles's scoring touch was accurate – Henry's helm filled with splinters from the broken lance. Charles swore he would never ride against the king again. When they next appeared in the lists, it was as a team of two, wearing identical silver beards.

Until the birth of Prince Edward in 1537, Henry did not have a legitimate male heir, so the children of his two sisters were potential successors. Charles and 'la reine blanche' had two daughters, a son called Henry, who died, and then another Henry, who was created earl of Lincoln. The creation signified the maturity of Henry's power, his dynastic grip. The last earl of Lincoln had been John de la Pole, the Yorkist claimant to the throne, killed fighting Henry VII at the battle of Stoke in 1487. His younger brother, Edmund de la Pole, earl of Suffolk, was executed in 1513; his brother William was securely shut in the Tower; another brother, Richard, was killed at Pavia in 1525. The ancient line had been erased, and Charles Brandon written in, no longer a parvenu but a feature of the Tudor landscape as solid as a Norman castle.

We don't know if the marriage was happy. Mary's health was frail. In the 1520s she came to court, but no longer danced. The shadow of the king's 'great matter' fell over the end of her life. As a royal lady, she was devoted to Katherine of Aragon, herself the daughter of two reigning monarchs. But she could make only mute protests – staying away from great occasions – when Henry began the long war that was to lead to Katherine's displacement by Anne Boleyn. Charles was required to play his part in harassing Katherine, who was sent off to the country with a reduced household. One of his missions ended when Katherine shut herself in her room and left him to shout at her through a locked door. He didn't enjoy this work, but he did it, just as he played his part in bringing Wolsey down. The chief agents may have been the men whom the French called 'le duc de Nortfoch et sa bande', but Suffolk marched in with Thomas Howard to confiscate the Great Seal, and declared: 'there never was legate nor cardinall, that did good in England.'

In the resulting power vacuum, the imperial ambassador thought that 'tous les grans d'Angleterre' would have to work together and Charles would be one of them. Norfolk, as the uncle of Anne Boleyn, was set to gain under the new regime. Relations between the two dukes were fragile, though Norfolk would later insist: 'I always called him cousyn Charles.' Anne Boleyn was more outspoken in her dislike. In 1531 she suggested that Suffolk was sleeping with one of his daughters. Charles in his turn is said to have told the king that Anne had slept with Thomas Wyatt – another redoubtable jouster. The Boleyn family took up religious reform, but Charles didn't quarrel with them on those grounds. He seemed to have no firm religious orientation of his own. Neither papist nor reformer, he wisely took his cue from the king.

In 1533 Mary Rose died. We know everything about her funeral, but nothing about what Charles felt. It was certainly a financial blow. Her French income would cease once the arrears were collected. Cromwell, the new chief minister, looked into the tangled matter of Charles's finances and a fresh settlement was reached between the duke and the crown. Debts were pardoned, the dead woman's liabilities were cancelled, Charles gave up his estates in Oxford and Berkshire and gained property in Lincolnshire, which would become the seat of his power. It was in this region that in 1536 a revolt broke out. Charles was still a new boy in the county, but during the Pilgrimage of Grace he was able to hold and pacify the region, moderating the belligerent and sometimes incoherent instructions from central government. It suited Henry to have Charles to keep a hand on a part of the country where there was continued potential for trouble, and Charles was capable. Through his career he was well served by a corps of advisers, by lawyers and accountants, auditors and surveyors. He worked amicably with Cromwell, whose letters to him are models of silky man-management. When Charles was called on to give up the prestigious office of earl marshal to Thomas Howard, Cromwell told him how glad he was to do it; such a sacrifice gave Charles, Cromwell said, the chance to show how much he cared about the happiness of the Duke of Norfolk, which clearly mattered to him more than any office in the world. It did the king's heart good to see Charles take it so well, and 'his subjects so lovingly and friendly, the one to love the other'. Moreover, if Charles got himself to court with 'resonable spede', he would be just in time to see Norfolk off to France in his new ambassadorial role: the effort is strongly advised, in case Henry take any foot-dragging as 'unkyndness', and meanwhile, 'the holye trynyte preserve your lordship in long lyffe and good helthe.'

A few months after the death of Mary Rose, Charles married an heiress of 14. Catherine Willoughby had been intended as his son's bride, but the second Henry died in March 1534, aged 10 or 11. Catherine was the daughter of one of Katherine of Aragon's ladies-in-waiting, who had married an English lord with extensive estates in East Anglia and Lincolnshire. Catherine and Charles quickly had a son, another

Henry, whose godfathers – sign of the times – were the king and Thomas Cromwell. This Henry survived his father and became duke of Suffolk in his turn, but died during a summer epidemic the year he was 16; his brother Charles's accession to the title was followed by his own death, within the hour. Their portraits by Holbein, made when they were small boys, were all that remained of them. Charles's title passed to Frances, his eldest daughter by Mary Rose; her daughter was Jane Grey, who ruled England for a matter of days and ended on the block. The drunken horseboy had not only married a queen, he had passed on his genes to another. Charles was no fool, but gave the impression of being barely able to spell his name; his granddaughter studied Latin, Greek and Hebrew, Chaldean and Aramaic. Jane Grey loved God; her grandfather loved his king. His later years were spent holding a mirror to reflect Henry's glory. His prestige inevitably waned with the passing of his royal wife, and in 1534 the Venetian ambassador wrote him off as not worth bribing. But he sat in Parliament and in the council, attended Garter ceremonies, helped to christen Prince Edward, bury Queen Jane, welcome Anne of Cleves and in 1542 investigate the adultery of Katherine Howard. In Cromwell's household reforms of 1539 he was given the post of lord steward of the royal household, renamed the Great Mastership. His health was declining by then, and Henry was obese and ill. Their occupations changed; in early middle age, jousting had given way to tennis and bowls, then to games of cards. But in the early 1540s, he acted as Henry's lieutenant in the north, and if it came to invading Scotland, he was willing: 'I dowt not to sustaigne not oonly that jornaye, but I trust many worse then that, as well as they that arr more yonger then I.' When Henry went to war in France again, Charles was back in harness. He directed the siege of Boulogne until Henry himself arrived and was able to make a triumphal entry as conqueror. After the king returned to England, the French in turn laid siege to the town, but back in England Charles was handsomely rewarded, and was lined up to go to the town's relief. But Henry concluded a peace, and succeeded in keeping Boulogne; Charles turned to organising the south of England for when that peace would break down and the French try to invade. He died suddenly, at Guildford, on 22 August 1545.

Charles Brandon's inner life, if he had one, is inaccessible to us. Gunn's thorough and discriminating history is built on recoverable facts. Charles is all persona and every inch of him is Tudor, as Tudor would be understood by the guests at Thornbury: he is a playing-card knight, flat and bright. In *The Tudors* he was played by Henry Cavill, soon to be cast as Superman in *Man of Steel*. In the RSC's *Wolf Hall* plays, he was impersonated by the towering and handsome Nicholas Boulton, who was snapped up between seasons by *Game of Thrones*, where he was beheaded in a gladiatorial arena in a spectacularly bloody fashion. Though Charles's career was packed with spectacular incident, it lacks the final flourish of an execution, which probably accounts for his comparatively low profile in Tudor pop mythology. A natural death, for one of Henry's councillors, seems an almost unnatural feat. Charles managed it because he was in no way Henry's rival, though he was his accredited double: as a commentator on the site the Tudor Enthusiast puts it, 'the original Charles Brandon is same fat ugly dude like henry the 8th himself, perhaps that's why he likes him so much.' Henry must sometimes have wondered what his ministers thought of him, not as a king but as a man – but from Charles he could count on straightforward admiration and gratitude. The Boleyns may have prospered because they were sexy and sneaky, Wolsey and Cromwell because they were smart, the Duke of Norfolk because of his inherited martial grit and double-tongued hypocrisy; Charles Brandon never forgot 'youre highnez only under God have brought hym to his estate'. He made few enemies unless he was ordered to make them. Often he swerved trouble when it was coming to meet him head on, and it is difficult to say whether this was 'tactical cunning' or 'ineffectual lethargy', as Gunn remarks. If he made a mistake, he was 'humble and soryfull'. Henry accepted what he had to give, his strong arm and 'gentill herte'. Charles lived up to his motto, 'loyaulte me oblige.' He spoke of the king as a lover, as Tudor men tended to speak of each other: as he told Wolsey in 1516, 'my hert and mynde be alwaye with hym, and daily appeteth and desireth to see his grace.' Charles died less than 18 months before the king, and is buried near him in St George's Chapel in Windsor. It was rumoured that Henry might snap up Charles's widow as his seventh wife, though in the event he decided to stick with Katherine Parr. He paid for Charles's lavish funeral, and didn't even try to recover the costs from the estate.

LRB (editorial)

From: LRB (editorial)
Sent: 3 March 2016 21:10
To:
Subject: Re:

Dear Hilary,

I'm sent to plague you again – I feel like a water-fly. This time though a small few questions about Brandon. Is it five wives he saw out, as it stands at present, or only four? We understood four, but with the bulls and the wards and the contracts and pre-contracts… And are we were right to call Mary Rose just Mary, and in saying it was William de la Pole who languished in the tower? There was some uncertainty too about who's the he when 'Cromwell told him how much he enjoyed making the sacrifice etc' – at first it reads as Cromwell. Perhaps some more from the letter would make it clear that this is what Cromwell and Henry are supposing of Suffolk?

Thank you, I keep thinking of Sense and Sensibility: all those Brandons swiving.

Alice x

LONDON REVIEW OF BOOKS
28 Little Russell Street
London WC1A 2HN
Tel: 020 7209 1101
Fax: 020 7209 1102
www.lrb.co.uk

03/03/2016

Fact-checking correspondence between
Hilary Mantel and the editors, 2016

LRB (editorial)

From: ▮▮▮▮▮▮▮▮▮▮▮▮▮▮
Sent: 4 March 2016 07:09
To: LRB (editorial)
Subject: Re:

Dear Alice,
Not at all: thank you for saving me from the de la Pole error - I'd already said that John was killed, then I have him in the Tower - yes, it's William who was the prisoner.

I mean five of Henry's wives, so five queens is correct - perhaps for clarity say 'five of Henry's queens,'

The use of calling her Mary Rose, as in the David Loades biog, is that it distinguishes her from the Mary Tudor who is Henry's daughter, and all the other Marys of the era, but there is only one in this story, so it's fine to prefer plain Mary if you like. I quite like her being Mary Rose because she's such a fairytale princess, dancing a king to death and marrying her gallant lover and doing weeping on a heroic scale. I think her making herself scarce as she grew older helped retain her mythological quality. It sounds a sentimental name to us, but I think Henry was sentimental about her, as she seems to have been the kind one in the family - she didn't even say anything horrible about the Boleyns , just took herself away from the situation. In real life, it's hard to think when her Christian name would have been used, and by whom - we don't know what Charles called her - probably 'Wife of the Day.'

foot of p 8, let's say:
... Cromwell told him how glad he was to do it; such a sacrifice gave Charles, Cromwell said, the chance to show how much he cared about the happiness of the duke of Norfolk, which clearly mattered to him more than any office in the world. It did the king's heart good to see Charles take it so well, and 'his subjects…'.
I'd love to quote more, as it is a Cromwell showpiece - blackly funny, if you know the personnel, and faintly sinister - but it is unpunctuated as dictated letters often are, so a bit hard to hack through. But that should clear up the ambiguity.

Many thanks for your kind and careful help. And for the mental picture of Charles Brandon striding into a Jane Austen novel.
love, Hilary

04/03/2016

A possible portrait of Margaret Pole
(c. 1535), National Portrait Gallery

How Do We Know Her?
The Secrets of Margaret Pole
2017

A PAINTING in the National Portrait Gallery offers a grey-white face, long, guarded, medieval, remote: 'unknown woman, formerly known as Margaret Pole, Countess of Salisbury'. It is painted on a dateable oak panel, and the dates suit the presumed subject, but the artist is anonymous. Where is Hans Holbein when you need him? The sitter might as well be carved, for all she suggests flesh or circulating blood. Put a different hood on her, and she could be a man – one of her own Plantagenet relations. She is the daughter of a duke and the niece of two kings, Edward IV and Richard III. On her wrist, emblematic, is a small barrel. Her father was Shakespeare's 'false, fleeting, perjured Clarence', who died in the Tower of London at the age of 29, attainted for treason and supposedly drowned in a butt of malmsey.

The barrel, though, may have been strung on Margaret after her death. The picture was cleaned in 1973, and study suggested that some original features have almost vanished. A pearl necklace is just a shadow now. The hands are the standard-issue long-fingered type; a black ribbon, added later, may conceal damage to the paint. Margaret – if it is she – wears coral and ermine. She would have been a widow when the portrait was painted, but she holds a sprig of honeysuckle, symbol of love and marriage.

Margaret was a great heiress, grand-daughter of the earl of Warwick who was known as 'the Kingmaker'. Born in 1473 into a world of bloody dynastic feuds, she survived under the first Tudor and thrived under the second, until she and her family, long suspected of plots against the regime, were destroyed. The French ambassador said she was 'above eighty years old' when Henry VIII had her beheaded, while the imperial ambassador said she was 'nearly ninety'. In fact she was 67. The chronology defeated observers, as if her life stretched back into a fabulous era when dragons roamed.

Susan Higginbotham's carefully written book comes with a misleading cover puff: 'At last, a biography of one of the most fascinating women of the Tudor period', who has 'too long been overlooked'.* But Margaret Pole, one of the great magnates of Tudor England, is not overlooked. In *The King's Curse* (2014) she was ground up by the great fictionalising machine that is Philippa Gregory, and in 2003 she was the subject of a major biography by Hazel Pierce: *Margaret Pole: Loyalty, Lineage and Leadership*. Pierce's book is thorough and scholarly, and her work is acknowledged in Higginbotham's biography, which is less detailed, but serious and judicious. Based in North Carolina, Higginbotham is a lawyer by background and has written several historical novels, spanning different eras. Through her website she keeps lively links with readers and writers. She is a close student of the sources, and careful not to stuff her novels with false excitements. Her fiction is stiff and chary, as if she is too constrained by her knowledge of the

* *Margaret Pole: The Countess in the Tower* by Susan Higginbotham (Amberley, 2016).

pitfalls to turn her characters loose in their own lives. Seldom distracted from voicing their headline concerns, her people give each other a lot of information, in unmodulated voices, each time they speak. Higginbotham is more comfortable with biography, but this has not deterred her publisher from dressing up her new book like a historical novel of the type she doesn't much like, with a moody wash of colour and a woman with trailing skirts and half a head. Margaret Pole's death, notoriously, was not a clean end. In some versions, the plucky old girl refused to kneel at the block, and the headsman had to pin her down. Even the more sedate accounts agree that, like Thomas Cromwell, she was hacked about by a second-string executioner. Higginbotham's narrative begins with this bungled beheading – so either the jacket designer was in the dark about the contents, or someone at her publisher has a mordant sense of humour.

Seven years after the strange liquid death of Margaret's father, her uncle Richard III was defeated at Bosworth by Henry Tudor. It is only in posterity's schoolroom view that Bosworth was the end of the Middle Ages or the end of anything; the noble families didn't think their wars were over, and indeed they were not, because in 1487 the new king was defending his throne at the Battle of Stoke Field. A Yorkist pretender had been crowned in Dublin, a child who claimed to be the Plantagenet heir, Edward, Earl of Warwick, Margaret's 12- year-old brother. Henry Tudor had the real Warwick in custody, and was able to produce him, so the rebellion came to nothing. Stoke was a decisive victory. Henry's adult opponents were dead or driven abroad. It was children who caused him a problem. The sons of Edward IV, 11 and 13 years old, had been held in the Tower by their uncle Richard III, and last been seen by Londoners in the summer of 1483. But no one could be sure they were dead, and not escaped abroad, or living under assumed names. The little Earl of Warwick remained alive and shut away. But for the rest of his reign Henry VII would be plagued by pretenders, persistently rising from the dead.

Because she was a girl Margaret did not represent the same threat. No one would stage a rebellion in her favour while there were male Yorkists to mount a challenge. Her early years are obscure. Her mother, the great heiress Isabel Neville, died in 1476 after giving birth to her fourth child; this last baby, like Isabel's first child, did not live. Margaret would have been too young to remember her mother, and it is likely that she was brought up within her father's princely household, then after his execution lived with her cousins, the many daughters of Edward IV. After Richard III seized the throne, he sent Margaret to Yorkshire with her brother. The two children were of use to him; their maternal family, the Nevilles, commanded allegiance in the north. After Richard was killed, Margaret came to court under the new regime, and in September 1486 she attended the christening of Arthur, the first Tudor prince. There are only glimpses of her in these years: 'my lady Margaret of Clarence'.

When she reached her teens, a marriage was arranged with Richard Pole, a modest landowner with solid Tudor connections, who had been rewarded for loyalty by being made constable of several Welsh castles. The date of the marriage is uncertain; 1487 is likely. Margaret was 14, and probably remained at court rather than living with her husband. The king's mother, Margaret Beaufort, was protective of young brides; her own body had been wrecked by a pregnancy at 13. It was five years after the likely date of Margaret's marriage that her first son was born. It was the beginning of a fertile new line. The remnants of the Plantagenets had no difficulty in breeding, while the Tudors were less lucky. Margaret's daughter Ursula would have 13 children, and three of her four sons would marry heiresses and have large families. Besides Ursula, four of Margaret's children lived to adulthood. Her husband's career flourished. He was made Knight of the Garter, and appointed chamberlain to the young Prince of Wales. Margaret may have been deprived of her dynastic importance, but her marriage was honourable and stable, and she retained her status, if not her family's great titles and wealth.

Her brother's royal blood, however, remained a danger. He had been shut up for most of his life and, one later chronicler said, 'could not discern a goose from a capon'. This phrase has been interpreted as meaning Edward was of low intelligence; it only means that he was unworldly, and Higginbotham sees this. His naivety meant that, when threats to the regime mounted, he was easily entrapped. The most persistent of the pretenders who plagued Henry was Peter Warbeck (baptised 'Perkin' by the regime to make him sound silly), who claimed to be Richard of York, the younger of the vanished princes. European rulers keen to destabilise England had promoted the claims of this plausible, glamorous young man, but by the summer of 1498 he was in the Tower, about to embark on the last act of his mysterious life. Contact was made with Warwick; a plot began, or perhaps was manufactured by agents provocateurs; just at this time, to increase the alarm of Henry

Tudor, another Warwick impersonator showed his face in Kent. The new pretender, Ralph Wilford, was arrested and killed before the conspiracy bred any action. But the king's horoscope was looking nasty and, according to a Spanish commentator, he aged twenty years in two weeks. It was time to be rid of Warwick. Henry was negotiating a glorious marriage for Prince Arthur, to a daughter of Ferdinand and Isabella. He needed to convince the Spanish he was secure in his kingdom. The alleged plot between the earl and Warbeck was flimsy and perhaps government-sponsored, but both men were tried and executed.

Margaret's brother was 24. It is unlikely she had seen him for many years, but in any case, mourning for a traitor was inadvisable. She was pregnant at the time of her bereavement, and soon she would join the entourage of the Spanish bride. When Prince Arthur held court in Ludlow with the 15-year-old Katherine of Aragon, Richard Pole was with him, and a friendship began between the bride and the chamberlain's wife which was to outlast Katherine's life and have deep and lasting consequences for Margaret Pole. The bridegroom, Arthur, was dead within months. His brother came to the throne in 1509 as Henry VIII, married the widowed Katherine, and in a first flush of goodwill began to repair the damage to Margaret's fortunes. When Richard Pole died in 1504 Margaret had had to borrow money to give him a suitable funeral. But three years into his reign, the young Henry VIII restored her to the greater part of her revenues and gave her back a family title, creating her countess of Salisbury in her own right. With the accession of the young king – uxorious, beautiful and benign – England seemed to have entered a golden age: and at his coronation, all the spectators, and presumably Margaret Pole with them, 'with great reverence, love and desire, said and cried: "Yea, yea!"'

It was, Pierce says, as if Margaret had won the lottery. She was now one of the richest people in England. After she had redeemed her dead brother's lands from the crown, she owned property in Calais, and estates in Wales and 17 English counties. She built herself a castle at Warblington, close to the sea on the Hampshire-Sussex border. It was sumptuously furnished and built of brick – a modern material – but moated, crenellated, archaic in form. Her London palace, Le Herber, stood in a busy mercantile quarter, approximately where Cannon Street Station is now, and she rented out the tenements around as workshops, stables and an inn. Inventories paint the picture: tableware of silver and gold, Venetian glass, mother of pearl, tapestries portraying the journeys of Ulysses and the discovery of Newfoundland; the countess herself, tall, stately, wears ermine, tawny damask, black satin and black velvet. Looking to her last end, Margaret commissioned a chantry at Christchurch Priory. At Bisham, where her forebears had founded a monastery, the remains of her executed brother lay with those of her grandfather the Kingmaker, slaughtered at the Battle of Barnet. Her son Arthur joined them, dying young, probably in the sweating sickness epidemic of 1528. Arthur had been a courtier, an able jouster and a great favourite with Henry, serving in his privy chamber. Margaret's whole family had been elevated with her on the wheel of fortune. Ursula married into the powerful Stafford family; of Margaret's sons, only Reginald did not marry; by the age of seven he was 'given utterly to God'. Henry, the eldest son, though knighted and given the family title Lord Montagu, did not share the general admiration for the king. But Margaret herself was an ornament to Henry. She was, Pierce says, 'intelligent, unquestionably virtuous, traditionally pious, and possessed an easy familiarity with the convoluted etiquette of a royal court'. By 1520, as an indication of the trust placed in her, she had been appointed lady governor to the Princess Mary, born in 1516 and the only child of the royal marriage to survive for more than a few weeks.

As the heir to the throne, Mary enjoyed a separate household, and in 1525 she was sent to Ludlow to hold court. The countess was to look after the little girl's health and diet, ensure that she did not wear herself out in learning French and Latin, and see that her immediate environment was kept spotless, 'so that everything about her be pure, sweet, clean and wholesome, as to so great a princess doth appertain'. Mary's food, Henry ordered, was to be served with 'joyous and merry communication'. Whether the countess was up to this is hard to say, but later the imperial ambassador was to declare that Mary regarded her as 'a second mother'. When Henry began proceedings to annul his first marriage, when Katherine was discarded and the Princess Mary downgraded to 'Lady Mary, the king's daughter', Margaret proved fiercely loyal and protective. In an effort to force their co-operation, Henry separated his wife and child, and Margaret – who was Mary's godmother – offered to serve the young girl at her own expense. She was no longer, though, the sort of influence Henry wished for his daughter. After his marriage to Anne Boleyn and the birth of their daughter, Elizabeth, Mary was sent to join the household of the infant princess. There, she was surrounded by connections of the Boleyn queen. Margaret was super-fluous; curtly, Henry wrote her off as a fool. If he had trusted her once, he no longer did so. The prestige of her ancient family, her traditionalist stance in religion, and her status as a peer in her own right – all these defined a woman who might wish to resist the new order. And her gender did not necessar-ily disqualify her from becoming leader of the opposition – if that was what she chose.

With Margaret's female peers, there is a gap between what they say and what they do, what they are and what they appear to be. In theory, after she married, a woman's personal prop-erty and real estate were at her husband's disposal. In pract-ice, pre-nuptial agreements, trusts and the legally sanction-ed breach of entails created some flexibility. Most aristocratic women outlived their husbands, and once a woman was widowed she was able to assert her independence and have a say in her family affairs, while cultivating the trope of the 'defenceless widow' in any dealings with the authorities. When historical novelists are looking for ways to empower their heroines they opt for making them hotshot herbalists or minxy witches. But literacy was their usual weapon, not spells, and many of them picked up enough legal know-ledge to fight their corner in civil disputes. As widows, or as deputies to living husbands, they handled complex legal and financial affairs with aplomb, while assenting – outwardly at least – to their status as irrational and inferior beings. Gaily agreeing that the chief female virtues are meekness and self-effacement, they managed estates, signed off accounts, bought wardships and brokered marriage settlements, all the while keeping up a steady output of needlework. In some cases, they conspired against the crown while claiming, if it went badly, that their weak female brains had been addled by male influence, and that 'fragility and brittleness' allowed their trust to be easily abused.

It was Gertrude Courtenay, Marchioness of Exeter, who claimed to be brittle and fragile; one of the most persistent of the aristocratic plotters against Henry, she was in trouble in 1533 for her contacts with Elizabeth Barton, the 'Nun of Kent', whose florid line in prophecy was discomfiting to the regime. The nun sought out eminent supporters, especially those who, like Margaret and like Gertrude's husband, had a claim to the throne, and pressed on them the contents of her visions: unless he went back to his wife and to Rome, Henry would expire in torments. Thomas More and Katherine herself were wise enough to steer clear of the nun. It seems Margaret was questioned about her contacts with Barton, but she came to no harm as a result and, unlike Gertrude, she escaped without grovelling. Whatever her private feelings at this point, in public she was pragmatic and circumspect. Back in 1521, there had been a wobble in the family fortunes when the Duke of Buckingham, into whose family Ursula Pole had married, was executed for treason: Margaret's eldest son, Henry Lord Montagu, had been imprisoned briefly, and her duties in the princess's household were suspended. Buckingham was alleged to have said that the lack of sons to carry on the Tudor line was God's punishment for the imprisonment and death of the young Earl of Warwick. Margaret kept silent on the matter. What a contemporary described as her 'nobility and goodness' soon put her back in royal favour. Ten years on, her situation was more difficult to negotiate. Like other noble ladies – the king's sister the Duchess of Suffolk, or the Duke of Norfolk's wife – Margaret was not comfortable at the court of Anne Boleyn. But Lord Montagu attended Anne's coronation – as he would later attend her trial. When Henry imposed an oath which recognised him as head of the church in England, the countess and her household complied. In 1886, Margaret would be beatified by Pope Leo XIII as a martyr to Henry's regime. But it is difficult to detect in her conduct the heroic virtues assumed by Rome, and easier to see self- protective caution at work. Elizabeth Darrell, later Thomas Wyatt's mistress, refused the oath; Lady Hussey, wife of one of Mary's household, was imprisoned because she would not accept Mary's exclusion from the succession and insisted on addressing her as a princess. But Margaret kept any dissident thoughts to herself, avoiding jeopardy until, in the summer of 1536, the actions of her son Reginald plunged her whole family into trouble.

Reginald was the most interesting and talented of Margaret's children, and the one to whom she was not close. He was the child Margaret had been carrying when her brother Warwick was executed. When Reginald was seven, and Margaret a widow with an uncertain future, she sent him to be educated at Sheen with the monks of the Charterhouse. Later, he would castigate her in the accents of a hurt child for what seemed to him abandonment, telling her that as she had given him up when he was so young, she should not interfere between him and his conscience. Family solidarity, the code of survival, did not mean much to Reginald, brought up under an alien roof; if he were to lose his earthly family, he said, he would still have the fellowship of the saints in paradise.

It was the king who had paid for Reginald's education at Oxford and later in Italy, where his noble connections gave him the entrée into the smartest humanist circles. He grew up cultivated and cosmopolitan, sensitive, lively-minded. He was keenly interested in theology, but he was not ordained; he was free to marry if he wished, and propagate a Plantagenet family. When Henry began to poll the European universities about the legality of his annulment, he chose Reginald to visit the Sorbonne, and had no fault to find with the way he carried out his mission. But Reginald stayed in Italy through the reign of Anne Boleyn – supposedly preparing a learned statement on the king's case. In the spring of 1536 the Boleyn family were destroyed, and the Pole family and other English grandees grouped themselves about the incoming queen, Jane Seymour. If Margaret played any part in the downfall of Henry's second queen, her role was so far behind the scenes that it has left no trace. But in late June she was back at court by the side of Queen Jane, and the king was looking forward to an era of peace and fertility. At this point, Reginald delivered him a nasty surprise, in the shape of a letter denouncing him as a schismatic, heretic and disgrace to Christendom: a Nero, a wild beast.

It was not so much a letter as a small book. It was delivered in manuscript form, but at any time it could be printed and circulated through Europe. Later that year, Reginald was summoned to Rome, made a cardinal and put in charge of organising a crusade against England – economic sanctions first, war if need be. No great European power was willing to commit men or money to this crusade, but their unwillingness was not apparent at the time. England became an embattled nation. The threat seemed even greater by 1538, when the two great powers, France and the emperor, signed a peace treaty which left them free to turn their attention to the pariah nation. Reginald was present at the treaty negotiations. The danger the Tudors saw lay not in the present disposition of the Pole family – who vehemently protested their loyalty – but in their claim to the throne, and in Reginald's actions while he was out of the jurisdiction. Henry and his ministers suspected Reginald of plotting to marry the king's daughter Mary, and unite her claim with his.

Henry wanted Reginald to come back to England and talk the matter over, but Reginald had the sense to keep his distance. As his disgrace deepened, Margaret withdrew from court. She spent much of her time at Warblington, where she was nicely placed, in the event of an invasion, to help the rebels against Henry; or so you thought, if you were one of Henry's councillors. Her many fortified houses and castles, the number of tenants she could turn out, the belligerent propaganda from abroad – all these brought the whole family into deep suspicion. Margaret reminded Reginald what they all owed to the Tudors, and urged him to give up his enterprise, to 'take another way' and serve the king: his renegade actions, she said, had plunged her into grief and fear, and 'trust me, Reginald, there never went the death of thy father or of any child so nigh my heart.' Thomas Cromwell, who spied efficiently on the whole family, tried to have Reginald abducted or assassinated. But Reginald, it seemed, always got a tip-off. His crusade against his native land was never launched, but many years later he would return, archbishop of Canterbury to Mary Tudor, and join in heresy-hunting and the burning of reformers. But for now he was out of Henry's reach, leaving his family as hostages.

Was the family sincere in deploring his disloyalty? 'Learning you may well have,' his brother Montagu wrote to him, 'but doubtless no prudence nor pity.' Reginald had compared himself to a surgeon ready to cut away diseased flesh from the body of England: not the most tactful metaphor, when your anointed king is dragging about with an ulcerated leg. Higginbotham follows Pierce in refusing to vilify Henry for his treatment of the Poles. Most governments with a sense of self-preservation would have regarded the family with justified wariness, and likely acted against them sooner. Their destruction came with a wave of arrests in the autumn of 1538. Margaret's youngest son, Geoffrey, probably under threat of torture, denounced not only his own family but the Courtenay clan and other prominent members of the old families. Afterwards, he made a botched suicide attempt. Margaret, warned of the threat he represented to her own interests and life, said: 'I trow he is not so unhappy that he will hurt his mother, and yet I care neither for him, nor for any other, for I am true to my Prince.'

At this point she was questioned rigorously by Henry's councillor William Fitzwilliam. 'Yesterday . . . we travailed with the Lady of Salisbury all day – before and after noon, till almost night.' Sometimes the questioners were mild, sometimes roughly spoken, 'traitoring her and her sons to the ninth degree – yet will she nothing utter.' Margaret continued not uttering, or uttering no proof of treason. Either her sons had not made her aware of their dealings, Fitzwilliam concluded, or she was an adept in brazen deceit. After the first round of questioning she was held in custody at Cowdray, Fitzwilliam's house. Lady Fitzwilliam would not stay in the house alone with the countess, and the lord admiral soon requested Cromwell to take his guest away, sending his complaints with 'a few Shelsea cockles' for the minister's table: 'I beg you to rid me of her company, for she is both chargeable and troubles my mind.' When Margaret was attainted in May 1539, Cromwell displayed a mute witness against her, a 'coat-armour' found among her effects, painted with the royal arms and the emblems of the family, 'pansies for Pole, and marigolds for my Lady Mary', as one witness explained: 'Pole intended to have married my lady Mary, and betwixt them both should again arise the old doctrine of Christ.'

But by then Lord Montagu was dead, executed along with the Marquis of Exeter and other opponents of the regime. It was not a bloodbath, but a selective cull, carried through by process of law. For at least five years, Montagu, Exeter and others had been passing information to the emperor through his ambassador, urging the invasion of England, and Reginald himself had assured the readers of his 1536 letter that a host of disaffected subjects were lurking within the realm, ready to support the invaders against Henry as soon as foreign troops landed. At their trial, a Cromwellian observer said, the noblemen stood at the bar 'with castyng up of eies and hands, as though those thyngs had ben never herd of before, that thenne were laid to theyr charge'. Margaret was perhaps guilty only by association, but at this distance it is impossible to tell. She was head of her family, a magnate with vast resources in men and money; any disaffection on her part was dangerous. Geoffrey Pole, who had given the government what it needed, was pardoned. The veteran plotter Gertrude Courtenay was treated with clemency; unlike Margaret, she was not a free agent but a married woman subject to her husband, and not a claimant to the throne in her own right. Margaret was not executed with her eldest son, but was held in the Tower for the last years of her life – the king paying her bills, outfitting her as became a great lady in furred petticoats and a satin nightgown. She was executed in 1541, the act of attainder rendering a trial unnecessary. It was a housekeeping matter, the French ambassador said; Henry, now with his fifth wife, Katherine Howard, wanted to make a progress north, and to empty the Tower before he set off, either by acts of mercy or the condemnation of detainees. On the scaffold, Margaret prayed for the royal family – all except Anne Boleyn's daughter, Elizabeth, whom she regarded as illegitimate. Then, her prayers completed, she faced the incompetent axeman.

In 1876, during restoration work on the chapel of St Peter ad Vincula, the bones of a tall, elderly woman came to light. The skeleton was not complete, but part of the skull had survived, and certain other bones. This is what Margaret is now, besides paper and ink, and the ruins of her palaces: pieces of breastbone and pelvis, a single finger bone and four vertebrae. Her thoughts, her motives, are so hidden, either by her inclination or by the work of time, that it is difficult for the most diligent biographer to put her together and make her walk and talk. Her life, marked by stunning reversals of fortune, is an irresistible subject, but it presents a familiar difficulty for the historian. Was she, at this point or that, doing nothing of interest at all – or was she doing everything, in a way that was almost supernaturally discreet? Margaret's later life, at least, is well documented, but we cannot approach her story from the inside. We know her, as we know so many of her contemporaries, through her inventories, through legal documents and official letters. Did she plot against the crown? Did she, as the regime alleged, burn the evidence that incriminated her? Or was there, as she claimed, nothing worth burning?

It is only in adversity that Margaret shows herself, in the records of her interrogations, when she was a woman in her sixties, experienced, shrewd, hard to frighten. Fitzwilliam despaired of getting anything out of her but denials, and paid her a twisted compliment in the way Tudor men did: 'We may call her rather a strong and constant man than a woman . . . she has shown herself so earnest, vehement and precise that more could not be.' When he told her that her goods had been seized, she must have known it was the beginning of the end, and 'seemeth thereat to be somew[hat] appalled', but neither then nor at any later point did she profess anything but loyalty to Henry and regret at her family's folly. Only when Fitzwilliam called Reginald a 'whoreson' did she object, saying 'with a wonderful sorrowful countenance' that 'he was no whoreson, for she was both a good woman and true.' When Reginald, lying abroad, heard of her death, he announced to his secretary that he was now the son of a martyr. He then disappeared into his private closet, and after an hour, 'came out as cheerful as before'.

LRB (editorial)

From:	▮▮▮▮▮▮▮▮
Sent:	23 September 2019 09:24
To:	LRB (editorial)
Subject:	Not much of a contributor

Dear Mary-Kay,
I hate telling you this, but even with the kind extension you gave me, I won't be able to finish a piece in time for the celebration issue. I wanted to write a piece of memoir, but everything that's happening- copy-editing , interviews, filming- is conspiring to stop me getting into a meditative frame of mind, and looking at what I have to do this next week I realise that the best course is to let you know and put the piece aside for a better time. If I try to force it, it won't find its natural shape.
I am so sorry. My book's not coming out till March, but then it is published the same week here and in US, in Holland and Germany. So I am already doing interviews for the media to store up. And making a documentary with Oxford Films - on Friday we are actually visiting Wolf Hall, which these days is covered in archeologists.
Let me just take this chance though to tell you how much I admire both you and the paper. I remember very well the first time we spoke on the phone. I couldn't hear a word and agreed to all sorts of things. Now time has rolled on and I am officially deaf and you no louder, but otherwise you are enhanced in every way.
Love, Hilary

Sent from my iPad

23/09/2019

Email from Hilary Mantel to
Mary-Kay Wilmers, 2019

About the LRB

The *London Review of Books* is Europe's leading magazine of culture and ideas. Published twice a month, it provides a space for some of the world's best writers to explore a wide variety of subjects in exhilarating detail – from art and politics to science and technology via history and philosophy, fiction and poetry. In the age of the long read, the LRB remains the pre-eminent exponent of the intellectual essay, admired around the world for its fearlessness, its range and its elegance.

As well as book reviews and reportage, each issue also contains poems, reviews of exhibitions and movies, 'short cuts', letters and a diary, and is available in print, online, and offline via our app. Subscribers enjoy unlimited access to every piece we've published since 1979, the year the magazine was founded, in our digital archive. It contains all of the articles in this volume, and many more that might have made the cut. Our website (lrb.co.uk) also features a regular blog, podcasts and short documentaries, plus video highlights from our events programme on both sides of the Atlantic, and at the London Review Bookshop.

A reader recently described the LRB as 'the best thing about being a human'. Make it the highlight of your fortnight, too, by taking out a subscription: lrb.me/sub

About 4th Estate

Founded in Notting Hill in 1984 on a shoestring budget and acquired by HarperCollins in 2000, 4th Estate is one of the most innovative imprints in the publishing industry, with a reputation for producing critically acclaimed and beautifully designed titles. We published Hilary Mantel's *Wolf Hall* trilogy, which made her the first woman and first British writer to win the Booker Prize twice. We are the home of Anthony Doerr, whose *All the Light We Cannot See* won the Pulitzer Prize in 2015. We publish the Samuel Johnson Prize-winning authors Lucy Hughes-Hallett and Philip Hoare, and the Costa Novel Award winner Jon McGregor.

We explore American life with authors such as Jonathan Franzen, Annie Proulx, Michael Chabon and Valeria Luiselli, and celebrate African and Asian literature with the likes of Chimamanda Ngozi Adichie and Tash Aw. We inspire cooks with books by Nigel Slater, Giorgio Locatelli and Anna Jones, and our non-fiction authors – Lena Dunham, Matt Ridley, Jia Tolentino and Hadley Freeman among them – influence the opinions and beliefs of readers around the world. We champion diverse British voices like Inua Ellams, Michael Donkor, Yomi Adegoke and Elizabeth Uviebinené, and seek out new ones with our annual BAME Short Story Prize. Our office bookshelves are lined with classics from writers like J.G. Ballard, Joan Didion, Penelope Fitzgerald, Arundhati Roy and Joyce Carol Oates. From fiction to cookery, biography to polemic, 4th Estate is the home of literature at its best.

All LRB covers by Peter Campbell.
Items on pages 7-8, 19, 29, 40, 63, 78, 88, 101, 102,
116, 138, and 153 from the *London Review of Books*
collection at, and reproduced courtesy of, the
Harry Ransom Center, University of Texas at Austin.